Healing with Limited Resources: Practical Psychotherapy for Real-World Contexts

Dr. Monalisa Nayak

notionpress.com

INDIA · SINGAPORE · MALAYSIA

ISBN
Paperback 979-8-90431-869-7
Hardcase 979-8-90431-870-3

Contents

Preface

Mental health care does not unfold in ideal conditions. It rarely happens in quiet therapy rooms with uninterrupted time, abundant resources and neatly defined boundaries. Instead, for many practitioners across India and similar contexts, it takes place in crowded government schools, under-resourced hospitals, rural primary health centers, community halls and sometimes even under a tree or through a mobile phone screen. This book emerged from that reality.

Healing with Limited Resources: Practical Psychotherapy for Real-World Contexts is born out of a simple but urgent need, to make psychotherapy workable where it is needed the most. In many parts of the world, particularly in low- and middle-income settings, the demand for mental health support far exceeds that availability of trained professionals, infrastructure and time. Practitioners are often required to do more with less time, fewer tools, limited privacy, minimal systemic support. Yet, within these constraints, meaningful psychological change is not only possible, it's happening every day.

This book attempts to focus on what is feasible, adaptable and effective in constrained environments. A central theme running through this work is adaptation. Evidence-based practices are important, but their impact depends on how well they can be translated into real-world context. This means simplifying intervention without diluting the essence, using culturally relevant language, working with families and communities and often relying on non-specialist through task shifting and peer-support models. Another key emphasis is on accessibility and equity. Mental health care cannot remain a privilege available only to those who can afford it. It must reach all people from all walks of life. This book aims to support practitioners in extending their reach to these populations in ways that are ethical, respectful, and contextually grounded.

The approaches described here are not rigid protocols, but starting points. They are meant to be adapted, reshaped and refined based on the needs of the individuals and communities you work with. Ultimately, effective psychotherapy in low-resource settings is not defined by perfection but by responsiveness, creativity and deep commitment to human dignity.

I would like to thank all the MSc Clinical students, CMR University to contribute to this book chapters which shows their curiosity for mental health care to support healing with Limited Resources.

Chapter 1

Psychotherapy for Exam Anxiety in Government Schools

– P. Shwetha

Introduction

The schools of low-and middle-income regions run by the government are in a paradox. They show the governmental interest in universal education and enhance its accessibility, but are strained systemically. There is often overcrowding, insufficient teaching materials, and psychological service. In most districts, one counsellor serves a number of hundreds of students, which is noted to be nowhere less than half that in some districts. As a result, academic achievement is perceived as the primary mechanism of socioeconomic mobility, which increases psychological stress over exams.

Most of the students in these institutions belong to economically vulnerable families. Many of them are first-generation students whose academic systems are new to them and they have no guidance of former experiences on how the new system should be. In such situations exams are not simply tests of understanding but are viewed as determining the future of the family and the emotional significance that grades become so great that the purposes of the exams are not met.

Predisposition to Development Change in Adolescence

The adolescents between 14-17 are the most affected by the exam anxiety. This is the stage of development when the identity is formed, the sensitivity towards peer judgment is increased, and abstract thinking grows. Although adolescents have mature cognition which helps in future planning, the same enables them to think of the worst situations, which they can easily imagine. Performance anxiety is enhanced by added sociocultural pressure.

Empirical research reveals that there is a close interrelationship between adolescent anxiety, academic stressors and perceived parental expectations (Zeidner 1998). In addition, anxiety and low academic performance are mutually reinforcing, and this results in a vicious cycle because anxiety causes low scores, which in turn stimulates anxious thinking.

Institutional Pressure and Culture of Examination

Board exams are often used to give the student eligibility to higher-secondary or vocational streams in government schools. There is pressure on teachers to get high pass rates which may unwillingly generate anxiety in students. Remedial assistance is predominantly academic; students who are emotionally challenged are usually referred to additional tuition, rather than emotional-regulation approaches.

Case Vignette

MN(Meena) is a 16-year-old Grade 11 student in a government girls higher-secondary school in a semi-urban district. She stays with her father and mother with two younger siblings in a two-room house.

Her father is a driver of an auto-rickshaw and has an odd schedule, and her mother is a house-cleaner. The family income is not very predictable, but education is always considered as a way to improve life. MN has been referred to as the hope of the house. MN has had an academic record that is very good in history and has been praised by teachers as a hardworking student and she has been mentioned as a role model by the family members. Approximately six months prior to the board exams, Meena started feeling anxious particularly in mathematics. The initial symptoms were mild restlessness preceding tests which later deteriorated to physiological hyperarousal-palpitations, sweating, tremors, and stomach discomfort.

Cognitively, MN expresses some repetitive automatic thoughts like, if I do not get a score of 90, I will lose everything, and, my parents have given too much, and I will not fail. She constantly practices possible errors, in particular during the night, and has reduced her sleep to five hours. Although she knows the contents, she does not take a risk when it comes to application tests and skipped a whole section on a mock examination due to the fear of making a mistake. On the emotional level, she swings between fear and guilt and considers anxiety a weakness, not a stress response. Teachers accuse her of being overthinking and her parents urge towards increased discipline. This is because she tried to have a tearful emotional outburst in the run-up to a math test, which evoked the thought that one wrong move would ruin her future.

The case of MN depicts the interaction of cognitive distortions, somatic anxiety, perfectionism and socio-cultural pressures. It also shows how psychological distress is not visible even among high-achieving students in government schools.

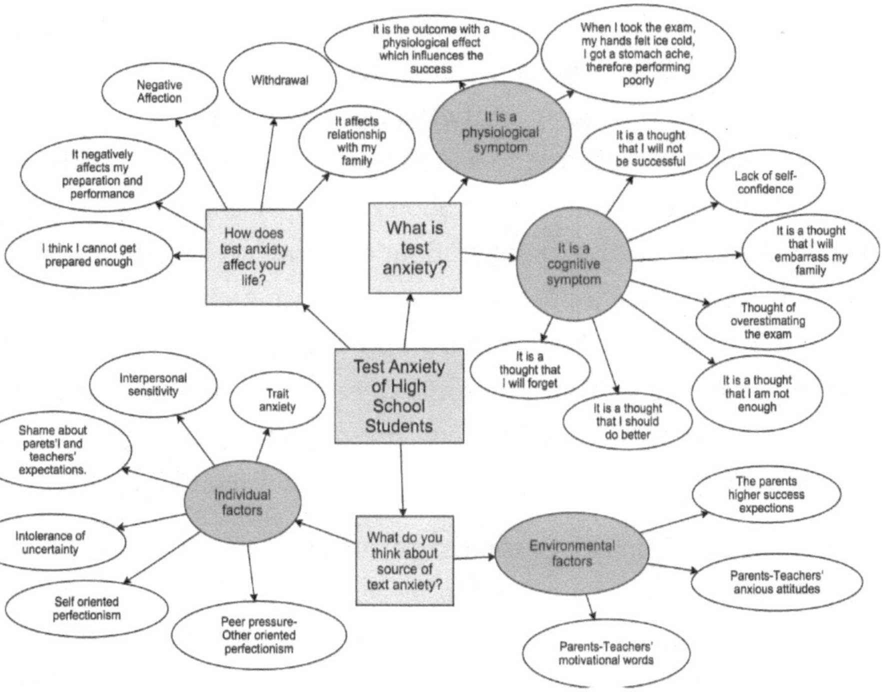

Figure 1: Understanding Test Anxiety of High School Students

Problems in Mental Health that are prevalent in this context

Anxiety during Examination as a Multidimensional Phenomenon

Situational anxiety is not all about exam anxiety. It consists of cognitive, emotional, physiological and behavioural components which interact. The mental component has intrusive worry and negative self-appraisal. The physiological component is the excessive stimulation of the autonomic nervous system. Common behavioural responses are avoidance, procrastination or the use of safety behaviour like seeking more reassurance. Zeidner (1998) views test anxiety as a combination of worry and emotionality, with the former taking the most negative impact in performance since it occupies working-memory space. This cognitive interference brings an added disadvantage in government schools where the preparation time is already constrained by household obligations.

Maladaptive Perfectionism and Conditional Self-worth

Unconditional positive regard entails a non-judgments stance, while conditional positive regard involves the use of evaluative judgments (Ackerman et al., 2017). Maladaptive perfectionists can be the students who attempt to work hard in resource constrained environments. Their school life becomes a combination of family demands. These students do have core beliefs that are rigid that include things like: My value is solely determined by achievement according to the cognitive models of anxiety that Beck (2011) has developed. They are under high risk since they have both internal and external standards.

Subclinical Depressive Symptomatology

Low mood, lack of pleasure and exhaustion may be effects of chronic exam anxiety. It is verified in the meta-analytic work (Hofmann et al., 2012) that anxiety and depression tend to be co-occurring. Stress over an extended period in adolescents can become hopeless resignation in the absence of coping mechanisms. It is important to identify the problem at school early enough to prevent its escalation to more serious issues.

Significant Constraints and Limitations

Structural and Resources Constraints

There are structural constraints to the provision of psychotherapy in government schools. A lot of schools do not have specific counselling rooms. Academic class conflicts decrease the frequency of sessions. In most cases counsellors have to combine both therapy with administrative work. These realities imply that interventions are to be brief, structured and group based.

Stigma and Cultural Beliefs

The term "Mental" is often perceived as a moral or character deficiency. Students are afraid of being considered weak or powerless.

Academic coaching is sometimes preferred by parents more than psychological assistance. Thus, framing therapy should be focused on performance improvement and coping with stress, but not on pathology.

Time Pressure and Examination Schedule

Interventions have to be within academic schedules. Prolonged open-ended therapy is not realistic. The model must thus be time constrained but must remain evidence-based practice.

Justification of Contextually Adapting Model

In state schools we have to reconcile both empirical rigor and utility. The most popular treatment of youth anxiety is the Cognitive-Behavioural Therapy (CBT) (Kendall et al., 1997; Hofmann et al., 2012). However, 12-16 session single protocols are hardly applicable in high load environments. A brief group CBT model of eight sessions can be proposed which is a combination of Narrative Identity Reconstruction and Performance Simulation Exposure. The special contribution is the Reframe Protocol of Examination Narrative. It combines formalized CBT with narrative therapy to assist students in changing their attitudes to performance-determined worth to that of a growing student. This takes care of the social-cultural load that is associated with performance in exams in government schools.

Low-financial resources psychotherapy plan

Therapy Format

Semi-structured group intervention.

- Group size: 8-10 students
- Session duration: 60 minutes

- Total sessions: 8
- Supplementary: 1 person intake and 1 booster prior to the end of examination.

Screening and Intake

Brief, standardized anxiety measures and teacher referrals are used to screen the students. In the course of the intake, the clinicians evaluate severity, co-occurring symptoms, and risk factors. In case there are severe cases of depression, the referral pathways are based on WHO school mental-health recommendation (World Health Organization, 2021).

Design and Content of the Session

Session 1: How to Deal with Exam Anxiety: This meeting presents psychoeducation. The physiological response to stress is presented to the students with the help of recognized examples, e.g., sport competition. Anxiety is presented as an effective survival mechanism but once too much, it becomes a problem. The model of cognitive-interference of test anxiety is defined in a simplistic way: worry occupies the working memory (Zeidner, 1998). Students fill in a rating of distress in different academic scenarios in an instrument known as the Anxiety Thermometer.

Session 2: Trigger Mapping and Anxiety: The participants undergo a body-mapping exercise to identify the physical symptoms in examinations. These symptoms become externalized which lowers self-stigma. The triggers are classified into cognitive, environmental, and interpersonal. Indicatively, Meena cites parental expectations as a mental stimulus that is associated with internal pressure and not direct criticism.

Session 3: Discovering Automatic Thoughts: The theory provided by Beck (2011) teaches students the prevalent forms of cognitive distortions catastrophizing, mind-reading, and all-or-nothing thinking. They fill in simplified records of thought, which differentiate facts and interpretations.

Session 4: Cognitive Restructuring and Balanced Thinking: The participants are taught to come up with balanced alternatives to the maladaptive thoughts. The role-play scenarios are simulations of exams, and the group discussion tests prove the evidence. The goal is cognitive flexibility and not unrealistic positivity. It has been demonstrated that cognitive restructuring creates anxiety reduction (Hofmann et al., 2012).

Session 5: Physiological Control and Emotion Regulation: Diaphragmatic breathing and short-progressive muscle relaxation is introduced to the students. These training activities are practiced and assigned as homework. It is also centered on their application, prior to and during examinations, in order to maximize performance instead of being applied as purely therapeutic methods and, therefore, stigma is minimized.

Session 6: Behaviour and Exposure Hierarchy Research: Treatment of avoidance behaviour is founded on the principles of graded exposure resting on the empirically supported youth anxiety treatment (Kendall et al., 1997). Students develop personalized exposure hierarchies to feared exam scenarios and they are advised to advance through the hierarchy in that order by integrating breathing methods with exposure.

Table 1: Sample Exposure for Exam Anxiety

Level	Task	Anxiety Rating
1	Solve 10 essay questions alone	3
2	Timed practice test at home	5
3	Full mock exam with peers	7
4	Simulated board exam setting	9

Session 7: Laboratory, Simulation of the Examination: This element will involve a full-length simulated test in well-organised but non-stressful circumstances. Before the test, the students perform breathing exercises and coughing card cheques. This is followed by a debriefing session, which discusses cognitive responses, changes in emotion and effectiveness of coping. This is an exposure that leads to mastery and decreased anticipatory fear.

Session 8: Reframe Protocol Examination Narrative: A student draws up a Resilience Timeline of the hardships and achievements that he has achieved in the past. Then they compose a letter to self in one year after the tests, which is not about the exam performance but about development. This narrative intervention supports identity more than performance and it speaks to conditional self-worth. The students are also advised to move through the levels slowly with exposure and breathing methods.

Table 2: Intervention framework for eight-sessions

Session	Core Focus	Primary Techniques
1	Psychoeducation	Anxiety model, normalization
2	Awareness	Body mapping, trigger identification
3	Cognitive Skills I	Thought monitoring

(contd.)

Session	Core Focus	Primary Techniques
4	Cognitive Skills II	Cognitive restructuring
5	Regulation Skills	Breathing, relaxation
6	Behavioural Activation	Exposure hierarchy development
7	Performance Simulation	Mock examination laboratory
8	Identity Integration	Resilience timeline, future self-letter

Ethical and Cultural Issues

Confidentiality in Group meetings

It is a clear confidentiality agreement that is developed at the beginning. Students get to know about the boundaries of confidentiality particularly in terms of probable damage. Psychological safety is achieved through group norms which are developed jointly.

Informed Consent

Parental and student consent are required to be written. The aim, format and voluntaryism of the programme is discussed plainly. Students will be guaranteed not to lose academic status because of the refusal to participate.

Family Engagement Culturally Sensitive

In most of the government schools, success is linked to family development. Parental aspirations should not be invalidated in the process of therapy, but rather they should be motivated by enhancing fear. Families can be taught adoptive strategies of support whenever time is available.

Boundary Management

School-based therapists have to explain their position. Dual relationships are kept to a minimum. The students are provided with clear information on the sessions and channels of communication.

Referral and Risk Management

School health guidelines would require the referral of the students who exhibit severe depression or suicidal thoughts to specialized services (World Health Organization, 2021). Ethical practice is composed of documentation and supervision.

Outcome Evaluation

Validated measures are used to get pre- and post-intervention anxiety. The quantitative data is supplemented by teacher reports on the participation and avoidance behaviors. Students can make informal qualitative feedback which can be a good measure of perceived benefits.

Conclusion

It takes discipline and creativity to design psychotherapy on exam anxiety in government schools. Evidence-based practice should be adapted, and it is evident that brief CBT that has been culturally reframed and supplemented with the narrative identity work is not only possible but also transformative as demonstrated in this model. The procedure echoes a basic clinical teaching, which can be well encapsulated by the statement that psychological interventions in low-resource contexts must be arranged in accordance with the priorities of accessibility, relevance and empowerment rather than theoretical purity. In these settings, precision, adaptability and sensitivity towards the lived environment are essential to good therapy.

References

Abdulbaqi, J., & Uzun, G. O. (2024). Effect of the Students' Test Anxiety Prevention Program on Students' Experiences of Test Anxiety: A Mixed-Methods Experiment. Sage Open, 14(4).

Beck, J. S. (2011). Cognitive behavior therapy: Basics and beyond (2nd ed.). Guilford Press.

Erkan, A., Doğan, U., & Adıgüzel, A. (2017). Sources of test anxiety: A qualitative approach.

Hofmann, S. G., Asnaani, A., Vonk, I. J. J., Sawyer, A. T., and Fang, A. (2012). The efficacy of cognitive behavioral therapy: A review of meta-analyses. Cognitive Therapy and Research, 36(5), 427 to 440.

Kendall, P. C., Flannery Schroeder, E., Panichelli Mindel, S., Southam Gerow, M., Henin, A., and Warman, M. (1997). Therapy for youths with anxiety disorders: A second randomized clinical trial. Journal of Consulting and Clinical Psychology, 65(3), 366 to 380.

Lee, S. S., Victor, A. M., James, M. G., Roach, L. E., & Bernstein, G. A. (2016). School-Based Interventions for Anxious Children: Long-Term Follow-Up. Child psychiatry and human development, 47(2), 183–193.

World Health Organization. (2021). Guideline on school health services. World Health Organization.

Zeidner, M. (1998). Test anxiety: The state of the art. Plenum Press.

Chapter 2

Low-Resource Counselling for Bullying and Peer Conflict in Schools

– Kapoor Rashee Raj

Introduction

This chapter is about a government secondary school located in a semi-urban region of India that serves children of lower socio-economic status; all of whom attend school for the first time. The student body consists of 800 students in grades 6 through 10. No infrastructure support exists for the school; classrooms are often overcrowded, with 50-60 students per class; no full-time psychologist is working at the school. A teacher is assigned as a part-time "counsellor" after having completed a short-term training program.

Bullying and peer conflict occur regularly among the student population, but there are few reports of this behaviour being reported. Forms of bullying include verbal, social exclusion, cyber (using mobile phones), and infrequent physical violence. Students have little if any understanding of how to regulate their emotions, and there are few, if any, skill-building opportunities for resolving conflict. The majority of parents are daily-wage workers and therefore do not have the time to participate in discussions regarding mental health at school; parents have little or no knowledge about how to discuss mental health with their children.

Counselling services (when available) occur in a corner of the staff room; there is little to no privacy available for students during that time; and, due to time constraints, each student is given 20–30 mins. for counselling. Most of the referrals are made by teachers, and self-referrals made by students are, very rarely, the reason for seeking help.

Case Vignette

AK, a 13-year-old girl in Grade 8, was referred to the school counsellor by her teacher because she has been crying excessively and appears to be reluctant to join in on any group activities. She stated that three of her classmates have been making fun of her appearance and not including her in their group projects; she was afraid that if she complained about what they were doing, she would face retaliation. Given the limited time and space available for the school counsellor, the counsellor planned a short series of four structured sessions that would include psychoeducation, teach her emotional regulation skills, and providing assertiveness training.

Common Mental Health Issues in This Context

Bullying and peer conflict in low-resource school settings are associated with multiple psychological difficulties.

Anxiety and Social Withdrawal

Students who are bullied often develop anticipatory anxiety, fear of attending school, and hypervigilance in peer settings. Somatic complaints such as headaches and stomach aches are common. Social withdrawal further increases vulnerability to peer victimization.

Depressive Symptoms and Low Self-Esteem

Repeated peer rejection contributes to feelings of worthlessness, sadness, and hopelessness. Adolescents may internalize negative peer messages, leading to identity confusion and self-doubt. In some cases, passive death wishes or self-harm ideation may emerge.

Aggression and Conduct Problems

Not all affected students internalize distress. Some externalize it through reactive aggression. Bullying victims may become perpetrators in other peer contexts, perpetuating a cycle of conflict.

Research consistently demonstrates that school bullying is linked with anxiety, depression, academic decline, and long-term psychosocial maladjustment (Arseneault, 2018; WHO, 2020). In low-resource settings, these effects may remain undetected due to limited screening systems.

Limitations

Designing counselling in this context requires acknowledgement of systemic barriers:

Limited Privacy

Sessions are often conducted in shared spaces. Students may fear being seen entering counselling, leading to stigma.

Time Constraints

High student-to-teacher ratios permit only brief sessions (20-30 minutes), typically 3-5 meetings at most.

Lack of Trained Professionals

Schools may lack licensed psychologists. Teachers functioning as counsellors may have minimal training in structured interventions.

Stigma and Minimization

Bullying is often normalized as "children being children." Parents may dismiss emotional distress as oversensitivity.

Language and Cultural Barriers

Students may struggle to articulate emotions verbally. Emotional vocabulary is often limited, requiring simple and culturally adapted explanations.

High Caseload

One counsellor may manage 20–30 referrals per month, making long-term therapy impractical. These constraints necessitate brief, structured, skill-based, scalable interventions.

Low-Resource Psychotherapy Plan

A Brief CBT-Informed Supportive Counselling Model combined with problem-solving and group psychoeducation is recommended. This model is chosen because:

1. CBT is structured and time-limited.
2. Skills can be taught quickly.
3. It is adaptable to non-specialist delivery (WHO, 2016).
4. It targets both emotional regulation and behavior change.

Session Structure

Format: 4 individual sessions (20-30 minutes each)

Optional: 1 follow-up session after 3 weeks

Supplement: 1 classroom-level psychoeducation session

Assessment

1. Olweus Bully/Victim Questionnaire.
2. Illinois Bully Scale.
3. Child Behaviour Checklist.
4. Peer Relations Questionnaire.

Session	Focus	Key Goals
Session 1	Assessment & Psychoeducation	Normalize emotions, explain bullying dynamics
Session 2	Emotional Regulation Skills	Teach grounding & calming techniques
Session 3	Cognitive & Assertiveness Skills	Address negative thoughts, practice assertive responses
Session 4	Problem-Solving & Safety Plan	Develop a coping plan, identify a support system

Key Techniques

Psychoeducation

Explain bullying as a behaviour problem of the aggressor, not a flaw in the victim. Use simple diagrams showing the "Thought-Feeling-Behaviour" triangle.

Example: "If someone says something hurtful, your mind may say, 'I am useless.' That thought creates sadness and withdrawal. We can learn to change our thoughts."

Grounding and Emotional Regulation

Teach simple breathing exercises

1. 4-4 breathing (inhale 4, exhale 4).
2. Muscle relaxation (tighten-release method).

3. 5-4-3-2-1 Technique - Using the 5-4-3-2-1 technique, you will purposefully take in the details of your surroundings using each of your senses. Strive to notice small details that your mind would usually tune out, such as distant sounds, or the texture of an ordinary object.
    a. What are 5 things you can see? Look for small details such as a pattern on the ceiling, the way light reflects off a surface, or an object you never noticed.
    b. What are 4 things you can feel? Notice the sensation of clothing on your body, the sun on your skin, or the feeling of the chair you are sitting in. Pick up an object and examine its weight, texture, and other physical qualities.
    c. What are 3 things you can hear? Pay special attention to the sounds your mind has tuned out, such as a ticking clock, distant traffic, or trees blowing in the wind.
    d. What are 2 things you can smell? Try to notice smells in the air around you, like an air freshener or freshly mowed grass. You may also look around for something that has a scent, such as a flower or an unlit candle.
    e. What is 1 thing you can taste? Carry gum, candy, or small snacks for this step. Pop one in your mouth and focus your attention closely on the flavors
4. Body Awareness - The body awareness technique will bring you into the here-and-now by directing your focus to sensations in the body. Pay special attention to the physical sensations created by each step.
    a. Take 5 long, deep breaths through your nose, and exhale through puckered lips.
    b. Place both feet flat on the floor. Wiggle your toes. Curl and uncurl your toes several times. Spend a moment noticing the sensations in your feet.

c. Stomp your feet on the ground several times. Pay attention to the sensations in your feet and legs as you make contact with the ground.

d. Clench your hands into fists, then release the tension. Repeat this 10 times.

e. Press your palms together. Press them harder and hold this pose for 15 seconds. Pay attention to the feeling of tension in your hands and arms.

f. Rub your palms together briskly. Notice and sound and the feeling of warmth.

g. Reach your hands over your head like you're trying to reach the sky. Stretch like this and bring your arms down and let them relax at your sides.

h. Take 5 more deep breaths and notice the feeling of calm in your body

These require no materials and can be practiced in class discreetly.

Cognitive Restructuring (Simplified)

Instead of full cognitive therapy, use basic thought-challenging questions:

Is this 100% true?

What would I say to a friend in this situation?

Replace: "I am ugly and no one likes me"

With: "Some students are teasing me, but not everyone dislikes me."

Assertiveness Training

Role-play simple assertive statements:

"Stop. I don't like that."

"Please don't speak about me that way."

Teach the difference between passive, aggressive, and assertive communication.

Problem-Solving Skills

Use a 4-step model:

1. What is the problem?
2. What are 3 possible solutions?
3. What might happen with each?
4. Choose one and try it.

Peer Support Mapping

Help student identify:

One safe friend

One trusted teacher

One adult at home

Classroom-Level Prevention

Conduct one 40-minute session covering:

1. What is bullying?
2. Bystander responsibility
3. Respectful communication

Evidence shows school-wide interventions reduce bullying prevalence (Olweus, 1993; WHO, 2020).

Ethical and Cultural Considerations

Confidentiality

Explain limits clearly:

"I will keep this private unless someone is in danger."

Given limited privacy, schedule sessions during free periods to reduce stigma.

Parental Consent

For minors, obtain written parental consent where possible. In low-literacy contexts, verbal consent with documentation may be necessary.

Cultural Sensitivity

Avoid imposing Western individualistic assertiveness norms. Adapt assertiveness to culturally respectful communication styles. Example: Instead of direct confrontation, teach: "I feel hurt when this happens."

Non-Labeling Approach

Avoid labelling students as "victims" or "bullies." Focus on behaviour, not identities.

Safety Protocol

If bullying involves physical harm or suicidal ideation:

a. Inform the school administration.
b. Refer to higher mental health services if available.
c. WHO (2016) recommends stepped-care approaches in low-resource settings.

Conclusion

Designing therapy for a low-resource school setting **emphasizes** that effective intervention does not always require intensive, long-term psychotherapy. Structured, brief, skills-based approaches can significantly reduce distress when adapted to contextual realities. The process highlights the importance of flexibility, cultural sensitivity, and systems-level thinking. It reinforces that school mental health must move beyond individual therapy toward preventive, scalable models that empower students, teachers, and peer systems.

References

American Psychological Association. (2020). Publication manual of the American Psychological Association (7th ed.). APA Publishing.

Arseneault, L. (2018). Annual research review: The persistent and pervasive impact of being bullied in childhood and adolescence. Journal of Child Psychology and Psychiatry, 59(4), 405-421.

Olweus, D. (1993). Bullying at school: What we know and what we can do. Blackwell Publishing.

World Health Organization. (2016). Problem management plus (PM+): Individual psychological help manual. WHO Press.

World Health Organization. (2020). School-based violence prevention: A practical handbook. WHO Press.

Chapter 3

Supporting First-Generation Learners: Brief Therapy in Rural Schools

– Rose Mary Rajesh

Introduction

In rural areas, schools are the only places where young people can get help with their education and emotions. A lot of students in these schools are first-generation learners, meaning they are the first in their families to go to school. These students often come from families where their parents did not go to school and cannot help them with schoolwork or emotional problems. Rural schools usually do not have a lot of resources. Teachers have to teach students at the same time, and it is hard to find people who are trained to help with emotional problems. School counsellors may only visit sometimes. They have to help many students, so they do not have a lot of time for each one.

First-generation learners face a lot of pressure. They have to deal with school work and also help their families with things like chores or work on the farm. Many students feel like they have to do well in school because their family is counting on them. Given these problems, brief therapy sessions in school can really help students feel better and do better in school. These sessions have to be practical, respectful of the students' culture, and able to fit into the time and space in rural schools._

Common Mental Health Issues in This Context

Students who are first-generation learners in schools often have a lot of emotional problems. One common problem is anxiety about schoolwork. Many students worry about tests, grades, and disappointing their families. Because their parents may not understand the school system, students often feel like they have to deal with school stress on their own. This anxiety can cause problems like trouble sleeping, difficulty concentrating, and avoiding schoolwork. Another problem is self-esteem and self-doubt. First-generation learners may compare themselves to students who come from families that value education more. They may feel like they are not as good as others or be embarrassed to ask questions in class. Over time, these feelings can make them less motivated and more likely to feel like they're not good enough. A third problem is stress and emotional distress. Students may struggle to balance school work with family responsibilities or financial pressures. Some may think about dropping out of school to work and support their families. Emotional symptoms like sadness, irritability, and loss of motivation can happen when students feel overwhelmed.

These emotional problems can hurt both school performance and overall well-being, making it essential to provide help in schools.

Limitations

One big problem is that there are no trained mental health professionals. Many rural schools do not have a full-time counsellor, so teachers or visiting psychologists have to provide support when they can. This means therapy has to be short, structured, and easy to deliver.

Another challenge is the lack of appropriate spaces for counselling. Schools may not have dedicated rooms for therapy sessions, so conversations may happen in classrooms, staff rooms, or outside, where people may interrupt. Keeping things confidential in these settings can be hard.

Time is also a problem. Counsellors may only have 10-20 minutes per student. They have to help many students in a short time. Long-term therapy is rarely possible.

Cultural and social factors can also limit help. In some communities, talking about problems is seen as a sign of weakness. Students might not want to share their difficulties because of stigma or fear of being judged.

Language barriers can also affect therapy. Some students may prefer to speak in their native language rather than the formal language used in school. Therapy approaches need to be flexible and respectful of cultures.

Because of these challenges, brief therapy approaches that focus on coping skills and emotional support are particularly useful in rural school settings.

Low-Resource Psychotherapy Plan

The proposed plan uses a Cognitive Behavioral Therapy (CBT) approach combined with supportive counselling. CBT techniques are helpful because they focus on identifying thoughts, managing anxiety, and developing practical coping strategies. Supportive counselling creates a space where students feel heard and understood.

This approach is suitable for schools because it is structured, time-efficient, and focused on practical skills that students can use on their own.

Session Structure

The intervention can be delivered in three to four sessions, each lasting about 20-30 minutes.

Session 1: Building Trust and Understanding*:* The first session focuses on building trust and understanding the students' concerns. The counsellor listens to the students' experiences. Provides information about stress and anxiety. The student learns that feeling worried about school is common and manageable.

Simple relaxation techniques like deep breathing exercises may be introduced to help reduce anxiety.

Session 2: Identifying Thoughts and Building Coping Skills*:* In the session, the counsellor helps the student identify negative thoughts related to school performance. The student is encouraged to question these thoughts and consider balanced alternatives. Practical strategies like breaking study tasks into steps, creating a basic study schedule, and seeking help from teachers are discussed.

Session 3: Problem-Solving and Confidence Building*:* This session focuses on developing problem-solving skills. The counsellor and student work together to identify challenges and possible solutions. The student practices thinking about problems in steps.

Positive reinforcement is used to build confidence and highlight the students' strengths.

Session 4: Review and Future Planning: If time allows, a follow-up session reviews progress and reinforces coping strategies.

The counsellor encourages the student to continue using learned techniques and to seek help if new difficulties arise.

Key Techniques to be Used

1. Psychoeducation helps students understand the relationship between thoughts, emotions, and behaviors. When students learn that anxiety is a response to pressure, it often reduces feelings of loneliness.
2. Breathing and grounding exercises are tools that can help manage immediate stress during exams or challenging situations.
3. Cognitive restructuring helps students challenge beliefs about their abilities and replace them with more realistic perspectives.
4. Problem-solving training allows students to approach difficulties systematically rather than feeling overwhelmed.
5. Strength-based encouragement helps students recognize their resilience and achievements, which is particularly important for those who may have limited academic role models.

Case Vignette

Anandi is a 15-year-old student in a rural government high school. She is the first person in her family to attend secondary school. Recently, her teachers noticed that she had become quieter in class and her test scores had begun to decline. When the school counsellor spoke with her, Anandi shared that she was constantly worried about failing her exams. She also felt pressure from her family, who hoped she would become the first graduate in the household.

She reported difficulty sleeping. Often felt nervous before tests. Believed that she was not as capable as her classmates and was afraid of disappointing her parents.

A brief counselling intervention was planned within the school setting. During the session, the counsellor explained how stress and anxiety can affect concentration and reassured Anandi that many students experience similar concerns. In the following sessions, the counsellor helped her identify thoughts about her abilities and replace them with more balanced ones. Simple breathing exercises were also introduced to help her relax before exams.

Over the course of three sessions, Anandi learned to break her study tasks into goals and ask teachers for clarification when needed. She reported feeling more confident and less overwhelmed by her responsibilities.

Ethical and Cultural Considerations

Providing support in rural school settings requires careful attention to ethical principles and cultural sensitivity.

1. Confidentiality is a concern, especially when counselling takes place in shared spaces. Counsellors must explain the limits of confidentiality. Ensure that personal information is protected as much as possible.
2. Informed consent should also be obtained before beginning counselling. In school settings, this may involve both the student and their parents or guardians.
3. Cultural sensitivity is particularly important. Counsellors must respect values, family structures, and community norms. For example, family expectations regarding education may strongly influence a student's experiences.

4. Language also plays a role. Counsellors should communicate in a way that's accessible and respectful of the students' linguistic background. Finally, counselors should be aware of power dynamics between teachers, counselors, and students. Students may feel hesitant to speak if they fear academic consequences.

Conclusion

Creating a therapy plan for a school with limited resources shows how important it is to make psychological help work in the real world. Mental health professionals often have to work in places where time, space, and staff are limited. This project shows that we can still give people support through short, structured, and culturally sensitive therapy sessions. It also shows that we need to be flexible, creative, and understanding when working with people who are vulnerable, such as students who are the first in their families to learn.

References

Beck, J. S. (2011). *Cognitive behavior therapy: Basics and beyond* (2nd ed.). Guilford Press.

Patel, V., Saxena, S., Lund, C., Thornicroft, G., Baingana, F., Bolton, P., & UnÜtzer, J. (2018). The Lancet Commission on global mental health and sustainable development. *The Lancet, 392*(10157), 1553–1598.

World Health Organization. (2021). *Guidance on community mental health services: Promoting person-centered and rights-based approaches.* WHO.

Hofmann, S. G., Asnaani, A., Vonk, I. J., Sawyer, A. T., & Fang, A. (2012). The efficacy of cognitive behavioral therapy: A review of meta-analyses. *Cognitive Therapy and Research, 36*(5), 427–440. UNESCO. (2020). *Inclusion and education: All means all.* UNESCO Publishing.

Chapter 4

School-Based Interventions for Adolescent Depression

– Jessa Elza Joby

Introduction

Schools are one of the most important environments in the lives of adolescents. Adolescents spend a large part of their day in schools, where they come in contact with teachers, peers, and other staff members of the school. Therefore, schools play an important role not only in the academic development of their students but also in the emotional and psychological development of their students. In many instances, schools are the first to identify emotional and behavioral problems in adolescents. This chapter deals with the school setting, especially government schools or institutions that have limited mental health resources. In many of these schools, access to professional psychological services may be limited or nonexistent. The teachers of the students may be the first to identify behavioral changes in their students, such as avoidance of activities, changes in mood, and decreased academic performance.

Adolescence is a period of life between the ages of 13 and 18 years. It is a period of great emotional, social, and psychological changes. At this period in life, adolescents face increased demands in terms of academics, social pressures, identity issues, and family issues. All these factors may contribute to emotional problems for adolescents. Therefore, since adolescents may not seek help from mental health professionals in their communities, school-based interventions are crucial. Such an intervention is important because it can help in the early identification of emotional problems and provide adolescents with timely assistance for their problems. Even in a resource-constrained environment, simple but effective strategies can be implemented in a school setting to assist adolescents in their mental health.

Common Mental Health Issues in This Context

Students in a school setting may encounter several emotional and psychological issues, and among those, depression, academic stress, and peer relationship issues are some of the common ones identified.

Adolescent Depression

Depression is a major emotional and psychological problem for teenagers. Depression is described as a state of low mood, loss of interest in activities, fatigue, and difficulty concentrating. In a school setting, if a student is depressed, it may reflect in the student's declining academic performance, irritability, or withdrawal from social interactions with peers. If depression is not identified at an early stage, it may impact the student's emotional and psychological well-being.

Academic Stress

Academic pressure and demands from parents, teachers, and society may cause academic stress among students. Prolonged academic pressure may lead to anxiety, sleep disorders, irritability, difficulty concentrating, and feelings of inadequacy. Academic stress may also lead to depression if not managed properly.

Peer Relationship Issues and Bullying

Peer relationships play a vital role in the emotional and psychological development of an adolescent. While positive peer relationships may contribute to the emotional and psychological development of an adolescent, negative peer relationship issues, such as bullying, may impact the student's emotional and psychological well-being.

Limitations

Despite schools being an ideal environment for mental health support, several factors act as a challenge in providing effective mental health support.

Lack of trained mental health professionals

The absence of psychologists or counselors in schools, especially in under-resourced environments, is a limitation in providing adequate counseling services to students. The responsibility falls on teachers, and teachers are not trained in counseling.

Lack of privacy in counseling

The absence of a counseling room in a school setting may make students feel uncomfortable talking openly about their problems.

Time constraint

The school calendar is mostly dedicated to academic activities, leaving limited time for counseling activities. The students may feel uncomfortable missing classes to attend counseling sessions. The stigma associated with seeking counseling services is a limitation in providing counseling services to students.

Student-counselor ratio

The number of students and the limited number of counselors in a school setting may make it difficult to provide counseling services to every student in need.

Low-Resource Psychotherapy Plan

A practical approach for school settings is brief Cognitive Behavioral Therapy (CBT) combined with supportive counselling. CBT is widely used to help individuals understand the relationship between their thoughts, emotions, and behaviors. It helps adolescents recognize negative thinking patterns and develop healthier ways of coping with challenges. Supportive counseling would involve creating a comfortable environment in which students feel supported and understood. This would be particularly effective for teenagers who may feel isolated or misunderstood in society.

Session Structure

This intervention can be carried out in four to six sessions, each lasting around 30 to 40 minutes. The sessions can be carried out in individual or small groups, depending on the resources available. One possible format for the intervention is as follows:

Session 1: Building rapport and providing psychoeducation about depression and emotional health.

Session 2: Helping students identify negative thoughts and emotional patterns.

Session 3: Teaching cognitive restructuring techniques to challenge negative thinking.

Session 4: Developing problem-solving skills and coping strategies.

Session 5: Introducing stress management and relaxation techniques.

Session 6: Reviewing progress and discussing strategies for maintaining emotional well-being.

In addition, working in small groups with a few students is another effective intervention, where students can share experiences and support each other.

Key Techniques to be Used

There are a number of simple and evidence-based strategies that can be employed during this intervention. Psychoeducation can be used to enlighten students on what depression is and how it affects thoughts, emotions, and behavior. Cognitive restructuring can be used to enable students to identify negative thoughts such as "I am not good enough" or "I always fail." The counselor can then challenge these negative thoughts and change them. Problem-solving skills can be used to enable students to deal with problems or difficulties in a systematic and constructive manner. Students can be helped to identify problems, generate possible solutions, and evaluate these options. Relaxation and grounding can be used to enable students to deal with stress and tension. Behavioral activation can be used to enable students to get involved in meaningful and pleasant activities such as sports, creative pursuits, and hanging out with friends. All these strategies are simple and can be used even in a school setting with limited resources.

Case Vignette

Ananya, a 15-year-old student in a government high school, was referred to the school counsellor by her teacher, as her academic performance had been declining, and she had been socially withdrawing. She complained of feeling sad most of the time, losing interest in things she used to enjoy, and feeling pressured about her studies. The school had limited resources, and there was no private room for counselling. A brief intervention was planned, which included psycho-education on depression, identification of negative thoughts, and simple coping skills and relaxation techniques.

Ethical and Cultural Considerations

When providing psychological support in schools, it is important to abide by ethical principles and respect cultural values. Confidentiality is important, and students should feel comfortable to share their problems with the psychologist, but at the same time, students should be made aware that confidentiality may be broken if there is a potential harm to themselves or others. Informed consent is important prior to providing counseling, and this may involve consent from the student's parents or guardian, depending on the school's policies and the student's age. The psychologist should also observe professional boundaries, and the relationship should be student-centered. Moreover, cultural sensitivity is important, and students come from different cultural backgrounds and may have different beliefs regarding mental health issues. Respecting students' differences is important in establishing trust and providing a supportive counseling environment.

Conclusion

In designing a plan for a psychotherapy intervention in a school setting with limited resources, there is a need to appreciate the value of creativity in a mental health intervention setting. Despite limited resources, a student in emotional distress can benefit from a well-structured intervention plan. The potential role that schools can play in promoting positive mental health and in preventing serious psychological problems cannot be overstated. This intervention plan has also taught me that, in spite of limited resources, a student in emotional distress can benefit from a well-structured intervention plan, and that schools can play a significant role in promoting positive mental health and in preventing serious psychological problems.

References

Beck, J. S. (2011). *Cognitive behavior therapy: Basics and beyond* (2nd ed.). Guilford Press.

Patel, V., Saxena, S., & Lund, C. (2018). The Lancet Commission on global mental health and sustainable development. *The Lancet, 392*(10157), 1553–1598.

Stallard, P. (2019). *Think good – feel good: A cognitive behaviour therapy workbook for children and young people.* Wiley-Blackwell.

World Health Organization. (2021). *Guideline on school-based mental health interventions.* World Health Organization.

Weisz, J. R., & Kazdin, A. E. (2017). *Evidence-based psychotherapies for children and adolescents* (3rd ed.). Guilford Press.

Chapter 5

Group Counselling for Social Anxiety among High School Students

– *Bhumika R Pyati*

Introduction

Social Anxiety Disorder (SAD) is a psychological condition in which individuals experience an intense and ongoing fear of being negatively judged, criticized, or evaluated by others during social interactions. This disorder frequently begins during adolescence, a stage of development when peer relationships, social approval, and identity formation become especially significant. For many high school students, daily school life involves numerous social interactions such as giving classroom presentations, participating in group discussions, engaging in extracurricular activities, and communicating through digital platforms. For adolescents who struggle with social anxiety, these situations can provoke strong feelings of nervousness, embarrassment, and self-consciousness (Myers & Davis, 2018).

For students experiencing social anxiety, ordinary school activities may feel extremely challenging or even overwhelming. They may hesitate to raise their hands in class, avoid speaking with classmates, or withdraw from school events because they fear being judged or making mistakes in front of others. Over time, this pattern of avoidance can affect several areas of their lives, including academic performance, peer relationships, and emotional well-being. Research suggests that between 7% and 15% of adolescents experience noticeable symptoms of social anxiety, making it one of the most prevalent anxiety disorders among teenagers (Myers & Davis, 2018).

Group counselling has become an increasingly useful intervention for adolescents experiencing social anxiety within school environments. Participating in counselling groups allows students to interact with peers who share similar experiences and concerns. Realizing that others face similar struggles can help reduce feelings of isolation and promote a sense of understanding and acceptance within the group (Beidel et al., 2010). Early support during adolescence is particularly important, as timely intervention can prevent the development of more severe psychological difficulties later in life, such as depression, substance misuse, or long-term social withdrawal.

Social Anxiety

Social anxiety involves a strong fear of situations in which individuals believe they might be observed, evaluated, or criticized by others. Adolescents who experience this form of anxiety often worry excessively about appearing awkward, saying something wrong, or embarrassing themselves in front of peers. Because of these fears, they may avoid common social situations such as speaking in class, eating in public spaces like the school cafeteria, or participating in group activities (Pflug & Wittchen, 2008). This condition typically includes both physical and psychological symptoms. Physical symptoms may involve sweating, trembling, blushing, rapid heartbeat, or difficulty speaking clearly in social situations. At the same time, adolescents with social anxiety often develop negative thought patterns that strengthen their fears. For instance, they may assume that everyone around them is constantly watching or evaluating their behavior, or they may believe that even minor mistakes will lead to embarrassment or rejection. These thoughts contribute to a cycle in which anxiety leads to avoidance, and avoidance reinforces the anxiety over time (Pflug & Wittchen, 2008).

During the high school years, social anxiety can influence many aspects of a student's life. Students may struggle to build friendships, participate confidently in classroom discussions, or become involved in extracurricular activities. If these challenges persist without proper support, they may lead to additional psychological difficulties such as low self-esteem, depressive symptoms, and decreased academic engagement (Hashim & Othman, n.d.).

Theoretical Foundations of Group Counselling

Many counselling programs developed for adolescents with social anxiety are grounded in the principles of Cognitive Behavioral Therapy (CBT). CBT is widely recognized as one of the most effective therapeutic approaches for treating anxiety disorders. The primary goal of CBT is to help individuals identify unrealistic or negative thought patterns and replace them with more balanced and constructive ways of thinking. By modifying these thought processes, individuals can gradually develop healthier emotional reactions and behavioral responses (Beidel et al., 2010).

In addition to changing thought patterns, CBT-based group counselling often incorporates behavioral techniques such as gradual exposure and social skills training. Exposure exercises encourage students to slowly confront situations that usually cause anxiety, allowing them to build confidence and reduce fear through repeated practice. Social skills training focuses on strengthening communication abilities, including initiating conversations, maintaining appropriate eye contact, and expressing ideas confidently during interactions with others (Kipper, 2022).

Another theoretical framework that contributes to group counselling effectiveness is Yalom's concept of therapeutic factors in group therapy. According to this perspective, several elements within group settings promote positive psychological change. These include universality, group cohesion, interpersonal learning, and altruism. When adolescents realize that others in the group share similar fears and experiences, they often feel less alone and more understood. This sense of shared experience can strengthen group relationships and encourage participants to engage more openly in the counselling process (Hashim & Othman, n.d.).

Structured interventions such as the Skills for Academic and Social Success (SASS) program combine CBT techniques with group-based learning activities designed specifically for adolescents experiencing social anxiety. These programs typically include psychoeducation, role-playing activities, and gradual exposure tasks that allow students to practice social interactions in a supportive and controlled environment (Beidel et al., 2010).

Benefits of Group Counselling for High School Students

Group counselling offers several important advantages for adolescents dealing with social anxiety. One of the most valuable aspects of group counselling is the opportunity for peer support. When students interact with others who share similar fears and experiences, they often feel more understood and less isolated (Hashim & Othman, n.d.).

Another benefit is the opportunity to practice social skills in a supportive and non-judgmental environment. Through activities such as role-playing, group discussions, and feedback sessions, students can gradually improve their communication abilities and develop greater confidence in interacting with others. Observing how peers manage similar challenges can also help participants learn practical strategies for coping with anxiety.

Group counselling is also beneficial from a practical perspective within school settings. Since counselors can work with several students at the same time, group sessions make mental health support more accessible to a larger number of students. Studies suggest that CBT-based group interventions can produce moderate to significant reductions in social anxiety symptoms among adolescents (Kipper, 2022).

Furthermore, the supportive atmosphere of group sessions can help maintain motivation among participants. Seeing other group members overcome their fears and make progress often encourages students to challenge their own anxieties and continue applying the strategies they have learned.

Designing the Group Counselling Program

A well-structured group counselling program for adolescents with social anxiety usually includes between eight and twelve sessions, with each session lasting approximately 45 to 60 minutes. Groups typically consist of six to ten students between the ages of 14 and 18. Using a closed group format, where the same participants attend each session, helps build trust and encourages open communication among members (Kraft, 2024).

Before joining the counselling group, students may undergo screening using standardized assessment tools such as the Social Anxiety Scale for Adolescents (SAS-A). These assessments help counsellors determine whether group counselling is suitable for each student and identify individuals who may require additional individual support (Kipper, 2022).

Parents and teachers can also play a supportive role in the counselling process. Providing psychoeducation to caregivers helps them understand the nature of social anxiety and encourages them to support students in practicing coping strategies outside the counselling sessions. Homework tasks are often included in group counselling programs to help students apply newly learned skills in real-life situations.

Outline for Sessions

Sessions 1-2: Building Rapport and Psychoeducation: The first few sessions focus on helping group members feel comfortable and establishing trust among participants. Counsellors provide basic information about anxiety and explain the connection between thoughts, emotions, and behaviors. Interactive discussions and activities help students understand how negative thinking patterns can contribute to feelings of anxiety (Kraft, 2024). Icebreaker activities may also be used to encourage communication and create a relaxed group atmosphere.

Sessions 3-5: Social Skills Development: During these sessions, the focus shifts toward strengthening communication and interpersonal skills. Students practice skills such as initiating conversations, maintaining eye contact, listening actively, and expressing opinions clearly. Role-playing exercises allow participants to practice these skills in simulated situations while receiving constructive feedback from both the counsellor and fellow group members (Hashim & Othman, n.d.).

Sessions 6-9: Exposure and Behavioral Practice: Exposure exercises are an important component of CBT-based treatment for social anxiety. In these sessions, students gradually face situations that typically cause them discomfort. Activities may include giving short presentations, initiating conversations with peers, or participating in structured group discussions. Counsellors may use tools such as the Subjective Units of Distress Scale (SUDS) to help students track their anxiety levels during these activities (Beidel et al., 2010).

Sessions 10-12: Review and Relapse Prevention: The final sessions focus on reviewing the skills learned throughout the counselling program. Students are encouraged to reflect on their progress and identify strategies that have been most helpful in managing their anxiety. Participants may also create personal coping plans that outline how they will deal with future social challenges such as presentations, new social interactions, or school events (Kraft, 2024).

Evidence of Effectiveness

Research strongly supports the effectiveness of CBT-based group counselling for adolescents experiencing social anxiety. Studies indicate that structured group interventions can significantly improve social confidence and reduce symptoms of anxiety (Kipper, 2022). Programs such as the Skills for Academic and Social Success (SASS) intervention have reported improvement rates of approximately 70% to 80% among participants. Many students continue to show progress even after the program has concluded, suggesting that the coping strategies developed during counselling have long-term benefits (Beidel et al., 2010).

Students who participate in these programs frequently report increased self-confidence, improved ability to interact with peers, and greater involvement in academic and social activities. The skills they learn during group counselling can also help them manage stressful situations outside of the school environment.

Practical Implementations in Schools

For group counselling programs to be successful in schools, collaboration among counsellors, teachers, administrators, and parents is essential. Students who may benefit from counselling can be identified through teacher referrals, counselling assessments, or self-report questionnaires (Kraft, 2024).

Counsellors conducting these programs should be trained in both cognitive behavioral techniques and group facilitation skills. Scheduling sessions during free periods or after school can help minimize disruption to students' academic responsibilities. Monitoring students' progress through questionnaires, discussions, and observations can also help evaluate the effectiveness of the program.

Ethical Considerations and Limitations

When conducting group counselling with adolescents, counsellors must follow important ethical guidelines. Informed consent should be obtained from both students and their parents or guardians before the counselling program begins. Counsellors must also emphasize confidentiality within the group to ensure that participants feel safe sharing personal experiences (Kraft, 2024).

Although group counselling can be beneficial for many adolescents with social anxiety, it may not be suitable for everyone. Students experiencing severe anxiety or more complex psychological conditions may require individual therapy or a combination of therapy and medication (Kipper, 2022). In some schools, challenges such as limited mental health resources or stigma surrounding counselling may also affect the implementation of such programs.

Conclusion

Social anxiety is a common psychological concern among high school students and can significantly affect their academic performance, social relationships, and emotional well-being if left unaddressed. Group counselling offers an effective and accessible way to support adolescents experiencing social anxiety within school settings. By combining cognitive-behavioral techniques, peer support, and structured skill-building activities, group counselling helps students develop confidence, strengthen social interactions, and learn practical strategies for managing anxiety. Implementing such programs in schools can play an important role in promoting adolescent mental health and helping students develop resilience that supports them throughout their lives.

References

Beidel, D. C., Turner, S. M., & Morris, T. L. (2010). Facing your fear: Group therapy for social anxiety disorder in adolescents. Journal of Anxiety Disorders.

Hashim, S. N. A., & Othman, Z. (n.d.). Adolescent social anxiety: The usage of cognitive behavioural approach in group counselling. Social and Psychological Academic Journal.

Kipper, E. (2022). Diagnosis-specific group CBT treating social anxiety in adolescents. Journal of Clinical Child and Adolescent Psychology.

Kraft, S. (2024). Anxiety group for teens group manual. Minnesota State University Moorhead.

Myers, F., & Davis, J. (2018). Understanding social anxiety disorder in adolescents. Adolescent Health, Medicine and Therapeutics.

Pflug, V., & Wittchen, H. (2008). Cognitive behavior therapy for generalized social anxiety disorder. Psychiatric Clinics.

Ryan, J. L., & Masia Warner, C. (2012). Treating adolescents with social anxiety disorder in schools. Child and Adolescent Psychiatric Clinics of North America, 21(1), 105–118. https://doi.org/10.1016/j.chc.2011.08.011

Hashim, S. N. A., & Othman, Z. (n.d.). Adolescent social anxiety: The usage of cognitive behavioural approach in group counseling. SPAJ UKM.

Kraft, S. (2024). Anxiety group for teens group manual (Master's thesis). Minnesota State University.Moorhead. https://red.mnstate.edu/cgi/viewcontent.cgi?article=1956&context=thesis

Myers, F., & Davis, J. (2018). Understanding social anxiety disorder in adolescents. Adolescent Health, Medicine andTherapeutics.

CBT Psychology. (2025). Group for teens with social anxiety.

Kipper, E. (2022). Diagnosis-specific group CBT treating social anxiety in adolescents. Frontiers in Psychiatry.

Pflug, V., & Wittchen, H. U. (2008). Cognitive behavior therapy for generalized social anxiety disorder. Psychiatric Clinics of North America.

Chapter 6

Addressing Behavioural Problems in Low-Resource School Settings

– Chaitanya Vankrothu

Introduction

Have you ever wondered whether a child who appears disruptive, inattentive, or withdrawn in the classroom might actually be struggling with emotional distress? In many classrooms, behavioural problems are often interpreted simply as discipline issues talking during lessons, refusing to complete assignments, arguing with peers, or avoiding class participation. However, these behaviours frequently reflect deeper challenges such as poverty, family stress, academic pressure, or unmet emotional needs. In many public schools, particularly in low-resource settings, classrooms may contain more than forty students with limited educational materials and high academic demands placed on teachers. Within such environments, some students display disruptive behaviour, others remain silent and withdrawn, and some gradually disengage from learning. These behavioural patterns are not isolated incidents but often reflect broader developmental and social circumstances.

Teachers in these schools frequently manage behavioural difficulties without formal training in psychology or mental health. As a result, responses are often discipline-focused rather than supportive or preventive. Traditional psychotherapy models designed for clinical settings are rarely feasible in such environments due to limited resources, lack of specialists, and time constraints. This chapter explores behavioural challenges commonly observed in low-resource school settings and discusses practical, culturally sensitive, and scalable psychological interventions that can be integrated into existing school systems. By understanding behaviour as a form of communication rather than simply misconduct, schools can support both students' emotional well-being and academic success.

Low-resource schools are educational environments that operate under financial, infrastructural, and human resource constraints. In India, particularly within government schools across southern states, these institutions often serve children from socio-economically disadvantaged communities. Schools frequently face challenges such as overcrowded classrooms, limited teaching materials, and high student–teacher ratios, while formal mental health services are largely absent. Students in these schools typically range from 6 to 16 years of age and many are first-generation learners. Their families may experience economic instability, seasonal migration, or employment in agriculture and informal labor sectors. These social and economic conditions influence children's emotional regulation, behaviour, and academic engagement.

Teachers in such settings perform multiple roles beyond teaching, including classroom management, emotional support, and conflict resolution. Despite these responsibilities, most educators receive little training in identifying or responding to psychological concerns among students. School counselors are rarely available, and referrals to external mental health services are often limited by cost, transportation barriers, and stigma. Recent studies estimate that approximately 13–15% of school-aged children in India experience emotional or behavioural difficulties, yet only a small proportion receive professional mental health support. In addition, national education surveys indicate that many government schools operate with student–teacher ratios exceeding 40:1, which further limits individualized attention. Research from low- and middle-income countries indicates that schools can serve as key locations for early identification and intervention for children's mental health concerns (Fazel et al., 2014; Jordans et al., 2021). Behavioural issues observed in classrooms such as aggression, inattentiveness, or social withdrawal, often signal unmet emotional or developmental needs.

Common Mental Health Issues in This Context

Behavioural difficulties in low-resource schools are rarely isolated psychological disorders. Instead, they often represent children's responses to environmental stressors, developmental challenges, and unmet emotional needs.

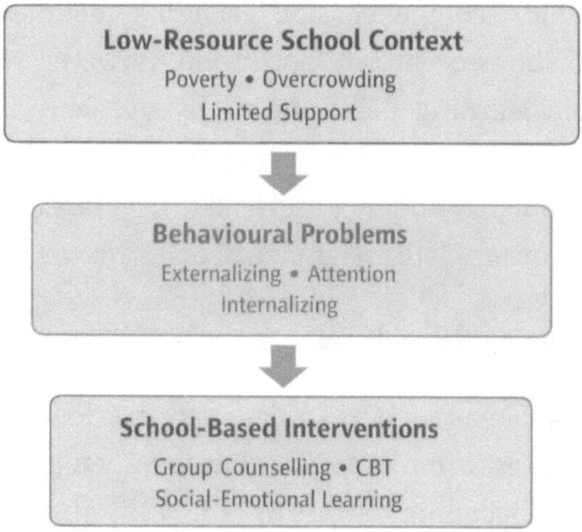

Figure 1: Conceptual framework illustrating the relationship between low-resource school contexts, behavioural problems, and school-based intervention strategies aimed at improving students' emotional well-being and academic engagement.

Externalizing Behaviour Problems

Externalizing behaviour are among the most frequently reported classroom difficulties. These behaviours include aggression, defiance, impulsivity, classroom disruptions, bullying, and refusal to follow instructions. Although these behaviours are often viewed as disciplinary problems, research suggests they may reflect emotional distress, frustration with academic difficulties, or stressful home environments. Children who experience inconsistent caregiving, financial hardship, or family conflict may have difficulty regulating their emotions. In overcrowded classrooms where individual attention is limited, disruptive behaviour may become a way to seek attention or express distress.

Attention Problems and Academic Difficulties

Attention problems and low academic engagement are also common in under-resourced classrooms. Students may appear distracted, restless, or unable to complete tasks. Teachers sometimes interpret this behaviour as laziness or lack of motivation. However, such behaviour may arise from learning difficulties, language barriers, or anxiety related to academic performance. Repeated academic failure may gradually reduce self-confidence and lead to avoidance behaviour such as absenteeism, incomplete assignments, or classroom disengagement.

Internalizing Emotional Problems

Internalizing problems such as anxiety, sadness, low self-esteem, and social withdrawal are often less visible but equally significant. Children experiencing socioeconomic stress or family instability may live with chronic emotional pressure without opportunities to express their feelings. Because these students rarely disrupt classroom activities, their emotional distress may remain unnoticed until it begins to affect academic performance or peer relationships. Understanding behaviour within its broader social and developmental context allows educators to view behaviour as communication rather than simply misconduct.

Major Constraints in Low-Resource Schools

Addressing behavioural difficulties in low-resource schools requires an understanding of the practical barriers that influence intervention efforts.

Limited Access to Mental Health Professionals

Most government schools do not employ trained psychologists or counselors. Teachers are therefore responsible for managing behavioural concerns despite limited training in mental health. Referral to external services is often difficult due to financial and geographic barriers.

Academic Time Constraints

School schedules are heavily focused on completing academic syllabi and preparing students for examinations. Teachers have limited time to conduct individual counselling sessions, making lengthy therapeutic interventions unrealistic.

Overcrowded Classrooms

Classrooms often contain 40–60 students or more. Such large class sizes reduce opportunities for individualized attention and make classroom management a major priority for teachers.

Mental Health Stigma

In many communities, behavioural problems are attributed to poor discipline or lack of Therapy Approach effort rather than emotional distress. Parents may hesitate to accept psychological interventions due to fear of stigma or social labeling.

Cultural and Linguistic Diversity

Government schools frequently include students from diverse linguistic and cultural backgrounds. Interventions must therefore be flexible and adapted to local cultural contexts.

Given these constraints, mental health programs in schools must be brief, group-based, culturally adaptable, and integrated into everyday classroom practices.

Low-Resource Psychotherapy Strategy

The initiative offers psychological support to under-resourced school systems via brief group therapy sessions aimed at teaching students' emotional regulation and problem-solving techniques without the necessity for comprehensive clinical treatment. The application of these strategies is feasible in educational environments that encounter limitations regarding time, physical resources, and the availability of mental health professionals.

This intervention integrates short-term Cognitive Behavioural Therapy (CBT) techniques with supportive counseling and components of social-emotional learning. The execution of small group sessions aids in reducing stigma while allowing a greater number of students to access psychological support through the resources already present in schools.

The program comprises eight to ten student groups that engage in six structured sessions, each lasting between 35 to 40 minutes, conducted on a weekly basis. The intervention can be carried out by trained educators and school counselors who are capable of facilitating sessions in schools that do not have access to mental health practitioners.

The sessions utilize several key methods for effective implementation. The content of the sessions includes psychoeducational resources on emotional and behavioral issues, along with activities designed to assist students in recognizing and expressing their feelings, as well as structured problem-solving techniques that incorporate the "Stop-Think-Act" approach.

The program instructs students in breathing techniques and grounding exercises to help them manage their stress and emotional reactions. It employs positive reinforcement alongside social skills training to encourage behaviors that foster successful teamwork and the development of friendships. The combined approaches of this program aim to improve students' ability to recognize their emotions, regulate their feelings, and cultivate social skills that contribute to their success in school and the maintenance of their mental well-being.

Hypothetical Case

Consider the example of Ravi, a 12-year-old student studying in a government school in rural South India. Ravi frequently interrupts lessons, refuses to complete assignments, and often argues with classmates. Teachers initially interpret his behaviour as disobedience. However, during a small group counselling program, Ravi reveals that his parents recently migrated for work, leaving him with relatives. He reports feeling lonely and struggling with school subjects, which makes him frustrated during lessons.

Through group sessions focused on emotional awareness and problem-solving, Ravi learns to identify his feelings and practice calming techniques when he becomes upset. Teachers also begin providing positive feedback for small improvements in his classroom behaviour. Over time, Ravi's disruptions decrease, and he becomes more engaged in class activities. This example illustrates how behavioural difficulties can reflect underlying emotional challenges that can be addressed through supportive school-based interventions.

Ethical and Cultural Considerations

Psychological interventions in schools must be implemented with careful attention to ethical and cultural factors. Confidentiality should be explained to students in simple, age-appropriate language. Informed consent must be obtained from both parents and students before participation in counselling activities. Teachers serving as facilitators must maintain professional boundaries and refer students experiencing severe distress to specialized services whenever possible.

Cultural sensitivity is equally important. Activities should incorporate local languages and culturally familiar examples. Presenting sessions as "life skills" or "well-being programs" rather than mental health treatment may reduce stigma and increase acceptance among families and school communities.

Conclusion

Behavioural problems in low-resource schools often reflect broader social, emotional, and developmental challenges rather than simple disciplinary issues. Factors such as poverty, family stress, overcrowded classrooms, and limited mental health resources significantly influence student behaviour. Despite these constraints, schools remain one of the most accessible environments for early psychological support. Brief, group-based interventions that integrate cognitive-behavioural techniques and social-emotional learning can provide practical and culturally appropriate support for students. Strengthening teachers' awareness of behavioural and emotional difficulties, along with implementing scalable school-based mental health programs, can play an important role in improving both the well-being and academic outcomes of children in low-resource educational settings.

References

Barry, M. M., Clarke, A. M., Jenkins, R., & Patel, V. (2013). A systematic review of the effectiveness of mental health promotion interventions for young people in low- and middle-income countries. *BMC Public Health, 13*, 835.

Bradshaw, M., Gericke, H., Coetzee, B. J., Stallard, P., Human, S., & Loades, M. (2021). Universal school-based mental health programmes in low- and middle-income countries: A systematic review and narrative synthesis. *Preventive Medicine, 143*(106317), 106317.

Fazel, M., Patel, V., Thomas, S., & Tol, W. (2014). Mental health interventions in schools in low- and middle-income countries. *The Lancet Psychiatry, 1*(5), 388–398.

Grande, A. J., Berdzenishvili, A., da Silva, V., & Moreira, A. (2023). School-based mental health interventions for children and adolescents: A systematic review and meta-analysis. *Frontiers in Psychiatry, 14*, 1012257.

Jordans, M. J. D., et al. (2021). Scaling up school mental health services in low-resource settings: Evidence from public schools. *International Journal of Mental Health Systems, 15*, 60.

Chapter 7

Brief Interventions for Attention and Concentration Problems in Classrooms

– Prajukta Pal

Introduction

This chapter focuses on government-sponsored secondary schools in India (Grades VI–X) across rural, semi-urban, and urban regions in different states and union territories. These schools serve approximately 118 million students (UDISE+, 2022), many of whom come from economically disadvantaged backgrounds, including Scheduled Caste and Scheduled Tribe communities, migrant families, and first-generation learners. Government schools typically have large class sizes of 35-60 students and rely mainly on lecture-based teaching. Many schools lack a full-time school counsellor, and in some cases, counsellors are shared across multiple schools. As a result, mental health services are rarely integrated into the school system. Although the Samagra Shiksha Abhiyan recommends school-based counselling, implementation varies widely across states (Ministry of Education, 2020).

Given these constraints, brief, structured, and low-cost psychological interventions that can be delivered to small groups of students are more feasible. This chapter presents a brief intervention programme aimed at improving attention, concentration, and academic engagement among adolescents through short group-based sessions delivered within the school setting.

Common Mental Health Issues in This Context

Attention-Deficit and Executive Dysfunction Presentations

The most prevalent clinical concern referred within government school settings involves persistent inattention, impaired inhibitory control, and deficits in working memory consistent with ADHD, predominantly inattentive presentation (DSM-5-TR; American Psychiatric Association, 2022). Epidemiological evidence cites global prevalence at 5% to 7% in school-aged children (American Psychiatric Association, 2022), with Indian studies yielding comparable rates (Grover et al., 2021). In the absence of formal diagnostic infrastructure, presentations are typically identified through teacher-report of off-task behaviour, failure to sustain effort across academic tasks, and chronic underperformance, rather than through structured clinical assessment. Subclinical attentional dysregulation attributable to sleep deprivation, nutritional insufficiency, and chronic psychosocial stress is substantially more prevalent and constitutes the primary target population for the present intervention.

Comorbid Anxiety and Cognitive Interference

Performance anxiety, characterized by high levels of anticipatory worrying, somatic hyperarousal, and avoidance of evaluative academic situations, represents a major but often undetected comorbidity in this group. Anxiety plays a role in cognitive interference by draining working memory resources through ruminative thinking and hypervigilant threat detection, which in turn exacerbates pre-existing deficits in EF (Clark & Beck, 2011). The complex relationship between anxiety and inattention in the high-stakes testing context of Indian secondary education is a two-way street and should not be ignored in any comprehensive formulation.

Depressive Symptomatology and Motivational Deficits

A clinically relevant group of students can be characterized by dysthymic symptoms, which include anhedonia, cognitive slowness, diminished self-efficacy, and behavioral withdrawal from academic engagement. These symptoms are often misattributed by educators and school staff to students' dispositional laziness and/or voluntary non-compliance. Neuropsychologically, depression-related symptoms affect prefrontal regulation of attentional control and dopaminergic modulation of motivational processes (American Psychiatric Association, 2022), resulting in a presentation that is identical to primary ADHD but requires differential clinical management that prioritizes behavioral activation before building cognitive skills.

Key Constraints and Limitations

The delivery of evidence-based psychological intervention in government school settings across India is substantially shaped by structural and systemic barriers that require explicit integration into clinical planning. Table 1 maps the primary constraints to their clinical impact and corresponding adaptive strategies.

Table 1: Structural Constraints and Adaptive Clinical Responses Across Indian Government School Settings

Constraint	Clinical Impact	Adaptive Strategy
Large class sizes (35-60 students)	Impedes individualised case formulation and therapeutic rapport	Universal SDQ screening; small-group CBT delivery (6-8 students)

Constraint	Clinical Impact	Adaptive Strategy
Absent or shared counsellor	Insufficient therapeutic contact hours; no clinical supervision	Manualised five-session protocol; peer co-facilitation model
No private clinical space	Breach of therapeutic frame; reduced client disclosure	Scheduled library or post-school sessions; confidentiality briefing
Mental health stigma	Treatment avoidance; caregiver non-consent	Psychoeducational framing as cognitive skills training
Linguistic and literacy diversity	Assessment tool invalidity; inaccessible psychoeducation	Pictorial, low-literacy materials; local language adaptation
Rural infrastructure deficits	No digital tools; irregular school attendance	Paper-based, session-independent take-home materials

Low-Resource Psychotherapy Plan

Theoretical Orientation and Clinical Rationale

The intervention is informed by a Brief Cognitive Behavioral Therapy (brief CBT) model adapted specifically for a school-based intervention (Stallard, 2019). The decision to utilise a CBT framework is informed by its established effectiveness in ADHD symptomology, performance anxiety, and co-occurring depressive symptomatology in children and young people, its appropriateness in a trans-diagnostic case formulation framework, and its suitability in a structured group intervention format. With regard to students demonstrating motivational withdrawal and depressive symptomatology, Behavioral Activation (BA) techniques are utilized in Session 2 to interrupt operant avoidance patterns prior to introducing cognitive techniques. Adapted Mindfulness-Based Attention Training (MBAT) techniques to increase sustained attention and metacognitive skills are also utilized in brief formats throughout the intervention. The intervention's theoretical model of attentional dysregulation is informed by models of executive dysfunction, cognitive appraisal, and avoidance behavior, and is amenable to modification in a structured skills acquisition format in a therapeutic context.

Session Structure and Format

The intervention programme consists of five structured group sessions, each lasting 45 minutes and conducted weekly over a period of five weeks. Groups include six to eight students who are identified through teacher-administered screening using the Strengths and Difficulties Questionnaire (SDQ) (Goodman, 1997). Each session follows a consistent three-part structure: a brief check-in and review of between-session practice (5 minutes), the main psychoeducation and skills training component (30 minutes), and a closing segment focused on summarising key learning and assigning practice activities for the following week (10 minutes). When additional support is required, up to two individual booster sessions may be provided to reinforce the strategies introduced during the group programme. Table 2 presents a session-by-session overview of the intervention.

Table 2: Five-Session Clinical Intervention Overview

No.	Clinical Focus	Techniques and Clinical Content	Duration
1	Psychoeducation and Therapeutic Alliance	Biopsychosocial formulation of inattention; neuropsychological rationale for executive dysfunction; normalisation of ADHD-spectrum presentations; collaborative goal-setting using motivational interviewing principles; introduction of SDQ self-report	45 min
2	Metacognitive Monitoring and Behavioural Activation	Self-monitoring of attentional states using structured attention logs; identification of antecedent triggers for off-task behaviour; behavioural activation scheduling to counter avoidance and motivational withdrawal; introduction of token reinforcement contingencies	45 min
3	Cognitive Restructuring	Elicitation of maladaptive cognitive schemas (e.g., "I am stupid," "I cannot control my mind"); Socratic questioning and guided discovery to challenge distorted appraisals; development of balanced alternative cognitions; construction of personalised coping cards for use under cognitive load	45 min

4	Executive Function Skills Training	Psychoeducation on working memory and inhibitory control deficits; implementation intentions (if-then planning) to reduce prospective memory failures; structured task decomposition; graded exposure to sustained-attention tasks with progressive duration; diaphragmatic breathing as physiological self-regulation technique	45 min
5	Relapse Prevention and Generalisation	Review of internalised coping repertoire; identification of high-risk situational triggers for attentional dysregulation; development of a written maintenance plan; consolidation of therapeutic gains; booster session scheduling for students meeting criteria for continued support	45 min

Key Clinical Techniques

Biopsychosocial Psychoeducation

Session 1 offers a psychoeducation module that is developmentally tailored to place inattention within a biopsychosocial model. It covers topics such as the neurobiological substrates of executive dysfunction, the role of stress-related cortisol dysregulation in attentional impairment, and the role of academic avoidance in sustaining problems. Psychoeducation is provided through pictorial work sheets developed to match differing literacy skills and is conveyed through the local language of instruction. Reframing inattention from a personality to a neuropsychological basis is considered a major cognitive intervention with goals of reducing self-stigma and enhancing therapeutic alliance.

Metacognitive Self-Monitoring.

Students use a structured attention log to record their attention state, antecedent environmental conditions, and consequent academic behavior at three time points each day. This method operationalizes metacognitive monitoring of executive function, enables self-regulated learning through the identification of individually optimal attention windows, and produces idiographic data for collaborative functional analysis in the next session.

Cognitive Restructuring via Guided Discovery.

The maladaptive core beliefs and automatic negative thoughts concerning academic self-efficacy, such as “My mind is broken” or “I will always fail,” are explored with the use of the Socratic method and discovery. The ABC model (Activating event, Belief, Consequence) provides a cognitive framework for appraisal and attribution. Personalized coping cards, which enhance the development of balanced alternative thoughts, are created and used as cognitive aids in high-demand academic contexts.

Executive Function Skills Training.

Session 4 targets specific executive function deficits through the use of implementation intentions to alleviate prospective memory problems, task decomposition to reduce cognitive load during complex academic activities, and graduated exposure to longer periods of sustained attention. Diaphragmatic breathing is introduced as a method of psychophysiological self-regulation to manage sympathetic nervous system activity, which has been associated with attentional dysregulation in anxiety-related presentations.

Relapse Prevention and Therapeutic Consolidation.

The final session operationalises a relapse prevention framework in which students identify high-risk situational triggers for attentional dysregulation, map available coping responses from their internalised therapeutic repertoire, and construct a written maintenance plan. Generalisation of therapeutic gains across academic settings is facilitated through peer modelling and teacher-coordinated reinforcement of in-session skills.

Monitoring Outcomes and Progress

Monitoring progress is important to determine whether the intervention leads to meaningful improvement in students' attentional functioning and academic engagement. Pre and post-intervention screening using the Strengths and Difficulties Questionnaire (SDQ) can be used to identify changes in attention-related behavioural difficulties. Teacher ratings of classroom engagement, task completion, and sustained attention during lessons can provide additional behavioural indicators of improvement. Students may also report subjective changes in their ability to focus, complete homework, and manage distracting thoughts. These multiple sources of feedback help determine whether the intervention strategies are effectively supporting students' attention regulation within the school environment.

Case Vignette

Malti, a 14-year-old female in Grade IX, was referred for progressive academic deterioration and classroom inattention over one semester, concurrent with her mother's hospitalisation for a chronic illness. Clinical interview in Hindi revealed generalised anxiety with prominent cognitive intrusions, sleep-onset insomnia, and diurnal fatigue consistent with a stress-related adjustment presentation. Differential formulation identified attentional impairment as secondary to anxiety-driven cognitive interference rather than primary executive dysfunction, distinguishing this presentation from ADHD and directing treatment sequencing accordingly. Behavioural activation was prioritised in Session 2 to address activity withdrawal, followed by cognitive restructuring targeting catastrophic appraisals of her mother's prognosis and their perceived irreversibility. A structured worry containment protocol, designating a bounded daily worry period to reduce ruminative intrusion during study, was introduced in Session 3. By Session 5, Malti reported homework completion on four of five days and described a subjective reduction in intrusive ideation during classroom instruction, indicating successful generalisation of cognitive regulatory strategies.

Ethical and Cultural Considerations

Informed Consent, Assent, and Confidentiality

In accordance with established ethical standards (American Psychological Association, 2017), parental or guardian informed consent is required for all students below 18 years, with developmentally appropriate assent obtained from the student. Given variable caregiver literacy across Indian school communities, consent procedures must be conducted verbally in the relevant regional language and not rely exclusively on written documentation. Students are explicitly informed of the limits of confidentiality, including mandatory disclosure obligations under the Protection of Children from Sexual Offences (POCSO) Act (2012) and the Juvenile Justice (Care and Protection of Children) Act (2015). The inherent constraints of the school setting on the therapeutic frame, including the absence of a dedicated clinical space and the group delivery format, must be disclosed prior to the elicitation of any personal information.

Boundaries and Role Clarity

The school counselor's role is also structurally complex because they are both a mental health worker and an institutional worker. This creates the potential for role violations and conflicts of interest. School counselors must maintain role clarity and are not to be pressured by the institution to produce evaluative reports or to violate session confidentiality. Role clarity also requires the scheduling of sessions and the prohibition against informal contact outside of the session, which is particularly relevant in rural and small community settings.

Cultural Responsiveness and Equity

In addition, all such material would require cultural and linguistic adaptation specific to the communities to be served, rather than generic translations. In addressing the issue of attention problems, it would be necessary to rephrase such information in terms of culturally comprehensible models that emphasize neuropsychological and skills-based language rather than psychiatric nosology to reduce potential stigmatization among diverse communities of India. The collectivistic familial perspective that is typical of most Indian cultural groups would require caregiver involvement to be addressed by providing appropriate psychoeducation in the regional language of communication. Proactive, gender-equitable strategies would be necessary to address the underreferral of girls with inattentive symptoms. Caste-based social exclusion and the specific vulnerabilities of Dalit and Adivasi students would be relevant in addressing group composition and therapeutic relationships.

Conclusion

The development of a clinically grounded, manualised intervention for a structurally constrained context of government schools in India has helped to refine understanding of the irreducible minimum of effective brief psychotherapy. The discipline of relating clinical techniques with sufficient clarity to enable replication by non-specialist counsellors without private space, supervisory support, or digital resources has helped to clarify that therapeutic effectiveness in a low-resource context is not related to procedural complexity but to the strength of the therapeutic alliance, case formulation fidelity, and skills taught in terms of ecological validity. This also serves to illustrate a broader systemic point: no clinical intervention programme, regardless of design quality or cultural adaptation, can compensate for a lack of investment in a range of circumstances that are conducive to cognitive and emotional development in childhood, such as nutritional adequacy, class sizes, teachers' mental health literacy, counsellors' consistent deployment under Samagra Shiksha Abhiyan, and structural reduction of socioeconomic adversity, which is the main aetiological driver of attention and learning difficulties in the government school system of India.

References

American Psychiatric Association. (2022). Diagnostic and statistical manual of mental disorders (5th ed., text rev.). American Psychiatric Publishing.

American Psychological Association. (2017). Ethical principles of psychologists and code of conduct (2002, amended effective June 1, 2010, and January 1, 2017).

Clark, D. A., and Beck, A. T. (2011). Cognitive therapy of anxiety disorders: Science and practice. Guilford Press.

DuPaul, G. J., and Stoner, G. (2014). ADHD in the schools: Assessment and intervention strategies (3rd ed.). Guilford Press.

Goodman, R. (1997). The Strengths and Difficulties Questionnaire: A research note. Journal of Child Psychology and Psychiatry, 38(5), 581-586.

Grover, S., Aneja, J., Subodh, B. N., and Chawla, N. (2021). Prevalence and correlates of ADHD in children and adolescents in India: A systematic review. Indian Journal of Psychiatry, 63(1), 10-19.

Ministry of Education, Government of India. (2020). Samagra Shiksha: An integrated scheme for school education. Department of School Education and Literacy.

Reid, R., Trout, A. L., and Schartz, M. (2005). Self-regulation interventions for children with attention deficit/hyperactivity disorder. Exceptional Children, 71(4), 361-377.

Stallard, P. (2019). Think good, feel good: A CBT workbook for children and young people (2nd ed.). Wiley-Blackwell.

Unified District Information System for Education Plus. (2022). UDISE+ 2021-22: School education in India. Ministry of Education, Government of India.

World Health Organization. (2019). International classification of diseases for mortality and morbidity statistics (11th revision).

Chapter 8

Mental Health First Aid for Teachers: A Psychotherapy Informed Approach

– Chandan Gowda G

Introduction

Government schools in urban low-income areas of Bengaluru and New Delhi serve thousands of children and adolescents from migrant labourer and informal-sector families. These are not abstract demographics; many of these students carry the weight of unstable homes, economic uncertainty, and the quiet anxiety of watching their parents work in precarious conditions, all while being expected to perform well in school. Classrooms are typically overcrowded, often housing 50–70 students at a time, with limited infrastructure. The National Education Policy 2020 calls for socio-emotional learning, psychological well-being, and integrated counselling services within schools (Ministry of Education, 2020). However, the ground reality in many government schools remains far from this vision. Trained counselors or mental health professionals are rarely available, and students who need support often have nowhere to turn (Patel et al., 2021).

In this gap, teachers become the de facto first responders for student distress. Without formal psychotherapy training, they nonetheless identify warning signs, manage emotional crises in classrooms, and field disclosures of abuse or suicidal thoughts ,all alongside their teaching and administrative load. This kind of task-shifting, where non-specialists provide foundational mental health support, is not a workaround. It is a recognized global strategy recommended by the World Health Organization for expanding mental health access in low-resource settings (WHO, 2022).

Common Mental Health Issues in This Context

Depression

Depression is among the most frequently observed mental health difficulties in adolescent populations. Systematic reviews suggest that approximately 10–20% of Indian adolescents experience clinically significant depressive symptoms, pointing to a serious and often underaddressed public health concern within school settings (Malhotra & Patra, 2023).

Adolescence is already a turbulent period, a time of rapid emotional, social, and physical change. When you layer economic instability, parental migration, family conflict, and post-pandemic isolation onto that developmental vulnerability, the risk compounds significantly. Many of these students have grown up with inconsistent caregiving and chronic stress as a backdrop.

What makes depression in adolescents particularly easy to miss is that it rarely looks like textbook sadness. Instead, it can appear as irritability, social withdrawal, persistent fatigue, a loss of interest in school, or a cluster of somatic complaints ,headaches, stomach aches, and general malaise. In more severe cases, it can involve hopelessness, crashing self-esteem, and suicidal ideation. Early identification in schools is therefore not just helpful; it can be life-saving (Malhotra & Patra, 2023).

Anxiety Disorders

Anxiety disorders are the most prevalent mental health concern among adolescents globally. In India, prevalence estimates for anxiety symptoms among school-going adolescents range between 15% and 25%, a substantial proportion of any classroom (WHO, 2022). Three forms are especially common in this context:

Generalized Anxiety Disorder (GAD)

Persistent, hard-to-control worry about everyday matters, grades, family expectations, the future. Students may appear restless, fatigued, and unable to concentrate.

Examination Anxiety

High-stakes board exams like SSLC and CBSE create immense pressure. Students may experience cognitive blocks during tests, intense fear of failure, and physical symptoms such as nausea, sweating, or a racing heart.

Social Anxiety

A deep fear of being judged or embarrassed. These students avoid classroom participation, group tasks, or any situation where they might be evaluated by peers or teachers.

Exam-oriented schooling systems can intensify all of these. Constant academic evaluation, perfectionistic thinking patterns, and limited focus on emotional well-being create a climate where anxiety can quietly worsen over time affecting sleep, concentration, and long-term psychological functioning (WHO, 2022).

Externalising and Behavioural Problems

Conduct issues, peer aggression, and bullying affect approximately 5–15% of students in school settings (Patel et al., 2021). These behaviours, rule-breaking, verbal or physical aggression, classroom disruption, defiance are often treated as discipline problems. But that framing misses something important.

Most of the time, externalising behaviours are distress made visible. Contributing factors frequently include exposure to domestic violence, substance misuse in the family, community-level stressors, and persistent academic frustration. A student who acts out in class may be doing the only thing they know how to do with pain they have no words for. Recognising this doesn't mean excusing the behaviour it means responding to it in ways that actually help (Patel et al., 2021)

Key Constraints and Limitations

Structural Constraints

1. 50–70 students per classroom with as little as 5–10 minutes of individual teacher attention per week
2. No private counselling space for confidential conversations
3. Weak referral pathways to mental health professionals

Teacher Burnout

Research on Indian teachers highlights high levels of occupational stress, emotional exhaustion, and burnout, particularly in government school settings (Sharma & Dhar, 2023). Teachers are working more than 50 hours a week, balancing lesson preparation, grading, administrative documentation, institutional accountability, and now, increasingly, informal mental health support. Salaries in some regions hover around 20,000–40,000 per month modest compensation for this level of responsibility.

When teachers are themselves burned out, their capacity to notice and respond to student distress understandably diminishes. Sustaining any school-based mental health system requires attending to teacher well-being, not just student well-being (Sharma & Dhar, 2023).

Sociocultural Barriers

1. ***Stigma***: Mental illness is still widely framed as personal weakness or moral failure in many communities
2. ***Language***: Classrooms span Hindi, Kannada, Urdu, and various regional dialects
3. ***Gender***: Girls face disproportionate pressures, including household labour expectations that affect both their time and their access to support
4. ***Parental Reluctance***: Many families are resistant to psychological referrals, fearing social consequences

These realities make it clear that any effective intervention must be brief, scalable, culturally embedded, and deliverable without specialist resources.

Low-Resource Psychotherapy Plan

Therapeutic Framework

The proposed model integrates two complementary approaches: Youth Mental Health First Aid (MHFA) and Brief Problem-Solving Therapy (PST). Together, they form a transdiagnostic framework meaning it addresses multiple mental health presentations (anxiety, low mood, behavioural difficulties, stress) rather than a single diagnosis. This is critical in a context where teachers cannot always arrive at precise clinical formulations.

Youth MHFA provides the ALGEE action plan, a structured guide for teachers responding to student distress:

1. ***Assess risk***: Identify warning signs of serious distress, including suicidal thinking or safety concerns
2. ***Listen non-judgmentally***: Create a safe space for the student to share without fear of criticism or dismissal
3. ***Give reassurance and information***: Normalise the student's experience and offer basic psychoeducation
4. ***Encourage professional help***: Guide students toward counsellors, psychologists, or healthcare providers when needed
5. ***Encourage self-help and coping strategies***: Suggest accessible tools such as breathing techniques, problem-solving, or peer support

Brief PST has been adapted for delivery by trained lay counsellors in India through the PRIDE (PremIum for aDolEscents) trial, a randomised controlled study demonstrating significant reductions in adolescent mental health difficulties when brief problem-solving approaches were implemented in urban low-income schools (Michelson et al., 2020). PST builds a student's ability to define problems clearly, generate options, evaluate feasibility, and take action skills that generalize well beyond the school context.

The model follows a task-shifting and stepped-care logic: teachers provide low-intensity first-line support, and students requiring more intensive help are referred onward to qualified professionals (Michelson et al., 2020).

Session Structure

The intervention runs over five sessions of approximately 30–45 minutes each, delivered over four weeks. Sessions can be conducted individually or in small groups of 5–10 students. Teachers also conduct brief 10-minute weekly check-ins between sessions to review coping strategies and track progress. Workbook-based activities support self-reflection and reinforce learning between sessions.

Session	Focus	Techniques	Homework	Goal
1	Rapport & Risk Assessment	ALGEE framework; suicide screening (ASK-S)	Daily mood tracking diary	Establish trust; identify high-risk students
2	Problem Identification	Structured storytelling; stressor mapping	List top 3 personal triggers	Name the core problem clearly
3	Problem-Solving	Brainstorm solutions; simple decision matrix	Try one chosen strategy this week	Build agency and coping skill
4	Behavioural Activation	Small achievable goals; peer role-play	Daily activation log	Restore motivation and routine
5	Relapse Prevention	Warning sign identification; referral mapping	Personal weekly self-check plan	Equip student for independent coping

Key Therapeutic Techniques

Psychoeducation is the foundation. When students understand what stress or anxiety actually is, it stops feeling like a personal failing. Teachers can normalise emotional experiences by explaining them as the mind's response to prolonged pressure the way a muscle strains with overuse. Using culturally accessible language and metaphors reduces stigma and increases a student's willingness to seek help (WHO, 2022).

Grounding techniques are particularly useful for acute anxiety. The 5-4-3-2-1 sensory technique;five things you can see, four you can touch, three you can hear, two you can smell, one you can taste, anchors students in the present moment and interrupts cycles of anxious rumination. It requires no equipment and can be taught in minutes (WHO, 2022).

Collaborative problem-solving builds the core skill of PST: rather than offering solutions, the teacher guides students through defining a problem, generating options, evaluating them, and choosing an action. This builds agency and self-efficacy over time, which matters as much as solving the immediate problem (Michelson et al., 2020).

Behavioral activation targets low mood and withdrawal by encouraging small, achievable activities that restore a sense of accomplishment. Completing a single task, joining a classroom activity, or taking a short walk the scale is less important than the momentum it creates (Michelson et al., 2020).

Family-involved goal setting brings parents or caregivers into brief conversations to align expectations and build a consistent support system across home and school. Additional school-level support for peer support circles, classroom emotion vocabulary boards, trauma-informed routines, and teacher supervision circles for peer reflection can deepen the overall culture of emotional safety (Michelson et al., 2020; WHO, 2022).

Ethical and Cultural Considerations

Confidentiality and Risk Management

Students need to feel safe before they will open up. That means teachers must maintain genuine confidentiality and handle sensitive disclosures with discretion. Verbal assent from students and parental consent for minors should be sought before structured interventions or referrals.

Confidentiality, however, has boundaries. When a student discloses a risk of self-harm, suicidal intent, or abuse, those concerns must be escalated to appropriate professionals or authorities , not managed alone by the teacher. A clear, pre-established referral protocol is not optional; it is an ethical requirement. Teachers should know exactly who to call and how when serious disclosures occur (WHO, 2022; Michelson et al., 2020).

Professional boundary maintenance is equally important. Teachers should avoid dual-role entanglements for example, becoming overly personally involved in a student's home life or forming relationships that compromise professional judgement. Brief, transparent documentation of concerns and meetings supports accountability and protects both students and teachers (Michelson et al., 2020).

Cultural Sensitivity and Inclusion

In many communities represented in these schools, mental health difficulties are still associated with shame. The language used to introduce support matters enormously. Framing interventions as 'mind strength training,' 'exam readiness skills,' or 'stress management workshops' positions them as tools for growth rather than admissions of illness ,and significantly increases uptake.

Indian families tend to be collectivist in orientation, which means family involvement is often not just acceptable but expected. Brief structured conversations with parents can align home and school support rather than creating tension between them. Cultural narratives of resilience , drawn carefully from philosophical or spiritual traditions students identify with can also be used to frame coping and perseverance, provided they are offered without imposition (WHO, 2022).

Gender sensitivity must be explicitly built into these interventions. Girls in many of these communities carry disproportionate household responsibilities, face restricted mobility, and may be discouraged from discussing personal difficulties outside the family. Safe spaces where girls can speak freely, and acknowledgement of the real structural pressures they navigate, are not optional additions to the intervention they are what makes it equitable (WHO, 2022; Michelson et al., 2020).

Conclusion

Working through this intervention design made clear how much the setting shapes what is possible. There is no version of this programme that looks like a full therapeutic model and that is not a failure. It is the design constraint. The goal was never to replicate clinical psychotherapy in a government school classroom; it was to make something that is honest about what teachers can actually carry, and that still meaningfully helps students.

The most important shift this programme asks of teachers is a perceptual one: to see a disruptive student and ask what is happening for them, rather than only what they are doing. That reframing does not require advanced training. It requires some psychoeducation, genuine support for teachers, and institutional backing that treats teacher well-being as a prerequisite for student well-being not an afterthought.

What stays with me most is this: the evidence from programmes like PRIDE shows that even very brief, structured interventions delivered by trained non-specialists can meaningfully reduce adolescent mental health difficulties (Michelson et al., 2020). That is not a small thing. In contexts where professional resources are scarce and need is enormous, the capacity of a single well-supported teacher to shift the trajectory for a student in distress is worth taking seriously.

References

Malhotra, S., & Patra, B. N. (2023). Prevalence of depression among adolescents in India: A systematic review. Indian Journal of Psychiatry, 65(2), 123–132.

Michelson, D., Malik, K., Parikh, R., Weiss, H. A., Doyle, A. M., Bhat, B., Sahu, R., Grappy, N., Mathur, S., Sudhir, P., King, M., & Patel, V. (2020). Effectiveness of a brief lay counsellor-delivered, problem-solving intervention for adolescent mental health problems in urban, low-income schools in India: A randomised controlled trial. The Lancet Child & Adolescent Health, 4(8), 571–582.

Ministry of Education, Government of India. (2020). National Education Policy 2020. Patel, V., Saxena, S., Lund, C., Thornicroft, G., Baingana, F., Bolton, P., Chisholm, D., Collins, P. Y., Cooper, J. L., Eaton, J., Herrman, H., Herzallah, M. M., Huang, Y., Jordans, M. J. D., Kleinman, A., Medina-Mora, M. E., Morgan, E., Niaz, U., Omigbodun, O., ... UnUtzer, J. (2021). School mental health in India: Current scenario and future directions. Indian Journal of Psychiatry, 63(Suppl 2), S347–S359.

Sharma, R., & Dhar, R. L. (2023). Occupational stress and burnout among school teachers in India: A review. Frontiers in Psychology, 14, 1239587.

World Health Organization. (2022). Adolescent mental health.

Chapter 9

Peer-Support Models in Resource-Limited College Campuses

– Gattupalli Suchitra

Introduction

There are growing concerns for students' mental health in higher education, with significant numbers of students reporting distress. In the World Health Organization's international college student survey, a third of first-year students screened positive for at least one common anxiety, mood or substance use disorder as defined by the DSM-IV.

In the last decade, rising rates of college students experiencing symptoms of depression and anxiety have been observed.Globally, approximately 31% of college students screened positive for a mental health disorder over the course of the last year. It is now easily seen that accessing treatments for these disorders are difficult. Due to the low mental health literacy among students, they often do not realize the need for treatment. They usually believe that the symptoms of depression and anxiety are typical college stress and thereby need no appropriate treatment. But among the students who also recognize the need for mental health services,they also face barriers, such as accessibility and the efficiency of treatment and campus counselling centres, etc. However, many counselling centres across the country are under-resourced, and have difficulty reaching students in need and to operate in full capacity during much of the year.

The treatment gap refers to the group of individuals who meet the clinical criteria for a mental health disorder but do not receive formal care. In the context of resource-limited campuses, this gap is driven by a rise in demand that is beyond institutional capacity. Recent data shows that while mental health awareness has risen,the pace of treatment service delivery has not much of an improvement. .National surveys in 2025 report that approximately 37% of college students experience moderate-to-severe depression, and 32% face moderate-to-severe anxiety. However, in resource-constrained regions like India, the treatment gap for common mental disorders remains between 70% and 92%.This gap is most distinct among marginalized populations (e.g., first-generation or low-income students), where the lack of insurance or high out-of-pocket costs creates a silent crisis of untreated pathology. In recent systematic reviews, financial barriers were identified as the most frequent obstacle, reported in 69% of studies. Many campuses face a shortage of professionals, with some regions reporting only 0.75 psychiatrists per 100,000 people, well below the WHO-recommended 3 per 100,000. Because most systems are designed only for “crisis” or “clinical” intervention, students with “sub-clinical” issues like transition stress or loneliness are often turned away or deprioritized, leading them to drop out or worsen in the long run.

The First Responder phenomenon describes the reality that students in distress are almost especially disclosed to their peers or staff before ever contacting a professional clinic. Up to 75% of students turn to a peer first. The reasons of relatability and lack of judgement are the primary reasons for choosing peers as the first step in seeking help. Disclosure to a peer feels like a conversation, whereas disclosure to a clinic may feel like a formal intake process.

Peer-Support Models

Peer support interventions are increasingly adopted worldwide within mental health services and third-sector organisations (voluntary organisations, community organisations, colleges and charities). Although studies of peer support for mental health problems suggest that it is associated with positive effects on hope, recovery and quality of life, the effects on other outcomes such as symptoms, hospital admission and satisfaction are inconclusive. Peer support may have different benefits and harms depending on the population and setting in which it is used.

Low-Intensity Models (Peer-Led Psychoeducation)

They are designed for primary prevention and the broad distribution of mental health literacy. They focus on equipping the general student body with the tools to recognize early signs of distress. These include Mental Health First Aid (MHFA) workshops and peer-facilitated seminars, open talks, etc on stress management, sleep hygiene, and mindfulness. Research from 2025 highlights that MHFA training on campuses significantly improves supportive behaviors and increases the confidence of students to intervene when they witness a peer in a mental health crisis. These models are particularly vital in resource-limited settings because they require minimal clinical supervision and can be scaled through large-group workshops.

Medium-Intensity Models (Befriending and Support Groups)

Medium-intensity models move beyond general education toward targeted social connection. They are often used for students experiencing loneliness, mild anxiety, or transition-related stress. This involves pairing trained student volunteers with peers who may be socially isolated. Unlike casual friendship, this is a structured role where the supporter uses active listening to build resilience. These can be identity-based or issue-based groups (e.g., groups for international students or students with chronic illness). They foster meaningful connections, relationships that provide emotional closeness and a common bond, which are proven mediators for reducing symptoms of depression and enhances a sense of belonging.

High-Intensity/Paraprofessional Models (Trained Peer Counseling)

In these models, students function as paraprofessionals. They receive systematic, intensive training in basic counseling techniques and professional ethics. A defining feature of this model is the dual-role where the peer acts as a friend but follows a professional protocol supervised by licensed clinicians. Recent 2025 studies have developed competency scales to ensure that peer counselors possess the necessary communication sensitivity and role identity to support peers without experiencing burnout. This model is a cornerstone of task-shifting, as it allows professional counselors to focus on severe cases while peers manage low-to-moderate psychological distress.

Digital & Hybrid Models (Anonymous Chat and AI Augmentation)

Digital models use technology to remove the barriers of stigma and physical distance, providing 24/7 on-demand support. Use of pseudonyms and avatars allows students to discuss sensitive topics like self-harm or sexual health, without fear of judgment. Artificial Intelligence (AI) and Natural Language Processing (NLP) are now being used to augment human peer support. In hybrid models, AI monitors peer-to-peer chats to indicate high-risk language, ensuring that clinical safeguarding is maintained even when human moderators are offline.

Implementation and Inclusivity

Inclusivity in peer support programs creates safe, equitable, and welcoming environments for diverse participants by valuing shared lived experiences, fostering empathy, and breaking down social barriers. Essential elements include training in cultural competence, accessible meeting formats, and personalized support for individuals with disabilities or unique needs. These programs boost self-confidence, improve social skills, and promote community integration.

Identity-Based Support

Traditional counseling services often struggle with"cultural mismatch, where marginalized students who have different stressors (e.g., systemic racism, acculturation, or heteronormativity) are misunderstood by clinical staff. Peer support relies on social identity theory, where students from marginalized backgrounds (First-gen, LGBTQ+, or International) find immediate safety in shared lived experiences. This reduces the explanation fatigue that often occurs when a student has to educate their therapist on their cultural background.

Indigenous and Localized Healing

In diverse and resource-limited settings, the Western medical model may clash with the local values of community and spirituality. Peer models can incorporate localized healing practices, such as talking circles or collective storytelling, which emphasize collective resilience over individual pathology. In many global contexts, peers act as cultural brokers who can bridge the gap between traditional family values and modern mental health practices. This is particularly effective in campuses serving Indigenous populations, where healing is viewed as a holistic reconnection to community and land rather than a private clinical encounter.

Stigma Mitigation

In many cultures, mental health struggles are viewed through the lens of family shame or weakness of character, creating a massive barrier to professional intake. Peers are uniquely positioned to bridge this shame gap. Because a peer is a social equal, a conversation about anxiety feels less like a medical admission and more like a shared human experience. Research from 2025 indicates that interacting with a peer who has successfully navigated a mental health challenge is the most effective way to reduce self-stigma. Peers act as living proof that mental health challenges do not define one's academic potential or social worth, which is vital in high-pressure, resource-limited academic environments.

Ethical Dilemmas

The Boundary Dilemma (Friend vs. Supporter)

The most significant ethical challenge in campus peer support is role blurring. Because peers are often in the same social circles or classes, maintaining a supportive yet objective distance is difficult. Training must emphasize that a peer supporter is a facilitator, not a friend and not a therapist. Ethical guidelines for 2025 - 2026 stress on the importance of matching protocols that avoid pairing students who have pre-existing social, romantic, or academic power imbalances (e.g., a Teaching Assistant supporting their own student).

Escalation Protocols

In resource-limited settings, peer supporters are often the first to encounter high-risk situations (suicidal ideation, self-harm, or psychosis). Effective programs use aRed-Yellow-Green light system. Peers are trained to recognize Red Light symptoms that require an immediate break in confidentiality to contact emergency services or professional on-call staff. Rather than simply giving a student a phone number, the warm hand-off involves the peer supporter staying with the student (physically or on a call) until a professional takes over. This reduces the dropout rate between disclosure and treatment.

Confidentiality vs. Mandated Reporting

Navigating the legalities of privacy is complex for non-professional supporters who may not be covered by the same privileged communication laws as licensed psychologists. Peer supporters must be trained to provide an Informed Consent statement at the start of any interaction, explicitly stating: *"I will keep what you say private unless I believe you are at risk of hurting yourself or others."* In digital/hybrid models, ensuring that chat logs are encrypted and stored according to local data protection laws (e.g., GDPR or local health privacy acts) is a growing ethical requirement for 2026 campus digital infrastructures.

Preventing Compassion Fatigue and Burnout

Peer supporters are at high risk for secondary traumatic stress. Ethical program management requires protecting the supporter as much as the seeker. Resource-limited campuses often use Group Supervision, where one clinician meets with 10–12 peer supporters. This provides a space for debriefing and ensures that no student is carrying the emotional weight of another's trauma alone.

Conclusion

In conclusion, the integration of peer-support models is not merely a budgetary necessity for resource-limited campuses, but a strategic necessity for fostering an inclusive and culturally competent mental health ecosystem. These models bridge the shame gap and mitigate explanation fatigue for different groups of populations by grounding support in shared lived experiences and localized healing traditions. However, the sustainability of these programs relies on careful ethical frameworks that address role-blurring, establish clear warm hand-off escalation protocols, and protect student supporters from compassion fatigue through structured group supervision. As we move through 2026, the successful campus will be one that views mental health as a collective community responsibility, utilizing peers as essential bridges between the student body and formal clinical care to ensure no student is left to navigate their psychological distress in isolation.

References

Auerbach, RP, Mortier, P, Bruffaerts, R, Alonso, J, Benjet, C, Cuijpers, P, et al. WHO world mental health surveys international college student project: prevalence and distribution of mental disorders. J Abnorm Psychol 2018; 127(7): 326–68.10.1037/abn0000362

Al-Khouja, M. A., & Corrigan, P. W. (2024). The impact of peer support on self-stigma: A systematic review and meta-analysis. *Stigma and Health*, 9(3), 241–255.

Basset, T, Faulkner, A, Repper, J, Stamou, E. Lived Experience Leading the Way: Peer Support in Mental Health. Together UK, 2010 .

Bravata, D. M., Russell, D. W., & Fellows, A. (2025). Exploring the impact of digital peer support services on meeting emotional health needs: Prospective cohort analysis. *JMIR Human Factors*, 12(1), e68221.

Brown, JSL. Student mental health: some answers and more questions. J Ment Health 2018; 27(3): 193–6.10.1080/09638237.2018.1470319

Cherian, A., Maji, S., & Singh, R. (2025). Student mental health crisis: Indian campuses rethink support. *Journal of Mental Health Insights*, 29(2), 55–61.

Eisenberg D, Golberstein E, Gollust SE. Help-seeking and access to mental health care in a university student population. Med Care 2007 Jul;45(7):594-601.

Eisenberg D, Hunt J, Speer N, Zivin K. Mental health service utilization among college students in the United States. J Nerv Ment Dis 2011 May;199(5):301-308.

Eisenberg D, Hunt J, Speer N. Help seeking for mental health on college campuses: review of evidence and next steps for research and practice. Harv Rev Psychiatry 2012;20(4):222-232.

Li, R., Hassan, N. C., Zhang, Q., & Ou, S. (2025). A systematic review on the impact of social support on college students' wellbeing and mental health. *PLoS ONE*, 20(7), e0325212.

Lipson SK, Lattie EG, Eisenberg D. Increased rates of mental health service utilization by US college students: 10-year population-level trends (2007-2017). Psychiatr Serv 2019 Jan 1;70(1):60-63.

Lipson, S. K., Diaz, Y., & Eisenberg, D. (2025). Mental health among first-generation college students: Findings from the national healthy minds study. *Journal of American College Health*, 73(1), 12–22.

Mhfaindia. (2025). *Addressing the shame gap: Cultural barriers to mental health in Indian higher education.* Mental Health Foundation of India.

Mhfaindia. (2025, May 27). India's mental health landscape in 2025: Ground-level insights. *Mental Health Foundation of India.*

Mowbray CT, Megivern D, Mandiberg JM, Strauss S, Stein CH, Collins K, et al. Campus mental health services: recommendations for change. Am J Orthopsychiatry 2006 Apr;76(2):226-237.

Neves, J, Hillman, N. Student Academic Experience Survey 2017. Higher Education Academy and Higher Education Policy Institute, 2017

Patmisari, E., Huang, Y., & Orr, M. (2025). Interventions supporting meaningful connections for people with serious mental illness: A concept-framed systematic narrative review. *BMC Psychiatry*, 25(1), 1-15.

Pinder-Amaker S, Bell C. A bioecological systems approach for navigating the college mental health crisis. Harv Rev Psychiatry 2012;20(4):174-188.

Shalaby, RAH, Agyapong, VIO. Peer support in mental health: literature review. JMIR Ment Health 2020; 7(6): e15572.

Smith, D. G., Giugni, M., Gulliver, A., & Banfield, M. (2026). Peer-led models focused on emotional distress and suicide prevention: A scoping review. *Journal of Public Health Research*, 31(1), 1041.

Walker, A., Tait-McCutcheon, S. L., & Gilbert, A. (2025). College students' disclosure of mental health problems on campus: The role of tutors and peers. *Disability & Society*, 40(2), 1–18.

Wong, K. Y., & Lau, J. S. (2025). Mixed-methods longitudinal evaluation of the mental health first aid (MHFA) training on university campuses: 2024–2027 study protocol. *BMJ Open*, 15(2), e125879.

Xiao H, Carney DM, Youn SJ, Janis RA, Castonguay LG, Hayes JA, et al. Are we in crisis? National mental health and treatment trends in college counseling centers. Psychol Serv 2017 Nov;14(4):407-415.

Walker, A., Tait-McCutcheon, S. L., & Gilbert, A. (2025). College students' disclosure of mental health problems on campus: The role of tutors and peers. *Disability & Society*, 40(2), 1–18.

Chapter 10

Community-Based Counselling in Rural Primary Health Centres

– *Riya N R*

Introduction

This chapter explores how brief psychological counselling can be integrated into rural Primary Health Centres (PHCs) in India. Mental health services are often limited in rural areas due to shortages of trained professionals and infrastructure. Community-based counselling models can help address common mental health concerns such as depression, anxiety, and stress. The chapter presents a low-resource psychotherapy framework that combines psychoeducation, behavioural activation, problem-solving strategies, and supportive counselling within PHC settings.

Access to mental health care remains a major challenge in rural parts of India. Many villages are far from specialized hospitals, and people often rely on basic government health facilities for most of their medical needs. In this context, Primary Health Centres (PHCs) play a very important role. They are usually the first place where people seek help for physical and emotional health problems.

A typical PHC serves around 20,000 to 30,000 people, depending on the region. These centres usually have one medical officer, a few nurses, and community health workers such as ASHA workers. Their main focus is often on maternal health, infectious diseases, immunization, and general medical care. Because of limited staff and infrastructure, mental health services are not always available. However, emotional distress and psychological difficulties are common in rural communities. People may experience stress related to financial problems, crop failures, family conflicts, or substance use. Unfortunately, many individuals do not receive proper psychological help because mental health specialists are rarely posted in PHCs.

In recent years, public health programs in India have begun to recognize the need for integrating mental health care into primary health systems. Under the District Mental Health Programme (DMHP), some efforts have been made to bring counselling and psychiatric support closer to communities. Even so, many PHCs still operate without a full-time psychologist.

Because PHCs are accessible and trusted by local communities, they provide a valuable opportunity for delivering basic counselling services. When simple and structured counselling approaches are integrated into these settings, mental health support can reach a larger number of people. Community-based counselling models are therefore an important step toward reducing the treatment gap in rural India.

Psychological Difficulties Commonly Seen in Rural PHCs

People visiting rural health centres often come with physical complaints. However, many of these symptoms are connected to underlying psychological distress. Understanding these common mental health concerns helps counsellors provide more appropriate support.

Depression and Low Mood

Depressive symptoms are frequently observed in rural populations, though they may not always be described in psychological terms. Individuals often report tiredness, lack of interest in daily work, body pain, or sleep problems. These complaints may be related to long-term stressors such as poverty, financial debt, or crop failure.

Women in rural households may also experience emotional exhaustion due to multiple responsibilities. Managing domestic work, childcare, and agricultural labour can create continuous stress. When such pressures remain unresolved, feelings of sadness and helplessness may develop.

Anxiety and Excessive Worry

Anxiety problems are also common but often misunderstood. People may complain about heart palpitations, dizziness, breathlessness, or a sense of restlessness. These symptoms sometimes lead individuals to visit the PHC repeatedly for medical examinations.

In many cases, these physical sensations are linked to persistent worries about family responsibilities, financial instability, or health concerns. Without psychological support, these worries can gradually affect a person's daily functioning and quality of life.

Alcohol-Related Problems

Alcohol misuse is another concern in several rural communities. Many men use alcohol as a way to cope with work stress, unemployment, or social pressures. Unfortunately, excessive alcohol use often leads to family conflict, financial difficulties, and domestic violence.

Family members, particularly women, may experience emotional distress because of these situations. Counselling services in PHCs can help individuals and families understand these patterns and explore healthier coping strategies.

Additional Sources of Distress

Rural communities may also face other challenges that contribute to psychological suffering. These include domestic violence, relationship conflicts, and in some regions, a higher risk of suicide associated with financial stress and agricultural losses. Addressing these issues requires culturally sensitive and accessible counselling approaches.

Challenges in Delivering Counselling in Rural Health Settings

Although PHCs are ideal points for community-based counselling, several practical barriers make mental health care difficult to provide in these settings.

Infrastructure Limitations

Many PHCs do not have dedicated rooms for psychological counselling. Consultations often happen in shared spaces where privacy is limited. This can make it difficult for individuals to openly discuss personal or family problems.Another challenge is the high number of patients visiting the PHC every day. Medical officers and nurses usually have only a short time to attend to each person. As a result, there is rarely enough time for detailed psychological conversations.

Limited Human Resources

A major barrier is the lack of trained mental health professionals. Most PHCs do not employ psychologists or counsellors. Health workers are often already busy managing medical responsibilities, leaving little time for mental health support.Because of this shortage, many mental health programs recommend a task-sharing approach. In this model, basic counselling skills are taught to nurses, social workers, or trained community health workers. These workers provide initial support while receiving supervision from mental health specialists.

Sociocultural Barriers

Stigma remains a significant issue in many rural communities. People may hesitate to seek psychological help because they fear being labeled as "mentally ill." Instead, they may prefer medical treatment for physical symptoms.Cultural beliefs about illness and healing also influence help-seeking behaviour. Some individuals may first consult traditional healers or religious leaders before approaching health professionals.Language diversity can also create communication challenges. Counsellors must be able to explain psychological concepts in simple language that people from different educational backgrounds can understand.

Practical Difficulties

Other everyday barriers also affect counselling services in rural areas. Some individuals may have difficulty travelling long distances to the PHC for repeated sessions. Literacy levels may be low, making written materials less useful. In addition, irregular follow-up visits can interrupt the counselling process.

Despite these difficulties, brief and structured interventions can still provide meaningful support when adapted to local realities.

Low-Resource Counselling Model for Rural PHCs

To address these challenges, a brief and structured counselling model can be implemented within PHCs. This approach focuses on simple psychological techniques that can be delivered within a short time frame.

The model draws from several evidence-based approaches, including elements of cognitive-behavioural therapy, supportive counselling, and problem-solving therapy. It also follows principles from the World Health Organization's mental health gap action programme (mhGAP), which promotes psychological interventions in non-specialized health settings.

Counselling sessions are typically brief, lasting about 30 minutes each. The intervention may include four to six sessions depending on the individual's needs and availability.

Importantly, this model can be delivered not only by psychologists but also by trained nurses, social workers, or supervised community health workers. This task-sharing approach helps extend mental health care to underserved communities.

Suggested Counselling Process

The counselling process usually begins with building rapport and understanding the person's difficulties. Because many individuals may not be familiar with psychological counselling, the first step is to create a safe and supportive environment.

Initial Engagement and Psychoeducation

During the first meeting, the counsellor listens to the person's concerns and explains how emotional stress can influence physical health. Many people feel relieved when they realize that their symptoms are connected to stress rather than a serious medical illness.

Providing simple psychoeducation helps normalize emotional distress. The counsellor may explain that feelings such as sadness, worry, or exhaustion are common reactions to difficult life situations.

Identifying Problems and Setting Goals

In the next step, the counsellor helps the individual identify the main problems causing stress. Instead of trying to address everything at once, the person is encouraged to focus on one manageable issue. The counsellor then introduces simple problem-solving steps. These include identifying possible solutions, evaluating options, and selecting practical actions that the individual can try in daily life.

Encouraging Positive Daily Activities

Many individuals experiencing depression gradually reduce their daily activities. Counselling therefore includes behavioural activation, which encourages people to engage in small, meaningful tasks. Examples may include visiting a friend, spending time in a relaxing activity, or returning to routine household work. Even small changes can improve mood and restore a sense of control.

Teaching Coping Skills

Relaxation and breathing exercises can also be introduced to help reduce anxiety and physical tension. These techniques are simple to learn and can be practiced at home.

Grounding exercises may also be useful for individuals who experience overwhelming worry. These exercises help people focus on the present moment instead of getting lost in anxious thoughts.

Strengthening Social Support

Community relationships play an important role in rural life. Counsellors therefore encourage individuals to identify supportive family members, friends, or community groups who can provide emotional help. Discussing available support systems can reduce feelings of isolation and strengthen resilience.

Preparing for Future Stress

In the final stage of counselling, the counsellor reviews the strategies that were most helpful. Individuals are also encouraged to recognize early warning signs of stress so they can apply coping skills before problems become severe.

This process helps build confidence and promotes long-term emotional well-being.

Case Vignette

Lakshmi, a 35-year-old agricultural worker, complained of headaches, persistent fatigue, and trouble falling asleep when she went to a rural PHC. Following an examination, the physician found no evidence of a serious physical condition. Lakshmi revealed during the consultation that her husband's alcohol consumption and financial debt had been causing her to feel overburdened.

She was referred to the PHC for short-term counseling. The counselor assisted her in understanding the link between physical symptoms and stress over a number of sessions. Together, they came up with doable solutions to everyday issues, like asking family for assistance and organizing modest activities that lifted her spirits.

In order to lessen her anxiety, Lakshmi also learned how to relax. She eventually reported increased energy and better sleep. This illustration demonstrates how brief counseling sessions in PHCs can assist people in managing emotional distress even in environments with limited resources.

Ethical and Cultural Considerations

Providing counselling in rural communities requires careful attention to ethical and cultural factors. Maintaining confidentiality can be challenging in crowded PHCs. Counsellors may need to find creative ways to ensure privacy, such as using quieter corners or scheduling sessions during less busy hours. Informed consent should always be obtained before starting counselling. Because literacy levels may vary, explanations should be given in simple and clear language. In some cases, verbal consent may be more appropriate than written forms.

Gender sensitivity is another important aspect. In many rural communities, women may feel more comfortable speaking with female counsellors about personal issues. Respecting local norms helps build trust between the counsellor and the client.

Counsellors must also remain respectful of cultural and spiritual beliefs. Rather than dismissing traditional practices, mental health professionals can work alongside community values while promoting healthy coping strategies.Finally, maintaining professional boundaries is important in small communities where dual relationships are common. Counsellors should remain aware of their professional role while offering compassionate support.

Conclusion

When we think about counselling models for health settings, we see how important it is to be flexible when it comes to psychological practice. Rural health settings like Primary Health Centres or PHCs do not have all the equipment and staff that urban clinics have so they have to work with what they have. This does not mean that people in rural areas cannot get good mental health care. If we use methods to give basic training to the people who work there and work with the community we can make counselling a part of the primary health system. This way of working also shows that clinical psychologists have a role to play in making public health services better. Clinical psychologists can work with doctors and community health workers to make sure that people in areas get the mental health treatment they need.

In the end counselling that is based in the community and happens at PHCs shows that people can get the support they need even when resources are limited as long as the care is tailored to the local culture, is practical and is easy to access.

References

Dawson, K. S., Bryant, R. A., Harper, M., Tay, A. K., Rahman, A., Schafer, A., & van Ommeren, M. (2015). Problem Management Plus (PM+): A WHO transdiagnostic psychological intervention for common mental health problems. *World Psychiatry, 14*(3), 354–357.

Government of India. (2014). *National mental health programme.* Ministry of Health and Family Welfare.

Patel, V., Weiss, H. A., Chowdhary, N., Naik, S., Pednekar, S., Chatterjee, S., De Silva, M., Bhat, B., Araya, R., King, M., Simon, G., & Kirkwood, B. R. (2010). Effectiveness of an intervention led by lay health counsellors for depressive and anxiety disorders in primary care. *The Lancet, 376*(9758), 2086–2095.

Patel, V., Saxena, S., Lund, C., Thornicroft, G., Baingana, F., Bolton, P., ... Unützer, J. (2018). The Lancet Commission on global mental health and sustainable development. *The Lancet, 392*(10157), 1553–1598.

World Health Organization. (2016). *mhGAP intervention guide for mental, neurological and substance use disorders in non-specialized health settings* (Version 2.0). WHO Press.

Chapter 11

Psychoeducation and Supportive Counselling in Panchayat Settings

– Arya C V

Introduction

Panchayats are the lowest level of local self-governance in rural India and play an important role in community development and public service delivery. They often serve as local centers where people can access services related to health, education, and welfare schemes. Panchayats commonly work in collaboration with Primary Health Centres (PHCs), Accredited Social Health Activists (ASHAs), Anganwadi workers, and other community organizations to address various health needs of the rural population.

In recent years, awareness about mental health has slowly increased in rural communities. Because of this growing awareness, Panchayat settings are now sometimes used for mental health outreach programs, psychoeducation sessions, and basic counselling support. These settings are useful because they are familiar and accessible to community members, especially for individuals who may not have access to specialized mental health professionals.

The population served in Panchayat areas is usually rural and socioeconomically diverse. It includes agricultural workers, daily wage labourers, homemakers, elderly individuals, and adolescents. Educational levels may vary, and many people may not have access to trained mental health professionals such as psychiatrists or clinical psychologists. For this reason, Panchayat offices sometimes become the first place where individuals seek help when they experience emotional or psychological distress.

People may approach Panchayat offices during health camps, awareness programs, welfare meetings, or women's self-help group gatherings. In these situations, counselling support is often provided in informal settings such as community halls or meeting rooms. The counselling provided is usually brief and practical, focusing on helping individuals understand their difficulties and learn simple coping strategies. When required, individuals may also be referred to nearby health centres for further support.

Common Mental Health Issues

Several mental health concerns commonly appear during interactions at the Panchayat level. These issues are often connected to economic stress, family responsibilities, and social pressures.

Stress and Adjustment Difficulties

Many people in rural communities experience stress related to financial instability, agricultural uncertainty, unemployment, or family responsibilities. These stressors can affect an individual's emotional wellbeing and daily functioning. Common symptoms of stress include irritability, sleep disturbances, constant worry, and feelings of helplessness. Women in particular may experience higher levels of stress because they often manage both household responsibilities and financial pressures within the family.

Mild to Moderate Depression and Anxiety

Depression and anxiety symptoms are also commonly seen but often remain unnoticed or untreated. Individuals may report feeling sad, tired, or worried for long periods of time. They may also lose interest in activities they previously enjoyed. In rural communities, emotional distress is often expressed through physical symptoms such as headaches, body pain, or fatigue. This happens partly because mental health problems may still carry stigma, and people may feel more comfortable discussing physical complaints rather than emotional difficulties.

Family and Interpersonal Conflicts

Family-related issues are another common source of psychological distress. These may include marital conflicts, disagreements between family members, or stress related to caregiving responsibilities for elderly relatives.

Adolescents may also experience emotional stress due to academic pressure, expectations from family members, and social challenges. When these issues remain unresolved, they can contribute to anxiety, frustration, and emotional difficulties.

Limitations

Limited Privacy

Counselling may take place in shared community spaces where it is difficult to maintain complete privacy. Because of this, individuals may hesitate to discuss personal or sensitive topics.

Stigma and Low Mental Health Awareness

Mental health stigma continues to exist in many rural communities. Psychological problems may sometimes be explained as personal weakness, fate, or spiritual causes. These beliefs may discourage people from seeking professional help.

High Client Load and Limited Professionals

In many rural areas, only a small number of trained professionals are available to serve a large population. Therefore, counselling methods used in Panchayat settings must be simple, brief, and easy to implement.

Language and Cultural Diversity

Counselling must be provided in local languages and should respect local traditions and cultural beliefs. Approaches that are culturally sensitive are more likely to be accepted by the community.

Low-Resource Psychotherapy Plan

A brief supportive counselling approach combined with psychoeducation is suitable for Panchayat settings. This approach focuses on offering emotional support, helping individuals understand their problems, and encouraging practical coping strategies.Some basic cognitive-behavioural ideas may also be included to help individuals recognize negative thinking patterns and replace them with healthier ways of thinking.

Session Structure

A practical counselling structure may include:

1. 3-4 counselling sessions
2. 20-30 minutes per session
3. Individual or small group sessions conducted during community programs

Session Outline

Session 1-Rapport Building and Psychoeducation. The counsellor listens to the client's concerns and builds trust. Basic information about stress and emotional wellbeing is provided to help normalize the person's experiences.

Session 2-Coping Skills and Emotional Regulation. The counsellor introduces simple relaxation techniques such as breathing exercises and helps the individual identify personal strengths and available support systems.

Session 3-Problem-Solving Strategies. The counsellor helps the individual break down problems into smaller steps and explore practical solutions.

Session 4-Review and Referral. Coping strategies are reviewed and reinforced. If the individual requires further support, they may be referred to a PHC or mental health professional.

Key Techniques Used

Psychoeducation

Providing simple explanations about stress and emotions helps increase awareness and reduce stigma related to mental health.

Active Listening

The counsellor listens carefully and allows the individual to express their feelings without judgment.

Problem-Solving Skills

Clients are guided to identify problems and explore possible solutions.

Relaxation Techniques

Breathing exercises and grounding techniques can help reduce stress and anxiety.

Strength-Based Approach

Counsellors encourage individuals to recognize their strengths and available family or community support.

Case Vignette

M is a 34-year-old married woman who attended a mental health awareness camp at her local Panchayat office. She lives with her husband, two children, and her elderly mother-in-law. Along with managing most of the household work, she also works as a daily wage labourer during the agricultural season.

For several months, M had been experiencing frequent headaches, sleep difficulties, and constant worry. Her family was going through financial stress because of irregular agricultural income, and she felt overwhelmed trying to balance work and family responsibilities. At first, she believed the problem was only physical and visited a local clinic for her headaches.

During counselling, she was encouraged to talk about the stress she faced in her daily life. The counsellor explained how emotional stress can also lead to physical symptoms. She was introduced to simple techniques like deep breathing and short relaxation exercises. Through problem-solving discussions, M also identified small changes she could make, such as sharing some household tasks with family members and taking short breaks during the day.

After three sessions, M reported feeling less tense and more confident in handling her stress. She also started communicating more openly with her husband, which improved things at home. The counsellor encouraged her to continue using the coping strategies and informed her about nearby health services if she needed further support.

This case highlights how brief counselling and basic mental health awareness at the Panchayat level can help people manage stress, even where mental health services are limited.

Ethical and Cultural Considerations

Ethical practice is important even in community-based counselling settings.

Confidentiality

Counsellors should make efforts to ensure privacy and protect the client's personal information.

Informed Consent

Clients should understand the purpose of counselling and that participation is voluntary.

Professional Boundaries

Counsellors should maintain clear professional boundaries when interacting with community members.

Cultural Sensitivity

Counselling approaches should respect local beliefs, traditions, and family structures.

Conclusion

Designing mental health support programs for Panchayat settings shows the importance of simple, practical, and culturally appropriate approaches. Even basic counselling techniques such as empathy, psychoeducation, and coping strategies can help individuals improve their emotional wellbeing. Community-based mental health initiatives also help connect rural populations with formal healthcare services. Panchayats can therefore play an important role in increasing mental health awareness and providing early support to people experiencing psychological distress.

References

Corey, G. (2017). Theory and practice of counseling and psychotherapy (10th ed.). Boston, MA: Cengage Learning.

Kumar, A., & Tiwari, S. (2019). Community mental health services in rural India: Challenges and opportunities. Indian Journal of Social Psychiatry, 35(1), 3-10.

Patel, V., Saxena, S., Lund, C., Thornicroft, G., Baingana, F., Bolton, P., Unützer, J. (2018). The Lancet Commission on global mental health and sustainable development. The Lancet, 392(10157), 1553-1598.

Chapter 12

Task-Shifting: Training Community Volunteers in Basic Counselling Skills

– *Meghnaa Manvendra Kamath*

Introduction

Task Shifting refers to a systematic delegation of specific tasks from highly trained professionals to individuals with fewer formal qualifications but appropriate training and supervision. In mental health care, it involves transferring selected counselling and psychosocial support responsibilities from psychologist, psychiatrist or social workers to trained community members lay counsellors or volunteers, (World Health Organization, 2008).Redistribution of the responsibilities maximizes a viable human resource. Equipping the volunteers with foundational competencies such as active listening empathy, basic problem-solving support and referral skills while complex cases remain under supervision is essential. Task- shifting. Task-shifting is therefore structured and evidence-informed strategy aimed access to care with compromising quality (Patel et al., 2011)

Task shifting gained global attention during the HIV/AIDs crisis in sub-Saharan Africa in early 2000s, where severe shortages of physicians and nurses required innovative workforce strategies (World Health Organization, 2008).The model was later extended to mental health care. The Mental Health Gap Action Programme (mhGAP), launched by the World Health Organization in 2008, provided structured guidelines enabling non-specialist to deliver evidence-based mental health intervention in low-resources settings (WHO,2010).

Mental disorders account for a significant proportion of the global burden of disease, yet a larger treatment gap, particularly in low- and middle-income countries (Patel et al., 2018). Many countries report fewer that one psychiatrist per 100,000 population highlighting the urgent need for scalable solution.In countries such as Zimbabwe and India demonstrates that trained lay health workers can deliver structured psychological intervention for depression and anxiety (Chibanda et al., 2016; Patel et al., 2010). The findings underscore the global relevance of task-shifting in expanding access to mental health care.

Rationale for Task-Shifting in Low-Resource Settings

Low- resources setting faces multiple barriers to mental health services delivery, including limited funding, workforces' shortage, stigma and weak infrastructure. Task-shifting addresses these challenges by expanding the workforces, reducing cost, improving cultural associability and strengthening referral systems (Patel et al.,2011). By empowering trained community volunteers with basic counselling skills Under professional supervision, task shifting provides a pragmatic and equitable response to the global mental health treatment gap

The Mental Health Treatment Gap

Mental Health disorder is a crucial aspect of health and a leading cause of disability worldwide. Conditions such as depression, anxiety disorders, bipolar disorder and schizophrenia contribute substantially to years lived with disability and reduced quality of life. According to World Health Organization 2022, nearly one in eight people globally live with a mental health disorder. Depression alone is a leading cause of disability worldwide, significantly affecting individual's social functioning, productivity and physical health (Patel et al., 2018).

Over time the prevalence rate increased and significant burden, but the mental health area has received lesser attention and funding compared to other areas due multiple factors. The result is a substantial gap between those who need care and those who actually receive appropriate service. One critical factor contributing to the treatment gap is severe shortage of trained mental health professionals. In high income countries, services are often concentrated in urban centres, leaving rural and marginalized communities underserved. Psychologists, psychiatrists, psychiatric nurses and clinical social workers are insufficient in number to meet growing demand. This imbalance between need and workforce capacity creates a long waiting list, limited consultation time and inadequate follow-up care. The scarcity of professionals underscores the urgency of alternative service delivery models supervised task sharing approach (Patel et al., 2018).

Barriers to Accessing Counselling Services

Beyond workforce shortage, multiple structural and social barriers limit access to counselling services

1. Financial Barriers: High out-of-pocket cost and limited insurance coverage
2. Geographical Barriers: Long travel distance especially rural setting
3. Stigma and Discrimination: Negative societal attitude towards mental illness discourage help-seeking

4. Limited mental Health Literacy: Lack of awareness about symptoms and available services
5. Cultural factors: Preference for informal or traditional system

These barriers often intersect, disproportionately affecting individuals in low – resources environments. The World Health Organization emphasize that social determinant such as poverty, unemployment, gender inequality and exposure to violence further compound the risk of mental disorder while simultaneously limiting access to care

The Mental Health treatment gap has the most profound impact on vulnerable and marginalized groups. These include:

1. People living in poverty
2. Women all around the globe, facing different types of problems (like inequality, violence etc)
3. Children and Adolescents
4. Refugees and displaced population
5. Individual living with chronic illness
6. Ethnic and Linguistic Minorities

The cumulative effects of untreated mental health disorder contribute to school dropouts, unemployment, family instability, substance misuse and increased risk of suicide, like chain reaction. Addressing the treatment gap is therefore not only a health priority but also a social economic imperative.

Role of Community Volunteers in Mental Health Support

Community volunteers in mental health are lay individuals who offer psychosocial support within their own communities after receiving structured training and supervision. They are not licensed mental health professionals; rather trusted community members such as teachers, faith leaders, retired workers and youth leaders, peer supporters or community health workers. In many settings, volunteers are selected because of their respected social standing, commitment to services and ability to maintain confidentiality. Programs supported by organizations such as the World Organization, emphasize equipping these individuals with foundational counselling skills while ensuring a clear referral pathway for complex cases. (WHO, 2010)

The volunteers serve many different roles such as basic emotional support, psychoeducation, problem solving assistance, identification of risk factors and linkage to formal services when necessary. One of the significant strengths of the community volunteers is the trust they already hold within their local context. Because they share language, traditions, social norms and lived experiences with those they serve, they are often perceived as approachable and relatable. Cultural competences are inherently embedded in community-based works. Volunteers understand local idioms of distress, culturally specific expression of emotional suffering and community coping mechanisms. This cultural alignment enhances engagement and reduces stigma, particularly in settings where seeking formal mental health care may be viewed negatively.

Evidence from community-led intervention in countries such as Zimbabwe demonstrates that culturally grounded, lay-delivered counselling approaches can significantly reduce symptoms of common mental disorder (Chibanda et al., 2016). Trust and cultural resonance are key factors in such outcomes.

Advantages of Community- Based Support

Increased Accessibility

Services are delivered within familiar environment, reducing travels and cost barrier

Early Identification

Volunteers can recognize early warning signs due to close community contact.

Reduced Stigma

Informal support setting feels less clinical and intimidating.

Cost Effectiveness

Training volunteers requires fewer resources than expanding specialist workforces (Patel et al., 2011).

Strengthened Social Network

Community interventions reinforce collective responsibility and mutual support.

Research highlighted in *The Lancet Commission on Global Mental Health* underscores that task- sharing models can effectively expand service coverage while maintaining acceptable quality standards when adequate supervision is provided (Patel et al., 2018). Community volunteers play a valuable role; clearly defined boundaries are essential. Volunteers must understand the limits of their competence and avoid performing tasks requiring professional licensure, such as diagnosing psychiatric disorders or prescribing medication.

Key Ethical principles

Confidentiality

Safeguarding personal information.

Informed consent

Ensuring individuals understand the nature of support

Non - Maleficence

Avoiding harm through inappropriate advice or overreach.

Referral responsibility

Recognizing when to escalate cases to trained professionals.

Structured supervision systems, often guided by a framework developed by the World Health Organization, help maintain accountability and quality assurance (WHO,2010). Maintaining ethical clarity protects both clients and volunteers, ensuring that community-based health support complements rather than replaces professional care.

Foundations of Basic Counselling Skills

Basic Counselling skills is a crucial component of task- shifting initiatives in mental health care. These foundational skills enable volunteers to provide emotional support, facilitate problems – solving, and guide individuals toward appropriate services while maintaining ethical standards. According to the World Health Organization, non-specialist providers can effectively deliver psychosocial intervention when given structured training, clear guidelines and supervision (WHO ,2016).

Core Counselling Principles

Basic Counselling Principles

Basic Counselling practices are grounded in several key principles that guide interactions between volunteers and individuals seeking support. These include respect for human dignity, empathy, active listening, confidentiality and empowerment of individuals to make their own decisions. Counselling aims to help individuals explore their concerns, understand their emotional responses and develop constructive coping strategies.

A person-centred approach is frequently emphasized in counselling practices, highlighting the importance of respect, authenticity and unconditional positive regard in supporting individuals expressing distress (Rogers, 1957). Community volunteers are trained to focus on facilitating discussion and supporting problem-solving rather than providing direct advice or solutions

Active Listening

Active Listening is a core counselling skill that involves giving full attention to the speaker and demonstrating through verbal and nonverbal communication. It includes techniques such as paraphrasing, summarising, asking open-ended questions and acknowledging emotions.Active Listening helps individuals feel heard, validated and respected. When volunteers listen attentively without interruption or judgement, it encourages individuals to express their concerns more openly and facilitates deeper understanding of the issues they face. (Egan, 2014).

Empathy and Rapport Building

Empathy to the ability to understand another's feelings and perspectives. In counselling, empathy involves recognising emotional experiences and communicating this understanding in a supportive manner. Demonstrating empathy can significantly strengthen rapport between volunteers and individuals seeking help. :Rapport is building involves creating a supportive and respectful relationship where individuals feel comfortable sharing personal concerns. This process includes maintaining a calm and supportive tone, validating emotional experiences and demonstrating patience during conversation (Corey, 2017). Strong rapport improves engagement and encourages individuals to participate in the counselling process.

Non- Judgemental Communication

Non- Judgemental communication is essential for creating a safe counselling environment. Individuals may hesitate to discuss sensitive topics if they fear criticisms or negative reactions. Volunteers must therefore adopt an open and accepting attitude toward diverse experiences, beliefs and behaviours. Avoiding assumptions, respecting cultural differences, and maintaining neutrality are essential aspects of non-judgemental communication. This approach reduces stigma and encourages individuals to discuss their concerns honestly.

Confidentiality and Trust

Confidentiality are fundamental ethical principles in counselling practice. Individuals must be assured that personal information shared during counselling will remain private, except in situations where there is a risk of harm to themselves or others. Maintaining confidently helps establish trust and encourage open communication. The World Health Organization highlights coidentity as a key component of community- based mental health care and recommends clear guidelines for volunteers regarding ethical responsibilities and referral procedures (WHO, 2016).

Designing a Training Program for Volunteers

Developing an effective training program is essential for preparing community volunteers to deliver basic counselling support. Training programs should combine theoretical knowledge, practical skill-building, and continuous supervision to ensure quality care. The first step in designing a training program is conducting a needs assessment. This process identifies the mental health needs within the community, available resources and the skills required for volunteers to provide effective support. Needs assessments may include community surveys, focus group discussion, and consultation with health professional and community leaders, The information gathered helps determine the scope and focus of the training programs (Patel et al., 2011). Once needs are identified, a structured training curriculum can be developed, The curriculum typically includes such as mental health awareness, communication skills, stress management, psychological first aid and referral mechanisms.

Guidelines developed by the World Health Organization, American Psychological Association and to provide evidence-based frameworks for training non specialist health workers in mental health support. The duration of volunteer training programs varies depending on the level of responsibility assigned to volunteers. Introductory training may vary several days, while more comprehensive programs may extend over several weeks and additional refresher sessions.

Training sessions are structured into modules, allowing volunteers to gradually develop both knowledge and skills. Learning methods may include lectures, group discussion, case studies and interactive exercise.

Practical vs. Theoretical Components

A balanced training program includes both theoretical and practical components. Theoretical sessions provide foundational knowledge of mental health conditions, counselling principles and ethical principles. Practical sessions allow volunteers to apply their knowledge through case discussions, supervised practices and field-based learning. Combining theory with practice ensures that volunteers develop confidence in applying counselling skills in real-life situations.

Role-play and stimulation exercises are widely used in counselling training programs. These interactive methods allow volunteers to practice communication techniques, problem-solving skills and emotional support strategies in controlled learning environments among volunteers. Participants take turns in the role of counsellor and client, which helps them understand both perspectives. Trainer provides feedback and guidance, helping volunteers refine their skills and build confidence in handling real-life situations (Egan,2014)

Supervision and Ongoing Support

Effective supervision and ongoing support are essential components of task shifting initiative in mental health care. Community volunteers often have emotionally challenging situations and regular supervision ensures that they receive guidance, maintain ethical standards and continue to develop their counselling skills. Structured supervision systems recommended by the World Health Organization emphasize the importance of professional oversight to maintain quality and safety in community- based mental health services (WHO ,2016). Supervision provides volunteers with the opportunity to discuss difficult cases, receive feedback and strengthen their counselling skills. It also helps ensure that volunteers remain within their scope of practices and follow established ethical guidelines.

Regular supervision sessions allow trained professionals to monitor the quality of support provided, address challenges faced by volunteers, and reinforce best practices. In addition, supervision helps identify situations where an individual requires referral to specialized mental health services. Studies on task-sharing g intervention shows that consistent supervision significantly improves the effectiveness and reliability of community- delivered mental health care (Patel et al., 2011)

Model of Supervision

Different models of supervision can be supporting community volunteers. The most common approaches include:

Individual Supervision

One-on One meeting between a volunteer and trained supervisor to discuss cases and receives personalized feedback

Group Supervision

Volunteer meet together with supervisor to discuss experiences, sharing learning and address common challenges

Peer supervision

Volunteer support one another by discussing case and reflecting on counselling experiences

Remote supervision

In a setting with limited resources, supervision may be conducted through phone calls, online platforms, or digital communication.Each opportunity for reflection, skill development and emotional support. Combining different supervision methods often produces the most effective outcomes in community mental health programs.

Preventing Burnout and Compassion Fatigue

Community volunteers providing mental health support may be exposed to distressing stories and emotionally demanding situations. Without proper support, this exposure can lead to burnout or compassion fatigue. Burnout is characterized by emotional exhaustion, reduced motivation and decreased effectiveness in helping. Compassion fatigue refers to emotional strain experienced from repeatedly hearing about traumatic experiences. Supervision, peer support and self-care are important in preventing these challenges. Volunteers should be encouraged to maintain healthy boundaries, practice stress management techniques and seek assistance when they feel overwhelmed. Creating a supportive team environment and recognising volunteer's contribution can also improve resilience and motivation (Figley, 2002). Ongoing training and professional developmental opportunities help volunteers maintain and enhance their counselling skills. Continuous learning may include refresher workshop, skill building session, and exposure to new mental practices or community support strategies.

Ethical and Legal Considerations

Ethical and legal; consideration is fundamental in community- based counselling services. Volunteers must understand their responsibilities and adhere to ethical principles that protect the dignity, rights and safety of individual receiving support. Clear guidelines and training in ethical practices help maintain trust and accountability in metal health programs.

Informed Consent

Informed Consent refers to the process of ensuring that individuals fully understand the nature and purpose of the counselling support they are receiving. Before beginning any counselling interaction, volunteers should explain their role, the limit of their expertise, and the type of the support they can provide.

Individuals must voluntarily agree to participate in counseling sessions and should be informed that they can withdraw at any time. Ensuring informed consent respects personal autonomy and promotes transparency in counselling relationships (Corey. Corey & Callanan, 2015).

Confidentiality and Privacy

Confidentiality is a core ethical principle in counselling. Individuals must feel confident that the information they share will be protected and not disclosed without their permission.

Maintaining confidentiality helps build trust and encourages open communication. However, there are specific circumstances in which confidentiality may need to be limited, such as when there is risk of harm to the individual or others. Volunteers should be trained to understand these limits and follow appropriate reporting or referral procedures. Ethical guidelines from WHO emphasize the importance of maintaining privacy while ensuring community mental health intervention. Community volunteers play an important role in identifying individuals who require specialized mental health care. Since volunteers are not trained to diagnose or treat severe mental health disorders, a clear referral pathway must be established within the program.

Referral pathway ensure that individual experiencing severe symptoms, suicidal thoughts, substance dependence or complex psychological conditions receive timely assistance from qualified professional such as psychologists, psychiatrist or clinical social workers. Establishing strong links between community volunteer and formal health care systems improves continuity of care and ensures that individuals receive appropriate support when needed (Patel et al., 2018).

Monitoring and Evaluation

Monitoring and evaluation (M&E) are essential components of community-based mental health programs that use task shifting approaches. These processes help determine whether a volunteer is delivering counselling support effectively and whether the intervention is improving mental health outcomes within communities. Systematic monitoring also ensures accountability, program improvement and sustainability. Evaluating the skills acquired by volunteers during training is an important step in determining program effectiveness. Skill acquisition can be measured through various methods such as pre- and post- training assessments, observation of counselling sessions, role-play evaluations and competency checklists.

Supervisors may assess volunteers' abilities in key counselling areas including active listening, empathy, communication skills and ethical decision-making. These assessments help identify areas where volunteers maintain competences in providing basic counselling services. In addition to evaluating volunteer skills, it is important to measure the impact of counselling intervention on individuals receiving support. Client outcomes may include reduction in symptoms of stress anxiety or depression, improved coping skills and increased engagement with community support systems. Standardized screening tools, client feedback surveys, and follow-up interviews can be used to assess these outcomes. Research on task-sharing mental health interventions shows that community- based counselling delivered by trained non-specialist can lead to significant improvement in mental health outcomes when implemented effectively (Patel et al., 2018). Feedback mechanisms enable both volunteers and clients to share their experiences and perspectives about the program. Regular feedback sessions, supervision meetings and anonymous surveys can help identify strength and area for improvement. Encouraging open communication between volunteers, supervisor and community members promotes transparency and program responsiveness. Feedback also helps ensure that services remain culturally relevant and responsive to the needs of the community.

Limitations

Task- shifting has shown significant promise in addressing mental health services gaps, several challenges and limitations must be considered when implementing volunteer-based counselling programs. One of the primary concerns in task shifting models is to maintain consistent quality of care. Volunteers may have varying levels of education, experiences and comfort with counselling. Without adequate supervision and training, there is a risk of inconsistent service delivery. Regular supervisors, refresher training and standardized guidelines are therefore essential for maintaining the quality and safety of community-based mental health services.

In some communities, mental health problems may be misunderstood or stigmatized. Cultural beliefs and traditional practices may influence how an individual perceives mental illness whether they seek help. Community resistance can also arise if mental health intervention is perceived and external or culturally inappropriate. Engaging community leaders, integrating culturally relevant practices and promoting mental health awareness can help reduce resistance and increase acceptance of volunteer- based counselling programs.

Sustaining volunteer engagement over time can be challenging. Volunteers may face competing responsibilities such as employment, family obligation, or educational commitment.Lack of financial incentives or recognition may also contribute to high dropout rates. Providing supportive supervision, recognition, opportunities for skills development and small incentives can improve volunteer motivation and retention. Community volunteers may experience role overload if they are asked to handle too many responsibilities or complex cases beyond their training. This can lead to stress, burnout, and reduced effectiveness. Clearly defined roles, structure referral pathway and manageable workload are necessary to prevent volunteers from becoming overwhelmed and to ensure they operate within their scope of practices

Best Practices

Real-world examples demonstrate the effectiveness of the task-shifting approaches in expanding access to mental health care

One of the most widely recognized initiatives supporting task sharing in mental health is Mental Health GAP Action Programme (mhGAP) developed by World Health Organization. The program provides evidence-based guidelines and training material that enables non-specialist health workers to identify and manage common mental, neurological and substance use disorders in primary care settings (WHO,2016).

The program has been implemented in numerous countries and has contributed to expanding access to mental health services in resources -limited setting

Community Mental Health Model in India

Task sharing or shifting approaches have also been successfully implemented in India. Programs such as the MANAS trial demonstrated that trained lay counsellors working in primary health care settings can effectively deliver intervention for depression and anxiety disorder.

The task shifting model has the potential to extend beyond mental health services. Community volunteers can also contribute to programs addressing chronic disease management, health promotion, substance use prevention and psychosocial support in disaster and humanitarian settings.

Conclusion

Task shifting represents a practical and evidence based approach to address the global mental health treatment gap , particularly in low resources settings. By redistributing selected counselling responsibilities from highly trained professionals to community volunteers , task shifting will give access to essential mental health support while maintaining quality through structured training , supervision and clear referral systems . Task shifting should be viewed not as replacement for professional mental health service but as a complementary strategy that strengthens existing systems. By integrating community based support with formal healthcare structure it offers a scalable , culturally responsive and cost effective pathway towards improving mental health care access and outcomes globally.

References

Chibanda, D., Weiss, H. A., Verhey, R., Simms, V., Munjoma, R., Rusakaniko, S., Chingono, A., Munetsi, E., Bere, T., Manda, E., Abas, M., & Araya, R. (2016). Effect of a primary care–based psychological intervention on symptoms of common mental disorders in Zimbabwe: A randomized clinical trial. *JAMA, 316*(24), 2618–2626.

Corey, G. (2017). *Theory and practice of counseling and psychotherapy* (10th ed.). Cengage Learning.

Corey, G., Corey, M. S., & Callanan, P. (2015). *Issues and ethics in the helping professions* (9th ed.). Cengage Learning.

Egan, G. (2014). *The skilled helper: A problem-management and opportunity-development approach to helping* (10th ed.). Cengage Learning.

Figley, C. R. (2002). Compassion fatigue: Psychotherapists' chronic lack of self-care. *Journal of Clinical Psychology, 58*(11), 1433–1441.

Patel, V., Chowdhary, N., Rahman, A., & Verdeli, H. (2011). Improving access to psychological treatments: Lessons from developing countries. *Behaviour Research and Therapy, 49*(9), 523–528.

Patel, V., Saxena, S., Lund, C., Thornicroft, G., Baingana, F., Bolton, P., Chisholm, D., Collins, P. Y., Cooper, J. L., Eaton, J., Herrman, H., Herzallah, M. M., Huang, Y., Jordans, M. J. D.,

Kleinman, A., Medina-Mora, M. E., Morgan, E., Niaz, U., Omigbodun, O., ... UnÜtzer, J. (2018). The Lancet Commission on global mental health and sustainable development. *The Lancet, 392*(10157), 1553–1598. l, V., Weiss, H. A., Chowdhary, N., Naik, S., Pednekar, S.,

Chatterjee, S., De Silva, M. J., Bhat, B., Araya, R., King, M., Simon, G., & Verdeli, H. (2010). Effectiveness of an intervention led by lay health counsellors for depressive and anxiety disorders in primary care in India (MANAS trial): A cluster randomized controlled trial. *The Lancet, 376*(9758), 2086–2095. Rogers, C. R. (1957). The necessary and sufficient conditions of therapeutic personality change. *Journal of Consulting Psychology, 21*(2), 95–103.

World Health Organization. (2008). *Task shifting: Rational redistribution of tasks among health workforce teams: Global recommendations and guidelines.* WHO Press.

World Health Organization. (2010). *mhGAP intervention guide for mental, neurological and substance use disorders in non-specialized health settings.* WHO Press.

World Health Organization. (2016). *mhGAP intervention guide for mental, neurological and substance use disorders in non-specialized health settings (Version 2.0).* WHO Press.

World Health Organization. (2021). *Guidance on community mental health services: Promoting person-centred and rights-based approaches.* WHO Press.

World Health Organization. (2022). *World mental health report: Transforming mental health for all.* WHO Press.

Chapter 13

Group Interventions for Alcohol Use in Rural Communities

– *Nandana Santhosh*

Introduction

This chapter discusses group-based psychological treatments for alcohol use in rural communities, especially in village panchayat halls, primary health centers (PHCs), and communal areas in rural India. In many villages, drinking, particularly among adult men, is socially accepted. However, harmful drinking often results in family disputes, financial issues, domestic violence, health problems, and job loss.Rural communities typically have limited access to specialized services for addiction, psychiatrists, or clinical psychologists. When available, mental health professionals often cater to large populations with insufficient resources. Challenges like transportation issues, stigma, and financial difficulties further hinder the desire to seek help.

Group interventions offer a culturally appropriate and affordable solution in these settings. Rural areas often value community, making dialogue, shared experiences, and mutual support significant. Structured group counseling can thus be an effective way to tackle alcohol-related problems.

Case Vignette

Raghavan, a 38-year-old farm worker, was referred to the local PHC by a community health worker because of his frequent drinking and family issues. His wife expressed concern about financial instability and emotional distress stemming from his daily alcohol use. Initially, Raghavan denied he had a "problem," but he chose to join a men's support group at the panchayat hall. A six-session group intervention aimed at enhancing motivation, educating participants, and preventing relapse was organized for him and eight other men from the village dealing with similar issues.

Common Mental Health

In rural areas, alcohol use often coexists with other mental health challenges. The following issues are frequently seen:

Alcohol Use Disorder (AUD)

Hazardous and dependent drinking patterns are common. Many people rely on alcohol to cope with financial stress, crop failures, unemployment, or conflicts with others.

Depression and Psychological Distress

Long-term alcohol use is strongly linked to symptoms of depression, feelings of hopelessness, irritability, and sleep problems. In rural men, emotional distress often manifests as physical symptoms like fatigue and body pain.

Family Conflict and Domestic Violence

Alcohol misuse often leads to marital discord, emotional neglect, and, in some cases, intimate partner violence. Family members frequently endure secondary trauma and financial instability.

Limitations

Creating psychotherapy in rural areas requires an understanding of systemic and structural challenges:

Stigma and Denial

Alcohol issues are often downplayed or accepted. Seeking help is sometimes seen as a weakness.

Limited Mental Health Workforce

There may be only one counselor for several villages, limiting the frequency and length of sessions.

Lack of Privacy

Sessions may take place in shared community spaces without soundproofing, compromising confidentiality.

Irregular Attendance

Agricultural work, migration, or financial pressures may lead to inconsistent attendance.

Low Literacy Levels

Interventions should avoid complicated written materials and instead use verbal, visual, and hands-on methods.

Low-Resource Psychotherapy Plan

The intervention includes are

- Motivational Interviewing (MI) principles
- Brief Cognitive Behavioral Therapy (CBT) strategies
- Relapse Prevention Model
- Supportive and peer-based group processes

The aim is to reduce harm, boost motivation for change, and enhance coping strategies.

Session Structure

- Number of Sessions: 6 structured group sessions
- Duration: 60–75 minutes per session
- Group Size: 6–10 participants
- Frequency: Weekly
- Facilitator: Counselor or trained mental health professional (with support from a community health worker)

Session Outline

Session 1: Building Rapport and Psychoeducation

- Introduction and group rules (confidentiality, respect)
- Discussion on myths versus facts about alcohol
- Education on the physical and psychological impact of alcohol
- Exploration of the personal costs and benefits of drinking

Session 2: Motivation Enhancement

- Decisional balance exercise (pros and cons)
- Readiness ruler (0–10 scale)
- Identifying personal goals (family, health, finances)

Session 3: Understanding Triggers

- Identifying high-risk situations (peer pressure, stress, festivals)
- Emotional awareness exercises
- Introduction to alternative coping strategies

Session 4: Coping Skills Training

- Steps for problem-solving
- Stress management (deep breathing, grounding)
- Role-plays for turning down alcohol in social situations

Session 5: Relapse Prevention

- Recognizing early warning signs
- Planning for lapses versus relapse
- Developing personal plans to prevent relapse

Session 6: Strengthening Support and Closure

- Identifying supportive family and community members
- Encouraging accountability among peers
- Group reflection and planning for future actions

Key Techniques Used

- Psychoeducation using visual aids and storytelling
- Techniques from motivational interviewing
- Behavioral self-monitoring (simple tracking calendar)
- Relaxation and breathing exercises
- Group discussions and encouragement from peers
- Culturally relevant metaphors (e.g., "protecting one's harvest")

Ethical and Cultural Considerations

Confidentiality

In group settings in small villages, confidentiality is vital but challenging. Establishing clear group norms from the beginning is necessary. Participants should be aware of the limits of confidentiality.

Informed Consent

Consent should be explained verbally in simple terms due to varying literacy levels. Participation must be voluntary.

Cultural Sensitivity

Alcohol use may relate to norms of masculinity or social rituals. Interventions should avoid judgmental language and maintain a neutral stance.

Gender Considerations

Men may find it hard to express vulnerability. Facilitators should create a respectful environment that allows emotional expression without shame.

Boundaries and Dual Relationships

In rural areas, therapists might meet participants socially. It is crucial to keep professional boundaries clear.

Conclusion

Creating group psychotherapy for alcohol use in rural communities shows the need for flexibility, cultural respect, and practicality. Evidence-based methods like CBT and motivational interviewing need to be adjusted for local language, literacy levels, and social practices. Low-resource situations call for creativity, utilizing community spaces, storytelling, and peer support instead of formal clinical setups. This approach highlights that effective psychotherapy is defined not by elaborate facilities but by responsiveness to the context and connections among people.

References

Beck, J. S. (2011). Cognitive behavior therapy: Basics and beyond (2nd ed.). Guilford Press.

Marlatt, G. A., & Donovan, D. M. (2005). Relapse prevention: Maintenance strategies in the treatment of addictive behaviors (2nd ed.). Guilford Press.

Miller, W. R., & Rollnick, S. (2013). Motivational interviewing: Helping people change (3rd ed.). Guilford Press.

Patel, V., Weiss, H. A., Chowdhary, N., Naik, S., Pednekar, S., Chatterjee, S., De Silva, M. J., Bhat, B., Araya, R., King, M., Simon, G., & Verdeli, H. (2010). Effectiveness of an intervention led by lay health counselors for depressive and anxiety disorders in primary care in India. The Lancet, 376(9758), 2086–2095.

World Health Organization. (2016). mhGAP intervention guide for mental, neurological and substance use disorders in non-specialized health settings (Version 2.0). WHO Press.

Chapter 14

Addressing Stigma: Community Mental Health Outreach in Villages

– Nandana V Menon

Introduction

Villages often have limited access to formal mental health services, with primary health centres, Anganwadi centres, schools, and panchayat offices serving as the main points of contact for general health and community services.They often have minimal access to trained psychologists or psychiatrists, and mental health concerns are frequently addressed only when symptoms become severe. A structured psychological support is rarely available in these settings. The population typically includes individuals from different age groups who depend largely on agriculture, daily wage labour, or small scale occupations for their livelihood. Villages are close-knit social networks and have strong cultural traditions, where community relationships play an important role in daily life.

One of the major barriers of seeking mental health care in rural communities is stigma. Mental illness is frequently misunderstood and associated with shame, weakness, or supernatural causes. People experiencing psychological distress may hesitate to speak openly about their struggles due to fear of social judgment or exclusion. Families may also prevent them from seeking professional help as they worry about how it might affect their social standing in the community. Community mental health outreach programs aim to reduce stigma by bringing mental health awareness and support directly into the village environment. These outreach initiatives involve trained counsellors or community volunteers who provide psychoeducation, basic counselling, and referral services within the village itself. These programs may be conducted in collaboration with local leaders, self-help groups, school teachers, and community health workers. By integrating mental health awareness with existing community structures, outreach initiatives can help normalize conversations about psychological well-being. They can also empower community members to recognize signs of distress and seek help early.

Common Mental Health Issues in This Context

Several psychological concerns are commonly observed in rural village settings. These issues are often influenced by socioeconomic stressors, limited resources, and cultural beliefs.

Depressive and anxiety-related symptoms related to chronic poverty, crop failure, debt, family conflict, and caregiving burdens are highly prevalent in rural communities. It is often expressed as bodily complaints such as headaches, sleep difficulties, and generalized fatigue rather than as explicit mental illness. Rural populations may experience anxiety related to economic instability, crop failure, educational pressures among youth, or family conflicts. Due to stigma and lack of awareness, anxiety symptoms may go unrecognized or untreated. Individuals may perceive their distress as a personal weakness rather than a psychological condition.

Alcohol misuse is yet another concern reported in several rural communities. Excessive alcohol consumption can contribute to domestic conflicts, financial strain, and emotional distress among family members. Women and children in such households may experience chronic stress but have limited opportunities to seek help.

These issues highlight the need for accessible mental health support that is sensitive to the realities of rural life.

Key Constraints

Providing mental health services in village settings involves several challenges. One of the major barriers is stigma and cultural beliefs surrounding mental illness. Mental illness may be associated with shame or supernatural explanations such as spirit possession or curses. As a result, individuals may first seek help from religious or traditional sources rather than mental health professionals.

Another significant challenge is the limited availability of trained mental health professionals. Most villages do not have trained psychologists or counselors. Outreach programs may rely on visiting professionals or trained community volunteers, which limits the frequency and duration of services and they often have limited time during village visits because they must serve many individuals within a short period.

There is also a lack of privacy, where village environments often lack confidential spaces for counselling. Conversations may take place in community halls, health centres, or outdoor settings where privacy is limited. This can make individuals hesitant to share personal information.

Language and literacy barriers also present as many villagers may have limited literacy or may speak regional dialects. Standard psychological assessment tools and therapy materials may not always be easily understood.

Case Vignette

LK, a 32-year-old woman living in a rural village, had been experiencing persistent sadness, fatigue, and difficulty managing daily responsibilities after her husband migrated to the city for work. She often felt overwhelmed but avoided discussing her feelings because she feared being labeled mentally unstable. During a community mental health awareness program organized in the village panchayat hall, she learned about common signs of emotional distress and available support services. After the session, she approached the outreach counsellor privately and agreed to participate in brief supportive counselling sessions conducted during weekly village visits.

Low-Resource Psychotherapy Plan

A brief community based intervention combining psychoeducation and supportive counselling can be effective in rural outreach settings. Elements of brief cognitive behavioural techniques and problem solving therapy can also be incorporated to help individuals manage distress and develop coping strategies. These approaches are suitable because they can be delivered by trained counsellors or community health workers and can be adapted to the local cultural context. Since outreach visits to villages are often limited, the intervention can be structured into a small number of short sessions. Typically, the program may involve three to four sessions lasting about 30–40 minutes each, conducted during community visits or health camps. The first session focuses on building rapport, understanding the individual's concerns, and providing basic psychoeducation about stress and emotional wellbeing. The second session explores the person's main stressors and introduces coping strategies that can be used in daily life. The third session emphasizes problem-solving skills, strengthening social support, and encouraging the use of healthy coping mechanisms.

A short follow-up session may be conducted during a later outreach visit to review progress and provide additional guidance if needed.

Several simple but effective techniques can be used in these brief interventions. Psychoeducation plays an important role in helping individuals understand that emotional distress is a common human experience and not a personal failure. Supportive listening and emotional validation allow individuals to express their feelings in a safe environment, which can reduce feelings of isolation. Counsellors may also introduce problem solving strategies that help individuals identify practical steps to manage everyday challenges. In addition, relaxation techniques such as deep breathing or grounding exercises can help individuals cope with stress and anxiety. Encouraging participation in community groups, self-help groups, or trusted social networks can further strengthen emotional support systems. In cases where severe mental health concerns are identified, individuals may be referred to nearby hospitals or mental health professionals for further care.

Ethical and Cultural Considerations

Ethical practice is essential when delivering mental health services in community settings. In rural villages social networks are closely connected and privacy can be limited. Counsellors must be mindful of maintaining confidentiality, as individuals may hesitate to seek help if they fear their personal concerns will become known to others in the community. It is therefore important to explain the limits of confidentiality clearly and conduct conversations in the most private setting available.

Informed consent is another ethical aspect. Individuals participating in counselling or outreach programs should be informed about the purpose of the sessions, what the process involves, and that participation is completely voluntary. They should also be aware that they have the right to discontinue the sessions at any time without any negative consequences.

Cultural sensitivity is also a key consideration in rural mental health outreach. Many communities may have traditional explanations for psychological distress, including spiritual or cultural beliefs. Rather than dismissing these perspectives, mental health professionals should respectfully acknowledge them and introduce psychological concepts in a culturally understandable way. This approach helps build trust and makes interventions more acceptable to the community.

Using non-stigmatizing and simple language is another important strategy. Technical psychological terms may create fear or misunderstanding; therefore, counsellors should explain mental health using everyday language that is easier for community members to understand. The collaboration with community leaders and local workers such as teachers, ASHA workers, and panchayat members can strengthen the effectiveness of outreach programs. Their support can

help increase awareness, reduce stigma, and encourage community members to participate in mental health initiatives.

Conclusion

Creating a psychological intervention for rural villages emphasizes the adaptability and cultural sensitivity in psychological practice. While advanced therapy techniques may not always be feasible in low resource settings, simple approaches such as psychoeducation, supportive listening, and problem solving can make a meaningful difference. Additionally, community outreach shows that mental health care can be incorporated into regular community spaces rather than being restricted to clinical settings. Improving rural population's access to psychological support requires addressing stigma through awareness and education.

References

Gururaj, G., Varghese, M., Benegal, V., Rao, G. N., Pathak, K., Singh, L. K., ... NMHS Collaborators Group. (2016). National mental health survey of India, 2015–16: Prevalence, patterns and outcomes. National Institute of Mental Health and Neurosciences.

Patel, V., Saxena, S., Lund, C., Thornicroft, G., Baingana, F., Bolton, P., ... Unützer, J. (2018). The Lancet Commission on global mental health and sustainable development. The Lancet, 392(10157), 1553–1598.

Thornicroft, G., Mehta, N., Clement, S., Evans-Lacko, S., Doherty, M., Rose, D., ... Henderson, C. (2016). Evidence for effective interventions to reduce mental-health-related stigma and discrimination. The Lancet, 387(10023), 1123–1132.

World Health Organization. (2017). Depression and other common mental disorders: Global health estimates. World Health Organization.

World Health Organization. (2021). Guidance on community mental health services: Promoting person-centred and rights-based approaches. World Health Organization.

Chapter 15

Brief Counselling for Migrant Workers in Urban Settings

– Sahala Riaz

Introduction

The phenomenon of rapid urbanization and internal migration is one of the defining characteristics of many developing economies in the world, including India. In many cases, a huge population of people migrate from rural and semi-rural areas to urban cities in pursuit of job opportunities and a better quality of life. These migrant workers are often engaged in low income jobs such as construction workers, domestic workers, factory workers, street vendors, and transportation workers. While the migrant workers are provided with economic opportunities, they are often subjected to stressful living and working conditions, which might have a negative impact on their psychological well-being. Some of the challenges faced by migrant workers include social isolation, separation from family members, job insecurity, discrimination, and poor living conditions. These migrant workers often live in crowded labor camps with poor living conditions and lack of privacy and sanitation facilities.

The mental health interventions for migrant workers are usually conducted through community health centers, PHCs, NGO interventions, and mobile health teams. These mental health interventions are usually conducted under difficult circumstances with limited resources and a lack of trained mental health professionals and counseling facilities. In such circumstances, it is difficult to undertake long-term therapy with migrant workers.

As a result, brief counselling approaches have received more attention as a feasible approach in resource-limited settings. Brief counselling involves a short-term, structured approach to alleviate psychological distress while enhancing coping skills in a short period of time. This approach is important in working with migrant workers, who might not have a regular working pattern and easy access to health care services.

In this chapter, brief counselling interventions with migrant workers in urban settings are discussed, including the psychological distress, service delivery constraints, and psychotherapy approaches, as well as the ethical considerations of counselling migrant workers in resource-limited settings.

Description

Migration from rural areas to urban areas is a common social and economic phenomenon in many developing countries, especially in India. Many individuals are migrating from rural areas to urban areas in search of better economic opportunities, better living conditions, and financial security. Migrant workers are often hired in construction jobs, domestic work, manufacturing, transportation, street vending, and in the labor market, among other jobs. Though this is beneficial in many ways, it also presents many psychosocial issues that may affect the migrant worker's mental well-being. Migrant workers in urban areas are often found living in temporary accommodation, such as labor camps, shared accommodation, construction camps, or overcrowded rented accommodations, which may be in poor condition, lack amenities, and may not be very private or hygienic. Migrant workers are often required to work long hours in harsh conditions, with little security and low pay, making their lives very difficult.

The mental health services for migrant populations are usually delivered through community health centers, urban PHCs, mobile health services, NGO outreach services, and workplace health services. In many cases, mental health services are delivered with limited resources, including a lack of mental health professionals and high patient numbers. Counseling services are usually conducted in multipurpose rooms in health centers, outreach settings, and shared spaces with other health services.

Migrant workers are one of the vulnerable groups of people who experience separation from their families and social support networks. In many cases, migrant workers leave their families, including their spouses, children, and aging parents, in their hometowns and move to urban centers in search of jobs. Separation from their families often results in feelings of loneliness and homesickness among migrant workers. Migrant workers are often subjected to discrimination, exploitation, and unsafe working conditions, which can cause mental health problems.

The other problem is that migrant workers may lack awareness regarding mental health services and may not be able to identify their mental health issues. Emotional distress may also be manifested in the form of physical complaints, such as headaches, body pain, tiredness, or gastrointestinal disturbances. People may also refrain from seeking professional help due to their cultural beliefs regarding mental illness, since many individuals may be afraid of being labelled "mentally ill."

Case Vignette

Ramesh is a 28-year-old male who works as a construction worker and migrated from his rural village in northern India to the metropolitan city in search of employment. He is living in a crowded labor camp with other migrant workers and works at the construction site. In the recent past, Ramesh has been experiencing increased fatigue, headaches, and difficulty sleeping. He is concerned about his family and worries about his parents, as they depend on him for financial support.

Ramesh seeks medical attention at the community health clinic due to his physical complaints. During the medical consultation, the medical practitioner realizes that Ramesh is experiencing emotional and psychological problems. The medical practitioner asks Ramesh about his situation, and Ramesh reveals that he is feeling lonely and overwhelmed with work pressure and responsibilities. He is feeling hopeless about his future and thinks about quitting his job, but due to his financial responsibilities, he is unable to do so.

In this situation, a mental health professional working in the clinic may provide brief counselling sessions focused on emotional support, stress management, and problem-solving strategies that help Ramesh cope with the challenges of migrant life.

Common Mental Health Issues in This Context

Migrant workers are exposed to a range of stressors associated with migration, employment conditions, and social isolation. These stressors can contribute to various mental health difficulties, among which depression, anxiety, and adjustment-related stress are the most commonly observed.

Depression and Emotional Distress

Depression is one of the most prevalent mental health conditions among migrant workers. Feelings of sadness, loneliness, and emotional exhaustion often arise due to prolonged separation from family members and the absence of familiar social support networks. Migrants who are unable to return home frequently or communicate regularly with their families may experience intense homesickness and a sense of disconnection from their cultural roots.

Depressive symptoms may include persistent low mood, loss of interest in previously enjoyable activities, fatigue, sleep disturbances, reduced appetite, and feelings of hopelessness. However, these symptoms are often expressed indirectly through somatic complaints, such as headaches, muscle pain, stomach problems, or general weakness. Many migrants use culturally accepted terms such as "stress," "tension," or "mental pressure" to describe their experiences rather than explicitly identifying them as depression.

Financial difficulties can further exacerbate depressive symptoms. Migrant workers often face unstable employment, delayed wages, or unexpected expenses. The pressure to send money home to support family members may lead to feelings of guilt or inadequacy when financial expectations cannot be met.

Anxiety and Chronic Stress

Anxiety is another common mental health concern among migrant workers. The uncertainty associated with temporary employment, unsafe working conditions, and lack of legal protection can create persistent worry and fear. Workers may feel anxious about losing their jobs, sustaining workplace injuries, or failing to meet financial obligations.

Symptoms of anxiety may include excessive worry, irritability, restlessness, difficulty concentrating, and sleep disturbances. In some cases, individuals may experience panic-like symptoms such as palpitations, sweating, dizziness, and shortness of breath. These symptoms may lead migrants to seek medical attention for physical health problems rather than psychological concerns.

Additionally, migrants often experience chronic stress due to demanding work schedules, crowded living conditions, and limited opportunities for rest or recreation. Over time, chronic stress can contribute to emotional exhaustion, burnout, and decreased overall well-being.

Adjustment Problems and Social Isolation

Migration involves significant life transitions that require individuals to adapt to unfamiliar environments, languages, and cultural norms. Migrant workers may struggle to adjust to urban lifestyles, new work environments, and different social expectations. These adjustment difficulties can lead to frustration, irritability, and feelings of helplessness.

Social isolation is another important factor affecting the mental health of migrant workers. Many migrants have limited opportunities to build meaningful social relationships in their host communities. Language barriers and cultural differences may further restrict social interaction, leading to loneliness and emotional distress.

Some migrant workers may also develop maladaptive coping strategies such as alcohol or substance use to manage stress and loneliness. These behaviours can worsen mental health problems and contribute to additional social and occupational difficulties.

Key Constraints

There are a few constraints in providing psychotherapy to migrant workers in urban areas. These constraints affect the level and extent of psychotherapy that can be implemented.

Limited Infrastructure and Privacy

Mental health services provided to migrant workers in community clinics are limited in infrastructure, especially in providing separate areas for psychotherapy sessions. In most cases, psychotherapy is conducted in a shared room with other medical staff or in a makeshift shelter or in a workplace setting.

Time Constraints

Mental health professionals in the community setting are required to see a high volume of clients in a single day. Thus, psychotherapy is generally short-term and focused on addressing immediate issues.

Language and Communication Barriers

Migrant workers are diverse in their language and communication skills. Differences in language and communication may lead to misunderstandings between migrant workers and mental health professionals.

Stigma and Limited Awareness

Mental health stigma is a major limitation in providing psychotherapy to migrant workers. Migrant workers may be reluctant to seek psychotherapy services due to the stigma or fear of being discriminated against by their peers or in their communities because of their mental illness or lack of awareness about the services.

Economic Constraints and Irregular Schedules

Migrant workers often have unpredictable work schedules and limited financial resources. These factors can make it difficult for individuals to attend multiple counselling sessions or follow-up appointments. To cater to the mental health of migrant workers in resource-limited environments, a brief counselling approach incorporating supportive counselling and aspects of Cognitive Behavioural Therapy (CBT) has been suggested.

Low-Resource Psychotherapy Plan

The counselling approach focuses on brief, structured interventions designed to provide emotional support and practical coping strategies within a limited number of sessions. The primary components include:

Therapy Approach

The counselling approach focuses on brief, structured interventions designed to provide emotional support and practical coping strategies within a limited number of sessions. The primary components include:

- Supportive counselling
- Brief CBT techniques
- Psychoeducation
- Problem-solving strategies
- Stress management skills

Session Structure

A typical brief counselling intervention may include 4-6 sessions over a period of six to eight weeks.

Session 1: Assessment and Rapport Building.

The counsellor gathers information about the client's migration history, current stressors, emotional experiences, and coping strategies. The session focuses on establishing trust and providing initial emotional support.

Session 2: Psychoeducation and Emotional Awareness.

The counsellor explains the relationship between stress, thoughts, emotions, and behaviour. Clients are helped to identify emotional triggers and recognize early signs of psychological distress.

Session 3: Stress Management and Relaxation Techniques.

Clients learn simple relaxation strategies such as deep breathing exercises, progressive muscle relaxation, and mindfulness techniques to reduce anxiety and tension.

Session 4: Problem-Solving and Behavioural Activation.

The counsellor guides the client through structured problem-solving steps to address practical challenges related to work, finances, or social relationships. Behavioral activation encourages engagement in meaningful and rewarding activities.

Session 5-6: Consolidation and Relapse Prevention.

The final sessions focus on reviewing progress, strengthening coping skills, and developing long-term strategies for managing stress.

Key Techniques

Psychoeducation

Giving information on stress, emotions, and coping strategies helps in the normalization of mental health and the removal of any stigma.

Grounding Techniques

These are simple strategies that help in dealing with emotions and anxiety.

Behavioural Activation

Engaging in activities that are meaningful and enjoyable helps in improving mood and reducing symptoms of depression.

Cognitive Reframing

This helps the client change negative thoughts and adopt more balanced ways of thinking.

Social Support Enhancement

Communicating with family members and developing supportive relationships within the migrant community can help alleviate feelings of loneliness and emotional distress.

Ethical and Cultural Considerations

Confidentiality

It is important to maintain confidentiality; however, in a busy clinic setting, this can be challenging. It is therefore important to be open and clear about the boundaries and ensure that the conversation is held in the most private space.

Informed Consent

It is important to ensure the client is aware of the purpose of the therapy, the length of the therapy sessions, and the right to end the sessions at any time.

Cultural Sensitivity

A counsellor has to respect cultural beliefs and values associated with mental health, family relationships, and coping mechanisms. Cultural concepts can be incorporated to encourage clients to participate in therapy.

Professional Boundaries

Professional boundaries are essential, especially when working with close-knit migrant communities.

Equity and Non-Discrimination

Migrant workers should have access to mental health services regardless of their language, religious affiliations, and socio-economic status.

Conclusion

Implementing a counseling intervention for migrant workers underscores the need to make psychological interventions more practical and applicable in the real world. Mental health service providers working in resource-scarce environments need to be effective problem solvers who are flexible, culturally aware, and practical. The effectiveness of brief counseling models shows the potential of counseling to make a substantial difference in people's emotional lives, as long as they are delivered with empathy, respect, and cultural understanding. This experience underlines the need for accessible community-based mental health services to address the special needs of migrant workers.

References

Hooper, C. R. (2010). Ethical and professional challenges in mental health care in low- and middle-income countries. *International Review of Psychiatry, 22*(3), 245-251.

Jenkins, J. H., & DelVecchio Good, M. J. (2014). Global mental health and cultural psychiatry: Toward a more integrated approach. *Transcultural Psychiatry, 51*(6), 803-826. Miller, K. E., & Rasmussen, A. (2017). The mental health of civilians displaced by armed conflict: An ecological model of refugee distress. *Social Science & Medicine, 70*(1), 7-16.

Patel, V., Saxena, S., Lund, C., Thornicroft, G., Baingana, F., Bolton, P., Chisholm, D., Collins, P. Y., Cooper, J. L., Eaton, J., Herrman, H., Herzallah, M., Huang, Y., Jordans, M., Kleinman, A., Medina-Mora, M. E., Morgan, E., Niaz, U., Omigbodun, O., ... UnÜtzer, J. (2018). The Lancet Commission on global mental health and sustainable development. *The Lancet, 392*(10157), 1553-1598.

Steel, Z., Chey, T., Silove, D., Marnane, C., Bryant, R., & Van Ommeren, M. (2009). Association of torture and other potentially traumatic events with mental health outcomes among populations exposed to mass conflict and displacement. *Journal of the American Medical Association, 302*(5), 537-549.

Thornicroft, G., Deb, T., & Henderson, C. (2016). Community mental health care worldwide: Current status and further developments. *World Psychiatry, 15*(3), 276-286.

World Health Organization. (2016). *mhGAP intervention guide for mental, neurological and substance use disorders in non-specialized health settings (Version 2.0).* World Health Organization.

World Health Organization. (2022). *World mental health report: Transforming mental health for all.* World Health Organization.

Zimmerman, C., Kiss, L., & Hossain, M. (2011). Migration and health: A framework for 21st century policy-making. *PLoS Medicine, 8*(5), e1001034.

Chapter 16

Low-Resource Interventions for Domestic Violence Survivors

– Rakshitha A

Introduction

Most real-world environments deliver psychological treatment through urgent spaces which lack both time and privacy of traditional clinics. The chapter presents an urban NGO shelter home which offers temporary sheltering to women who escape domestic violence. The shelters provide essential support to survivors who lack social connections and financial resources and access to professional mental health treatment.

Women arriving at shelter homes typically do so following acute crises such as severe physical assault, threats to life, or forced removal from their homes. Many people who experience intimate relationship abuse suffer through lengthy periods of physical and emotional and sexual mistreatment. The entry process shows their emotional state through three main feelings which include fear and confusion and exhaustion and uncertainty about structured psychotherapy.

The delivery of mental health services in this setting consists of short and disjointed treatment sessions. A single or double professional team provides counselling services while dealing with extensive client needs from their communal work area. Legal obligations and childcare needs and safety issues cause regular session interruptions. Psychotherapy needs to change from its idealized format to techniques which meet actual psychological requirements through culturally appropriate methods (Patel et al., 2018). The goal establishes emotional support and validation during critical transitional periods instead of achieving complete trauma recovery.

Common Mental Health Issues in This Context

Domestic violence survivors develop psychological problems which result from their continual exposure to intimidation and domination and their complete disregard of personal feelings. Three primary issues arise within shelter environments which show an interconnected relationship to each other.

Depressive symptoms are widely observed and people commonly demonstrate them through their constant experience of sadness and their tendency to cry and their state of emotional numbness and their extreme tiredness and their perception of worthless existence. Survivors frequently internalize blame for the abuse, questioning their own actions or believing they failed to meet expected social or marital roles (Walker, 2009). The experience of depression becomes more severe through the loss of family relationships and social identity and economic security.

People experience anxiety throughout their lives with fear-based symptoms. Survivors exhibit hypervigilance and constant danger assessment after they escape from unsafe environments which involves them worrying about their personal protection and their children's safety and legal matters that will affect their future. Dutton and his colleagues (2006) found that people often experience sleep problems and become irritable and have trouble focusing and report physical symptoms which include headaches and body discomfort.

People show trauma responses which develop after they experience either multiple violent events or one extreme violent incident. The symptoms include intrusive memories and avoidance behaviors and emotional dysregulation and a constant feeling of danger. Survivors experience trauma symptoms which prevent them from functioning in their daily lives and from achieving emotional healing although not all of them fulfill the post-traumatic stress disorder diagnosis criteria (Herman 1992).

Key Constraints

Psychological intervention in NGO shelter homes is restricted by established boundaries which require active monitoring of ethical principles. The main obstacle exists because counselors need to handle their current caseloads while they only possess limited time to conduct brief client sessions. Therapy may be interrupted or discontinued because of the need to move between locations or because of safety concerns or legal matters.

The total absence of private space represents a major obstacle that needs to be dealt with. The counselling process usually occurs in public areas where complete protection of patient confidentiality remains impossible. The situation might prevent people from disclosing their feelings because they have special ties to their friends and family members who have been sexually assaulted.

Cultural and social barriers determine how people participate in different activities. Many societies treat domestic violence as a normal occurrence which should not be discussed outside the home. Survivors experience shameful feelings because they fear social judgment and face pressure to reunite with their abusive partners (Jewkes 2002). People face assessment challenges because they lack language skills and basic reading skills and they do not know psychological terms.

The need for basic verbal treatment methods which focus on relationship building emerges because organizations face resource shortages and they lack access to advanced treatment methods and specialist resources.

Low-Resource Psychotherapy Plan

The proposed intervention adopts a brief supportive counselling approach which utilizes both trauma-aware and cognitive-behavioural principles to provide its main therapeutic framework. The primary aim is emotional stabilization rather than intensive trauma processing. The method enables people to navigate dangerous situations because it provides protection together with safety and validation and empowerment, which people need to develop their coping abilities in difficult situations (Murray et al., 2011). The therapy helps survivors understand their emotional reactions because it needs to help them regain their sense of control.

Session Structure

The intervention requires 4 to 6 sessions which each session lasts about 30 to 40 minutes. The program adapts its session schedule according to when survivors feel emotionally ready to participate and when they are available. The program prefers individual sessions but it allows informal group interactions to provide supplementary support when necessary.

Key Techniques to Be Used

Psychoeducation helps survivors understand that their emotional and physical reactions are normal responses to prolonged stress and abuse. The process of normalization leads to decreased self-blame while they achieve better emotional understanding (Herman, 1992).

The program introduces grounding together with emotional regulation techniques through its slow breathing and sensory grounding methods to handle anxiety and trauma-related arousal. The techniques are affordable and easy to learn because they can be practiced independently by users (Tol et al., 2011).

The solution focuses on multiple problem-solving strategies because it needs to handle both parenting problems and daily life challenges. Survivors should select minor objectives because they will develop a feeling of authority through their achievement. Throughout therapy, supportive validation remains central. The counsellor consistently affirms that responsibility for the abuse lies with the perpetrator and acknowledges survivors' resilience.

Case Vignette

Lata, a 32-year-old woman, arrived at an NGO shelter with her two young children after leaving an abusive marriage. She described years of physical violence, verbal humiliation, and controlling behaviour by her husband. Meena experienced frequent crying and poor sleep and persistent fear and feelings of helplessness since she entered the shelter. The counselling sessions took place in a structured format which is most apt to Meena.

The first session produced an intervention plan which continued until its fifth session. The initial sessions established trust between the two parties while the session leaders taught participants about how trauma affects human behavior. Meena learned basic breathing techniques and grounding techniques to help her handle panic attacks and feelings of fear. The following sessions focused on assisting Meena with her childcare duties while developing her emotional management skills. Meena developed better emotional stability through continuous validation and support which helped her manage her current situation.

Ethical and Cultural Considerations

The practice of ethical work in domestic violence situations which lack sufficient resources requires workers to give special consideration to both protection of confidential information and the safety of their work. The World Health Organization 2013 requires counsellors to explain their confidentiality limits while implementing measures which safeguard protected information. The process of obtaining informed consent requires organizations to present information through simple language which enables survivors to comprehend their right to choose whether to participate in counselling. Survivors should never be pressured to disclose traumatic experiences before they feel ready.

Counsellors need to establish professional boundaries which protect their clients because they work in shelter settings where they must do multiple duties with their clients. The practice of cultural sensitivity enables professionals to understand how various cultural beliefs about marriage and gender roles and family honor impact the survivor experience. The interventions need to maintain respect for cultural practices while they work to change social standards which allow violence to occur and people to blame themselves.

Conclusion

The development of a psychotherapy intervention for low-resource environments helped me to learn fundamental lessons that overturned my preconceptions about therapy operations. The study demonstrated that psychological training uses fixed methods and extended treatment approaches as primary teaching methods yet actual work requires professionals to exhibit adaptable skills and maintain appropriate responses to different situations. The first lesson showed that people should always choose to create secure environments before attempting to reach deeper understanding. In settings marked by uncertainty and crisis, emotional containment and validation are often more therapeutic than insight-oriented work. The exercise demonstrated that minor interventions, which include basic grounding techniques and short periods of empathic listening, produce significant outcomes when resources are restricted.

The process established that psychotherapy requires basic conditions which enable therapists to deliver their work to clients. The need for real therapy practice had therapists to provide survivor-focused care which combined empathy with actual survivor experiences.

References

Briere, J., & Scott, C. (2015). *Principles of trauma therapy* (2nd ed.). Sage.

Campbell, J. C. (2002). Health consequences of intimate partner violence. *The Lancet, 359*(9314), 1331–1336.

Dutton, M. A., Green, B. L., Kaltman, S. I., Roesch, D. M., Zeffiro, T. A., & Krause, E. D. (2006). Intimate partner violence, PTSD, and adverse health outcomes. *Journal of Interpersonal Violence, 21*(7), 955–968.

Herman, J. L. (1992). *Trauma and recovery*. Basic Books.

Jewkes, R. (2002). Intimate partner violence: Causes and prevention. *The Lancet, 359*(9315), 1423–1429.

Murray, L. K., et al. (2011). Common elements treatment approach for adult mental health problems in low-resource settings. *Cognitive and Behavioral Practice, 18*(2), 173–185.

Patel, V., Saxena, S., Lund, C., et al. (2018). The Lancet Commission on global mental health. *The Lancet, 392*(10157), 1553–1598.

Tol, W., Barbui, C., Galappatti, A., et al. (2011). Outcomes of mental health interventions in humanitarian settings. *PLoS Medicine, 8*(5), e1001036.

Walker, L. E. (2009). *The battered woman syndrome* (3rd ed.). Springer.

World Health Organization. (2013). *Responding to intimate partner violence and sexual violence against women.* WHO Press.

World Health Organization. (2022). *Guidelines for the management of conditions specifically related to stress.* WHO Press.

Chapter 17

Psychotherapy for Street-Connected Youth in India: Ethical and Practical Challenges

– Nitin Benoy

Introduction

Street-connected youth in India experience layered psychosocial vulnerability arising from poverty, migration, family disruption, exposure to violence, substance use, and chronic exclusion from education, healthcare, and protection systems. Recent Indian evidence and policy guidance show that children in street situations are at heightened risk of exploitation, abuse, unstable living conditions, and significant emotional distress, while also facing major barriers to sustained mental health care. Within the Indian child protection framework, they are recognized as children in need of care and protection, requiring coordinated responses across shelters, outreach services, Child Welfare Committees, and community-based organizations.

This chapter applies a low-resource psychotherapy lens to street-connected adolescents in India, using the policy term "children in street situations" (CiSS) while recognising that some young people aged 18-19 may still be street-connected but no longer legally "children". The chapter assumes (because these details are unspecified) an urban, low-resource Indian setting; an age range of 12-19; and an NGO drop-in centre with street outreach near transport hubs and informal work sites. Indian child protection policy frames CiSS as a subset of "children in need of care and protection" under the Juvenile Justice system, with Child Welfare Committees as the statutory decision-makers for care, restoration, and rehabilitation pathways. A brief, trauma-informed, stepped-care psychotherapy plan is proposed that (a) prioritises safety and engagement using Psychological First Aid (PFA) principles, (b) delivers a short skills package centred on problem-solving and stress-management methods with evidence from Indian adolescent trials, and (c) "steps up" to public mental health services and safeguarding mechanisms when risk is high.

In India, "children in street situations" is a widely used framing that recognises diverse patterns of street connection (living alone on the street, working on the street but returning home, or living on the street with family). National guidance in India places CiSS within the Juvenile Justice (Care and Protection of Children) framework as children in need of care and protection (CNCP), emphasising that institutionalisation should be a last resort and that systems should first attempt family strengthening and safe restoration when in the child's best interests.

This chapter assumes an urban, low-resource service model typical of many Indian cities: an NGO drop-in centre offering food, bathing facilities, basic first aid, informal education support, and a quiet corner for brief counselling, alongside a small outreach team that does engagement contacts at hotspots (railway/bus stations, markets, traffic junctions, construction sites). This model aligns with the practical reality that many CiSS have irregular attendance, lack identity documentation, and are at risk of exploitation, requiring simultaneous psychosocial support and protection-oriented casework.

Case vignette

Rehan (15) sleeps near a railway station with a small peer group and does intermittent work loading goods. He reports being "on edge all the time", frequent anger outbursts, and trouble sleeping. He avoids a particular platform after being beaten by older youth there. He sometimes uses inhalants ("solution/whitener") to "numb the mind", and he is unsure whether he can return home because he fears being punished for leaving.

At the drop-in centre, Rehan agrees to talk but insists that "police should not know". The counsellor has 30 minutes, no guaranteed privacy, and no assurance of follow-up. A brief plan is created that prioritises immediate safety, stabilisation skills, and a small, achievable next step (linking him to a safer sleeping option that night and scheduling a short follow-up via outreach within 72 hours).

Common Mental Health Issues in This Context

Street-connected adolescents in India commonly present with trauma- and stress-related symptoms rather than neatly labelled disorders: hypervigilance, irritability, sleep disturbance, intrusive memories, and avoidance behaviours linked to violence, coercion, and chronic insecurity. Evidence from vulnerable Indian adolescent populations with histories of child work and maltreatment shows a high burden of mental health symptoms, including internalising problems and trauma-related presentations, with gendered patterns (girls reporting more PTSD and somatisation symptoms; boys more conduct-related symptoms). turn19view1

A second frequent cluster is depressive and anxiety presentations shaped by "everyday adversity"(poverty, family conflict, unstable shelter, social exclusion). UNICEF's India synthesis highlights that mental health challenges in CiSS are driven by exposure to violence/

trauma, unstable finances and living conditions, and limited social support; children describe stress, "tension", anxiety and depression-like experiences in ways that often blend emotional and practical concerns.In Indian clinical and community research, distress is also often communicated through culturally familiar idioms such as "tension" and through somatic complaints, which can influence engagement and assessment if clinicians rely only on diagnostic language.

A third common issue is substance use as coping, peer bonding, and survival strategy, particularly inhalant use and tobacco products among younger adolescents. An Indian cross-sectional study among street children in Guwahati (ages 5–18) found very high rates of substance use, with glue sniffing prominent among users—illustrating how early initiation and high prevalence can become embedded in street peer ecology. turn9view4 Clinically, substance use interacts with sleep, mood, aggression, and risk exposure, and often requires harm-reduction steps even when abstinence-focused treatment is not immediately feasible.

Limitations

Privacy and confidentiality are structurally fragile in outreach.PFA guidance stresses that helpers should seek privacy when possible and that privacy is essential for dignity and confidentiality when discussing sensitive harms such as sexual violence.In Indian outreach, conversations may occur in semi-public spaces, and young people may reasonably fear disclosure to police, employers, exploiters, or even family members, making "confidentiality" less a promise and more a negotiated practice with explicit limits.

Continuity is unreliable. CiSS may be mobile across hotspots and cities; attendance at a drop-in centre varies with work, policing, health, weather, and peer movement. UNICEF documents the long-standing difficulty of even estimating street-child populations nationally, underscoring how service planning must work under uncertainty and churn. Therefore, therapy must be designed so that each contact delivers standalone value and can be interrupted without destabilising the young person. Language, literacy, and idioms of distress affect assessment and technique delivery.

Tools that depend on reading/writing may fail; "tension", fear ("ghabrahat"), anger, and bodily symptoms may be more meaningful than psychiatric terms, and young people may not identify their experience as a "mental disorder".

This has direct practical consequences: psychoeducation must be concrete, normalising, and locally intelligible, while still allowing risk detection (self-harm, psychosis, severe withdrawal). High caseloads and few specialists require task-sharing with quality safeguards.

India's public system has scaled community mental health through programmes such as the District Mental Health Programme, with district teams including specialist roles but variable practical availability. For NGO settings, the main constraint is not only "few specialists" but also limited supervision capacity, making competency-based training and supervision approaches (e.g., WHO-UNICEF EQUIP) relevant to reduce harm and maintain fidelity in brief psychological interventions.

Low-Resource Psychotherapy Plan

Therapy approach. A pragmatic stepped-care approach is recommended: (1) immediate engagement and stabilisation using PFA principles ("look, listen, link") while avoiding coercive emotional processing; (2) a brief, transdiagnostic skills package focused on stress management and structured problem-solving; and (3) step-up referral guided by mhGAP-style identification of priority conditions (self-harm risk, psychosis, severe substance use disorders, safeguarding emergencies). This approach is chosen because Indian evidence shows that brief, lay counsellor–delivered problem-solving can improve adolescent-identified psychosocial problems and supports its role as a first-line intervention in stepped care.

Session structure. Four sessions of 30-45 minutes are planned over 2-4 weeks, delivered flexibly at the drop-in centre or via outreach. Because missed contacts are expected, each session is designed as a "complete unit": it begins with a risk/safety check-in and ends with one concrete next step plus a written/pictorial coping card. Where only a single contact occurs, Session 1 plus one chosen skill (grounding or problem-solving micro-step) constitutes a minimum viable intervention. This reflects PFA's emphasis on practical, humane support without pressuring disclosure, and adolescent trial evidence that brief problem-solving delivered over a short window can be beneficial.

Key Techniques

1. PFA micro-skills: safety assessment, practical help, and linkage to supports
2. Grounding and physiological down-regulation (paced breathing; 5-sense grounding)
3. Culturally adapted psychoeducation ("stress and tension live in the body; skills bring the body back under your control")
4. Structured problem-solving (define, brainstorm, choose, plan, review);
5. Behavioural activation ("get going, keep doing" logic drawn from scalable transdiagnostic models) but translated into realistic street routines

6. Harm-reduction planning for substance use (triggers, safer alternatives, emergency steps)
7. Social support mapping and help-seeking rehearsal.

Ethical and Cultural Considerations

Consent and safeguarding for minors without guardians. Many CiSS do not have an available caregiver to provide consent; ethical practice therefore relies on (1) the young person's informed assent/consent to the extent possible, (2) the "best interests" principle embedded in child protection frameworks, and (3) timely engagement with statutory mechanisms when protection decisions exceed the NGO's remit. turn19view2turn1search8turn4view1 For formal mental health treatment decisions involving "minors with mental illness", Indian law provides for a nominated representative (typically the legal guardian, unless a Board appoints another suitable person), which becomes relevant when stepping up into regulated mental health establishment care rather than brief NGO counselling.

Mandatory reporting and coordinated protection. In India, the POCSO Act includes procedures for reporting offences and penalties for failure to report, while also mandating rapid linkage to care and protection and notification to the Child Welfare Committee. In practice, NGO counsellors should explain (early and repeatedly) that confidentiality has limits when there is imminent risk, sexual exploitation, or serious harm, and should plan "how" reporting will happen with the young person to reduce betrayal and improve safety (e.g., where they will stay that night; who accompanies them).

Confidentiality in outreach and data/storage safety. Confidentiality is not only a conversation rule; it is a data-handling system. UNICEF's India study describes concrete safeguards (seeking assent, minimising identifying information, using password-protected folders, limiting access, and deleting files from personal devices after transfer), illustrating feasible practices even in fieldwork with vulnerable adolescents.

In 2023, India enacted the Digital Personal Data Protection Act, which requires "verifiable consent" of a parent/lawful guardian before processing digital personal data of a child and prohibits processing likely to cause detrimental effects on the child's wellbeing. 1 For NGO psychotherapy notes, a conservative "minimum necessary data" approach is ethically preferable: avoid collecting Aadhaar numbers unless required for a specific protection benefit, store identifiers separately from clinical notes, restrict access, and treat any digital sharing (messaging, photos, location data) as high-risk.

Boundaries when material aid is provided. When food, shelter, or legal help is linked to the same programme that offers counselling, inadvertent coercion is a live risk: youth may feel they must disclose trauma to "deserve" assistance. PFA guidance emphasises "do no harm", practical help, respect, and supporting people's agency rather than extracting narratives.

Operationally, programmes should separate eligibility for basic services from willingness to participate in counselling, keep gifts and money rules consistent, and document boundaries (home visits, social media contact, phone access) to protect both staff and young people.

Cultural idioms of distress and engagement. In India, "tension" often functions as an idiom that connects social adversity, bodily symptoms, and emotional suffering; many people report "tension" without describing themselves as having a mental illness, and may present primarily somatic complaints. turn18search7turn18search1 For street-connected youth, this suggests that culturally sensitive psychotherapy should begin with problem-areas the adolescent identifies (sleep, fear, anger, headaches, concentration, conflict), translate skills into everyday language, and avoid pathologising survival behaviours while still naming risks (self-harm, exploitation, severe dependence).

Gendered Risks and Differentiated Safety Planning

Indian evidence and synthesis consistently indicate gendered patterns: girls face disproportionate sexual harassment, assault, and exploitation risks, while boys may report higher rates of physical abuse in some samples; both patterns demand gender-responsive safety planning and referral. This also affects therapy logistics (who is present in sessions, safe travel routes, safe shelter options, and when involving family increases danger).

Conclusion

Designing psychotherapy for street-connected adolescents in India clarifies that "techniques" are only effective when embedded in protection, trust, and realistic service pathways. A low-resource plan must treat ethics (non-coercion, transparent confidentiality limits, safe data practices) as core clinical mechanisms, not administrative extras, and must translate evidence-based skills into locally meaningful idioms ("tension", sleep, anger, safety) while maintaining clear thresholds for safeguarding and step-up care.

References

Michelson, D., Malik, K., Parikh, R., Weiss, H. A., Doyle, A. M., Bhat, B., ... Patel, V. (2020). Effectiveness of a brief lay counsellor-delivered, problem-solving intervention for adolescent mental health problems in urban, low-income schools in India: A randomised controlled trial

National Commission for Protection of Child Rights. (2020). Standard operating procedure (SOP) for care and protection of children in street situations (SOP 2.0). Government of India.

Pandey, R., Gupta, S., Upadhyay, A., & Kumar, P. (2020). Childhood maltreatment and its mental health consequences among Indian adolescents with a history of child work. Journal of Child and Adolescent Trauma.

UN Committee on the Rights of the Child. (2017). General comment No. 21 (2017) on children in street situations.

UNICEF. (2024). Study of children in street situations in India.UNICEF India.

World Health Organization. (2011). Psychological first aid: Guide for field workers.WHO.

World Health Organization. (2016). mhGAP intervention guide for mental, neurological and substance use disorders in non-specialized health settings:

World Health Organization. (2018). Problem management plus (PM+): Individual psychological help for adults impaired by distress in communities exposed to adversity (generic field-trial World Health Organization. (2020). Doing what matters in times of stress: An illustrated guide. WHO.

Chapter 18

Trauma-Informed Counselling in Urban Shelter Homes

–Paravathy V

Introduction

Urban shelter homes can be defined as residential facilities that offer protection, care, and support to vulnerable individuals like abandoned children, homeless people, victims of domestic violence, and people who face severe social or economic problems. These shelter homes are often run by government departments, non-governmental organizations (NGOs), or community-based organizations. In most metropolitan cities, shelter homes can be considered emergency support systems for people who do not have a proper place to stay. The population of urban shelter homes is very diverse and may include people like children who face abuse or abandonment, teenagers who run away from home, women who face domestic abuse, and people who face poverty or homelessness. These people often face traumatic experiences like physical abuse, emotional abuse, loss of family support, or exposure to violence.

In shelter homes, there are limited facilities when it comes to providing mental health services. For instance, a counsellor may have limited time, space, and facilities to provide counselling to a client. Secondly, shelter homes are characterized by a high number of residents, thus increasing the workload of caregivers and counsellors. Despite these challenges, psychological support is very important because trauma has a huge effect on a person's life.

Trauma-informed counselling is a therapeutic approach that seeks to address a client's psychological and emotional well-being after experiencing a traumatic event. It is different from other therapeutic approaches because it seeks to address a client's feelings of safety, empowerment, trust, and sensitivity.

In urban shelter homes, trauma-informed counselling is very useful in helping residents regain a sense of security even when resources are limited.

Common Mental Health Issues in This Context

People who live in urban shelters often have mental health problems because of the bad things that have happened to them in their lives. Some of the most common mental health problems in this group are stress from trauma, depression, and anxiety. One of the psychological problems that people who live in a shelter home may have is stress from trauma. This is because most of the people who live there have been physically abused, emotionally neglected, or exposed to violence. People who live in shelters often have depression as well. People who live in shelters may feel hopeless, sad, and unmotivated in their lives. Some things that can make people depressed are being away from their family, not knowing what will happen in the future, and not being able to change their living situation. People who are depressed may also show signs of withdrawal from social activities, tiredness, and a lack of interest in their daily routine. A lot of these people also have anxiety disorders. They might be worried about their safety, their family, or what will happen in the future. People who are anxious may show it by being restless, having trouble focusing, or having physical problems like headaches or stomach pain. Adolescents residing in shelter homes may exhibit behavioural issues such as aggression, irritability, or challenges in adhering to rules. This behaviour is not deliberate; it is an expression of their emotional turmoil. A trauma-informed approach can help the counsellor understand why the person is acting the way they are and respond with kindness instead of punishment.

Key Constraints

There are some practical problems with doing psychotherapy in urban shelter homes. The lack of privacy is a big problem. The counselling room may be shared with other offices in shelter homes, which may not be very big. Clients might find it hard to speak up. Time limits are another big problem that needs to be thought about. The counsellor may have to help several residents, which could mean that each person only has a short amount of time during the session. Most of the time, only short sessions can be held.

1. A high number of clients is another big problem that needs to be thought about. Shelter homes are meant to house a lot of people with different mental health needs, and mental health workers may not have enough support staff. So, the mental health worker may have to handle emergencies and give basic emotional support to other people.
2. Stigma surrounding mental health may also influence the efficacy of counselling interventions. People who live in shelters might not want to get mental health help because of the stigma that comes with mental illness.
3. Language barriers might also affect the counselling interventions. Shelter homes are mostly located in urban areas and provide shelter to people with different linguistic

and cultural backgrounds. Language barriers might affect the counselling interventions because the mental health worker and the client might not speak the same language.

Considering all the challenges and limitations, it becomes essential to develop psychotherapy interventions that are flexible, time-effective, and easily adaptable to the shelter settings.

Low Resource Psychotherapy Plan

In the context of urban shelter homes, a trauma-informed supportive counselling approach along with brief cognitive- behavioral techniques (CBT) may be effective. This approach to counselling focuses on emotional safety, stabilization, and the building of coping skills. The first aim is not to engage in long-term psychotherapy but to help individuals gain a sense of control over their lives and emotional stability approach.

Session Structure

A brief intervention model can be implemented over three to five sessions, depending on the resident's needs.

1. Session duration:30-40 minutes
2. Frequency: Once per week or based on availability
3. Format: Individual sessions with optional small group activities.

This flexible structure allows counsellors to provide meaningful psychological support within the limitations of shelter environments.

Key Techniques Used

1. ***Psychoeducation***: The first step includes educating the residents about trauma and emotions. The counsellor helps the residents understand that emotions like fear, sadness, and anger are normal

reactions to trauma. This helps the residents overcome guilt and understand emotions.

2. ***Grounding and relaxation techniques*** :Basic grounding techniques can be used to cope with difficult emotions. Techniques like deep breathing, sensory experiences, and muscle relaxation can calm the body. These techniques are easy to use even outside the counselling room.
3. ***Emotional Validation and Supportive Listening***: A trauma-informed approach emphasizes empathy and Validation. Counsellors listen without judgment and acknowledge the client's feelings. This process helps build trust and promotes emotional safety.
4. ***Problem Solving Skills:*** Residents are guided to identify practical challenges they are facing and develop small, manageable solutions. For example, adolescents may work on strategies to manage conflicts with peers or improve daily routines.
5. ***Strength Based Approach:*** Counsellors highlight the individual's strengths and resilience. Recognizing personal strengths can increase confidence and promote hope for the future.

Case Vignette

Anjali, a 16-year-old girl, has recently been admitted to the urban shelter home after fleeing an abusive family environment. She was found to be withdrawn and avoided social interactions with the other inmates. She complained of nightmares and sleep deprivation, along with feelings of fear when reminded of her past experiences.

Due to a lack of counselling facilities in the shelter, a brief counselling plan following a trauma-informed approach was developed. During the first session, psychoeducation on trauma and normalization of emotions were provided to Anjali by the counsellor. In the second session, grounding techniques were taught to Anjali to help her cope with anxiety. In the third session, positive relationships in the shelter were identified, and coping techniques were taught to Anjali to help her cope with difficult situations.With time, Anjali slowly began to take part in the activities with the group. She also reported feeling a little more comfortable with the shelter's surroundings. Though Anjali's traumatic experiences needed long-term support, the intervention helped to stabilize her emotional state to a certain extent.

Ethical and Culture Considerations

Ethical considerations in the provision of counselling in shelter homes are vital. Some of the considerations include confidentiality. A counsellor needs to ensure that the information given to them by the residents is kept private. There could be limits to confidentiality in the case of safety or harm. Another consideration is informed consent. The client needs to understand the reason for counselling, the type of counselling, and the right to stop the counselling at any time. There is a need for consent from the guardians or authorities in the case of minors.

Professional boundaries need to be maintained in shelter homes since the residents may need to see the counselors often. Cultural sensitivity is another crucial factor to consider in shelter homes since the residents may come from different cultural backgrounds. A counsellor should always show cultural values, beliefs, and communication. The use of cultural examples in communication may promote engagement in therapy. Another factor to consider in trauma-informed care is the use of power. Some residents in shelter homes may have come from situations where they were unable to make their own decisions. A counsellor should promote collaboration in the therapy process.

Conclusion

The development of psychotherapy for low-resource settings underscores the need for flexibility and creativity in mental health service delivery. In urban shelter homes, for example, the therapist cannot afford to adopt the conventional long-term approach to therapy. Instead, the therapist has to adopt a brief, utilitarian approach, which focuses on safety, stabilization, and coping skills. This underscores the need for empathy, cultural sensitivity, and working with the community. In trauma-informed therapy, the brief interaction is significant for the person who has been through a traumatic experience.

References

Brymer, M., Jacobs, A., Layne, C., et al. (2012). Psychological first aid: Field operations guide. National Child Traumatic Stress Network.

Courtois, C. A., & Ford, J. D. (2016). Treatment of complex trauma: A sequenced, relationship-based approach. Guilford Press.

Herman, J. L. (2015). Trauma and recovery: The aftermath of violence—From domestic abuse to political terror. Basic Books.

Substance Abuse and Mental Health Services Administration. (2014). SAMHSA's concept of trauma and guidance for a trauma-informed approach. U.S. Department of Health and Human Services.

World Health Organization. (2013). Guidelines for the management of conditions specifically related to stress. WHO Press.

Chapter 19

Group Therapy for Women in Community Centres

– Pratha Sharma

Introduction

Mental health issues such as stress, anxiety, and depression are issues that everyone in this world is beginning to understand. Women in this world are facing a lot of stress because women have to do things every day. Women have to be parents, take care of their homes, and in some cases, women have to earn money to feed their families. If women do not have anyone to turn to, women can become very sad. Most women cannot turn to professionals for help when women are feeling sad or upset. Women cannot turn to professionals because people may think badly of them if they do not know about this option. Women cannot turn to professionals because women do not have enough money. There are no places where women can turn to talk to someone about their feelings. Some women are afraid to turn to these places for help. Community centers are very important in helping women with their health issues. People like to turn to these places to find their friends, learn things, and find jobs. These centers can be places to offer counseling services because they are happy and comfortable places to be. In these circumstances, group therapy can prove to be very beneficial.

If a whole lot of people are brought together with a therapist and they are encouraged to discuss what is going on in their lives, they can learn how to deal with their problems. Mental health problems like stress, anxiety, and depression can be helped with group therapy. Group therapy is good for women because they can see that they are not the ones with these problems. They can see that other women are going through these things. Corey said in 2016 that group therapy is very good in places where there are not resources because one therapist can help many people at the same time. Mental health issues like stress, anxiety and depression can be helped with group therapy, in community centers.

Community centers are often the focal points where women come together and engage in various activities such as events and skill-based training programs. In order to make women economically independent and empowered in society, many non-governmental organizations (NGOs) hold workshops in community centers. In these workshops, handicrafts, tailoring, and small-scale business are conducted. Despite the fact that women of different backgrounds and professions are involved in these workshops and activities, they all have similar experiences in their personal lives. Women are mostly stay-at-home moms and take care of all household chores and provide economic and emotional support for the family. They are mostly involved in family businesses and work part-time.

Women casually discuss their personal matters with each other when they are involved in these activities. In these circumstances, women discuss their personal problems with each other. These problems highlight the emotional problems women carry with them, which they don't publicly express.

Therefore, the community center presents an opportunity for the introduction of mental health services in a setting where women feel comfortable. This is because they usually converge in such settings, and the introduction of group therapy sessions in the same settings will help reduce the stigma associated with mental health services.

Common Mental Health Issues in This Context

Women who are involved in community center programs tend to face many psychological problems as a result of the pressure from their families, communities, and the economy. One such psychological problem is stress. Stress may also result from handling all the responsibilities at home. These responsibilities may include taking care of the kids, cooking, home management, and providing emotional support to all the family members.

The second psychological problem is anxiety. This is another psychological problem that can affect individuals. Stress can be the main cause of anxiety. Stress can be caused by the uncertainty of the future, family problems, children's education, and financial problems. Some physical symptoms of anxiety are headaches, lack of sleep, and tense muscles.

In addition, women in community centers can also suffer from depression. Depression is characterized by a poor mood and lack of motivation. Depression can be caused by the lack of fulfillment of women's emotional needs. However, women in family settings are likely to face social isolation despite their company of other people.

Communication of personal issues may at times not be encouraged by culture values, which may lead women to try to suppress their feelings. Recognizing these common mental health issues, therefore, highlights the need for readily available and encouraging therapy sessions in the community.

Limitations in Community-Based Settings

Despite the accessible and conducive environment offered by community centers for mental health support, there are some limitations in the provision of mental health interventions.

One of the main limitations is the lack of mental health professionals. In many cases, community centers are only able to provide support through visiting mental health professionals, who might only be able to provide support for a limited time.

Another limitation is the lack of private facilities for mental health support. In many cases, support is offered in a hall where other activities are taking place at the same time.

Another limitation is that of time for support. In most cases, women who come for support are expected to have other responsibilities, such as household chores, which may not allow them to spend too much time in support sessions.

Another limitation is that of mental health stigmas among women in the community. In most cases, mental health stigmas may not allow women in the community to openly share mental health issues for fear of how people in the community may perceive their condition.

Low-Resource Psychotherapy Plan

Simple strategies and psychological interventions that can be easily implemented over a short space of time are most appropriate for such a low-resource setting. For a low - resource setting a structured group therapy program based on supportive counselling and cognitive behavioral interventions is appropriate. The main aim of such an intervention are to spread awareness about mental health , physical health and promote emotional well-being. To increase knowledge about basic skills for managing stress To encourage sharing of experiences and helping each other To overcome daily problems help the members to develop problem-solving skills . The strategies used should be simple and easily applicable in day to day life, as the intervention is conducted in a community setting. Emphasis should focus on empowerment and not on treatment.

Session Structure

Group therapy with a short term plan which is designed should have 4 weekly sessions and the duration should be around 45-60 mins.

Session 1: Psychoeducation and Introduction: The first session's main criteria is to initiate trust among the participants. A judgment-free zone is established, and the participants are free to discuss themselves and reasons for attending the session. Some basic knowledge about stress, emotional well-being, and mental health is imparted to the participants. Participating and communication are the ground rules implemented for the group session.

Session 2: Stress Management Techniques: The second session focuses on methods which help in managing and reducing levels of stress. Deep Breathing exercises and mindfulness techniques are taught to the group to reduce the emotional tension, these techniques help in lowering the physical symptoms of stress and helps the mind to be calm.

Session 3: Problem-Solving Skills: The third session is all about identification and exploration of problems and help them find solutions to the problems, the participants are asked to identify the problem they encounter in their day to day life and how they can handle their responsibilities or their families.

Session 4: Reflection and Future Coping: The fourth session makes the participants reflect on the coping skills that were learned in the previous sessions. This session helps the participants to think of how they can proceed with the coping skills that were learned in the previous sessions. This session also makes the participants support one another even after the sessions.

Key Techniques

There are various therapeutic methods which can be applied in order to have an effective group therapy program. Psycho-education is applied to educate clients on the interrelation between stress, emotions, and physical well-being. Relaxation methods are applied to reduce physical stress. Group discussions are applied to allow clients to learn from each other. Problem-solving is applied to allow clients to learn how to deal with their problems. Peer support is also very effective for clients who are undergoing group therapy. The clients are able to learn from each other as they share their experiences and learn from those undergoing similar experiences. Group therapy has been proven to have therapeutic effects on clients. These are universality, interpersonal learning, and group cohesion, as stated by Yalom and Leszcz (2020).

Ethical and Cultural Considerations

Working with clients in a community group setting, there are various ethical and cultural considerations that should be considered . One of these is confidentiality. For clients to open up freely about their experiences, all clients involved in the sessions should agree to keep each other's experiences confidential and not discuss them beyond the sessions. Secondly, informed consent is vital before beginning the therapy program. All clients involved should understand the importance of the sessions and that they are doing it voluntarily.

Lastly, therapists should also show cultural sensitivity to clients. Cultural values, family structures, and gender differences may affect clients' perceptions of their emotional problems. Also, therapists should not use clinical language that stigmatizes clients. Instead, they should discuss clients' emotional well-being and ways of coping.

Case Study

A community center run by an NGO in Bengaluru had regular training programs for women in which training is provided in the field of tailoring and handicrafts. Women from the nearby localities used to participate in these training programs. While having casual talks with women attending these training programs, women started sharing their personal issues regarding their families, financial, and emotional problems.Women attending these training programs were home-makers and belonged to the age group of 25-45 years. One woman expressed her feelings of being tired as she had to manage her home and family on her own as her husband used to work long hours. The second woman expressed her problems of not being able to sleep due to arguments in her family. Despite working hard to bring up her family, the third woman expressed her feelings of not being valued and appreciated . Considering mental health services to be expensive and socially unacceptable None of the members received any psychological help in the past.The psychologist developed a short term group therapy program for the members which can help the members . The participants started to share their share of issues and experiences and then they began to support each other emotionally. They found it very peaceful to share about their experiences and they understood that they aren't alone in their battles. The group therapy created a feeling of safety among the group members.

Conclusion

Intervention programs on mental health in the community have also highlighted the need to adapt therapy to the specific circumstances and contexts. Resources and time constraints, as well as the social stigma of the community, might hinder the delivery of traditional therapy in the community. This case has, however, highlighted the possibility of providing effective psychological interventions with simple and structured group therapy. The community center provides a context in which the women feel comfortable and can be at home. Group therapy has also been recognized as an effective means of promoting social learning and fostering stronger social relationships in the community. Group therapy has also been recognized as an effective means of promoting the development of new coping skills and improving the emotional well-being of individuals. This approach has highlighted the need for community-based interventions and the possibility of adapting psychological interventions to the specific requirements of the community.

References

Burlingame, G. M., McClendon, D. T., & Alonso, J. (2011). Cohesion in group therapy. Psychotherapy.

Burlingame, G. M., Strauss, B., & Joyce, A. S. (2019). Change mechanisms and effectiveness of small group treatments. In M. J. Lambert (Ed.), Bergin and Garfield's handbook of psychotherapy and behavior change(7th ed.). Wiley.

Corey, G. (2016). Theory and practice of group counseling(9th ed.). Cengage Learning.

Kohen, D. (2001). Psychiatric services for women. Advances in Psychiatric Treatment, 7(5), 328–334.

World Health Organization. (2021). Guidance on community mental health services: Promoting person-centred and rights-based approaches. https://www.who.int/publications/i/item/9789240025707

Yalom, I. D., & Leszcz, M. (2020). The theory and practice of group psychotherapy (6th ed.). Basic Books.

Chapter 20

Mental Health Support for Daily Wage Workers

– Gautham Harish Elayaraja

Introduction

The daily wage worker is an essential part of the construction, agricultural, transport, domestic service, sanitation, and home manufacturing sectors in developing countries (Chen, 2012). However, despite their importance in increasing productivity, these workers do not enjoy the same rights as those who are formally employed (International Labour Organization, 2022). In India, millions of workers are engaged on a daily wage basis without job security, written contracts, paid leave, insurance, or pension benefits (International Labour Organization, 2022). Their livelihoods depend on the demand for labor on a daily basis; hence, illness, adverse weather, injury, or a downturn in the local economy can instantly nullify their earning capacity (Benach et al., 2014). This is a situation where economic survival is contingent on being constantly available for work (Marmot, 2015). Mental health among this population has been grossly neglected, as the discourse on labor has traditionally centered on physical health, compensation, and migration rather than mental health (World Health Organization, 2024). However, the constant state of uncertainty takes its toll on people over time, as they must plan for future expenditures without being sure that their earnings for the next day will be sufficient to cover them (Lund et al., 2018). Ongoing concerns about food security, debt, school fees, and housing costs all contribute to increased anxiety (Patel et al., 2018). Increasing evidence indicates that insecure work is a predictor of poor mental health even after adjusting for age and total poverty, indicating that job insecurity is an independent predictor of psychological distress.

Mental Health Conditions Among Daily Wage Workers

Depression and anxiety are most visible in the ranks of daily wage earners (Silva-Peñaherrera et al., 2022). Instead of screaming out symptoms, they feel fatigued, irritated, unfocused, hopeless, and have problems with sleep. Since wages depend on attendance, many workers struggle through in order to delay both diagnosis and treatment. Emotional suffering is often tolerated as simply part of growing up or living in poverty, rather than being recognized as a concern for health. Job-related trauma is also a significant source of problems. Workers in construction, agriculture, and sanitation are often forced to watch colleagues suffer serious injuries from accidents involving equipment, falls, electrical shock, toxic substances, or road accidents. Even if they appear uninjured, regular exposure to danger keeps them perpetually on edge and alert for the next threat. They may experience flashbacks, avoid certain activities, or remain nervously alert around similar tasks (Ballard et al., 2025).

Turning to substances as a means of coping is also very common (Banjari, 2021). After-work drinking is deeply ingrained in many work environments because it provides an instant escape from pain and emotional exhaustion. Tobacco and other locally available drugs are also widely used. However, regular use quickly empties pockets that could be filled with food or medicine, causes friction in family relationships, and can contribute to a long-term sense of depressive despair. This is a vicious cycle that links emotional distress, substance addiction, and economic instability (World Health Organization & International Labour Organization, 2022).

Informal Employment and Structural Risk

The informal economy establishes work relationships that fall outside the realm of formal legal and regulatory frameworks (Chen, 2012). Daily wage laborers are usually at the bottom of this hierarchy, where wages are negotiated in an informal manner and may be determined by contractors or middlemen. They have little negotiating power since employers can easily replace them. This condition is a major contributor to wage repression, delayed payments, and tolerance of poor working conditions (Benach et al., 2014). Income instability is one of the most important factors that contribute to distress (Lund et al., 2018). A worker may have several productive days in a row, only to find themselves unemployed due to rain, project delays, seasonal changes, or contractor decisions. Given the fact that many households lack savings, each of these events can quickly become a crisis. Individuals may resort to borrowing from informal lenders at high interest rates, leading to long-term debt that raises anxiety levels.

Financial instability also reduces perceived control, which is a major predictor of depressive symptoms in occupational health research (Karasek & Theorell, 1990). Housing and environmental insecurity are also sources of stress. Migrant workers usually live in temporary housing near their construction sites, in crowded and rented rooms, or in labor colonies with inadequate sanitation and privacy. Overcrowding leads to sleep disturbances, conflict, and poor emotional recovery from physically demanding work. Lack of access to support networks in their families further compromises their ability to cope when illness or financial problems occur (Benach et al., 2014).

Theoretical Perspectives

The Social Determinants of Health approach illustrates how mental illness in this population cannot be viewed in isolation from the larger picture of inequality (Lund et al., 2018). Mental health outcomes are very much shaped by factors such as income, housing, education, social protection, and people's feelings of inclusion by institutions. Daily wage workers are positioned in structurally disadvantaged positions on all these factors, so mental illness is not simply a matter of individual resilience breaking down; it is the result of being subjected to adverse social conditions (Marmot, 2015). The Job Demand-Control-Support model also illuminates the issue clearly (Karasek & Theorell, 1990). Daily wage work involves high physical demands and very little control. Workers do not get to choose their work, their hours, or their safety regulations. Managerial support is also likely to be sporadic, as contractor arrangements are short-term. High demand and low control mean that work is more stressful, increasing the risk of burnout, irritability, and depression (Ballard et al., 2025).

Barriers to Mental Health Support

Economic barriers remain the largest obstacle to being treated (Patel et al., 2018). Private psychiatric treatment and counselling remain unaffordable, while public treatment means a lost day of work. For daily wage earners, this directly impacts the survival of the family. Even if public treatment is free, the cost of transport and waiting times can be a deterrent. Geographic barriers are also important (World Health Organization, 2024). Mental health professionals are concentrated in large cities, while many labor settlement areas are in the periphery of cities or in rural areas. Migrant workers may not be aware of the availability of treatment or may avoid hospitals due to documentation requirements.

Cultural barriers continue to be important. Psychological manifestations are perceived as a lack of strength, fate, or a temporary bout of tiredness. Men, in particular, may fear that expressing distress could negatively impact their job prospects, as physical strength and endurance are inextricably tied to notions of masculinity in the labor context (Patel et al., 2018).

Intervention Strategies

Community-based mental health services are one of the most promising ways ahead (Patel et al., 2018). Frontline health staff can be trained to identify depression, anxiety, trauma, and harmful alcohol use in labor communities. Short counselling sessions conducted at outreach camps or local health clinics help reduce access gaps since they do not require specialist travel. Interventions in the workplace are also important (Ballard et al., 2025). If earnings are stable, rest breaks are provided, clean water and protective equipment are accessible, and a clear grievance process is in place, mental distress will decrease. Even small gains in work organization can increase workers' feelings of dignity and control. Social protection has major mental health advantages (International Labour Organization, 2022). Cash transfers, emergency wage support, accident benefits, subsidized insurance, and simplified welfare registration can help reduce fear of unemployment or illness. Sector welfare boards are most effective when barriers to membership for migrant workers are reduced. Mental health interventions through technology are a promising new frontier (World Health Organization, 2024). Telephone counselling, regionally adapted audio content, and mobile mental health education can reach workers who cannot access clinics. These interventions are particularly useful when literacy is low and work schedules are irregular.

Conclusion

Mental health in daily wage workers should be conceptualized as a structural labor issue and not merely an individual medical concern. Factors such as economic insecurity, unsafe working conditions, poor social protection, migration pressures, and stigma interact to produce a complex of conditions that repeatedly put workers at risk of poor mental health. Unlike regular employees, daily wage workers experience persistent uncertainty regarding income, employment, and healthcare access, making family planning challenging and increasing emotional distress. These conditions contribute to anxiety, depression, reduced coping ability, and the development of maladaptive coping behaviors such as substance abuse. The evidence reviewed in this paper illustrates that mental health outcomes for daily wage workers are impacted by structural issues of inequality, including poor housing conditions, debt bondage, and lack of labor protection. Effective change, therefore, must be addressed through a comprehensive approach that includes better labor regulation, community mental health care access, simplified welfare benefits, and effective enforcement of workplace safety standards. Community mental health programs are particularly important because they remove obstacles created by treatment costs and distance to care (World Health Organization, 2024). The mental health and well-being of daily wage workers must be protected as a means of enhancing not only individual health but also family, labor, and social health.

References

Ballard, D. W., Davenport, T., & Harvey, S. B. (2025). Mental health at work: A practical framework for employers. *Frontiers in Public Health, 13*, 1521842.

Banjari, S. (2021). Effect of lockdown on mental health of daily wage workers. *Journal of Evidence Based Medicine and Healthcare, 8*(14), 891–895.

Benach, J., Muntaner, C., Chung, H., & Benavides, F. G. (2016). The health-damaging potential of new types of flexible employment: A challenge for public health researchers. *International Journal of Health Services, 46*(4), 706–720.

Benach, J., Vives, A., Amable, M., Vanroelen, C., Tarafa, G., & Muntaner, C. (2014). Precarious employment: Understanding an emerging social determinant of health. *Annual Review of Public Health, 35*, 229–253.

Chen, M. A. (2012). *The informal economy: Definitions, theories and policies* (WIEGO Working Paper No. 1). Women in Informal Employment: Globalizing and Organizing.

International Labour Organization. (2022). *Mental health at work: Policy brief.*

Karasek, R., & Theorell, T. (1990). *Healthy work: Stress, productivity, and the reconstruction of working life.* Basic Books.

Lund, C., Brooke-Sumner, C., Baingana, F., Baron, E. C., Breuer, E., Chandra, P., Haushofer, J., Herrman, H., Jordans, M., Kieling, C., Medina-Mora, M. E., Morgan, E., Omigbodun, O., Tol, W., Patel, V., & Saxena, S. (2018). Social determinants of mental disorders and the Sustainable Development Goals: A systematic review of reviews. *The Lancet Psychiatry, 5*(4), 357–369.

Marmot, M. (2015). *The health gap: The challenge of an unequal world.* Bloomsbury.

Patel, V., Saxena, S., Lund, C., Thornicroft, G., Baingana, F., Bolton, P., Chisholm, D., Collins, P. Y., Cooper, J. L., Eaton, J., Herrman, H., Herzallah, M., Huang, Y., Jordans, M. J. D., Kleinman, A., Medina-Mora,

M. E., Morgan, E., Omigbodun, O., UnÜtzer, J., & van Ommeren, M. (2018). The Lancet Commission on global mental health and sustainable development. *The Lancet, 392*(10157), 1553–1598.

Silva-Peñaherrera, M., Santiá, P., & Benavides, F. G. (2022). Informal employment and poor mental health in a sample of 180,260 workers from 13 Iberoamerican countries. *International Journal of Environmental Research and Public Health, 19*(13), 7800.

World Health Organization. (2024). *Mental health at work.*

World Health Organization, & International Labour Organization. (2022). *Mental health at work: Policy brief.* World Health Organization.

Chapter 21

Integrating Psychotherapy into Primary Health Care: A Low-Resource Model

– Katepalli Gayathri Padmini

Introduction

The primary health care (PHC) system is the first point of contact for the majority of people requiring healthcare services. PHC systems include government clinics, community health centers, and rural health facilities, which provide basic medical care, preventive care, and treatment of common illnesses. In low and middle-income countries, PHC systems play a vital role in providing healthcare services to people, as they would otherwise remain deprived of basic medical care.

Mental health conditions are a major cause of the burden of disease, and mental disorders are one of the leading causes of disability worldwide. Patel et al. (2018) emphasized the fact that mental disorders are a major cause of disability and a significant burden on the healthcare system, particularly in low-resource countries. However, there is a scarcity of mental healthcare services, and a large treatment gap exists, particularly in low and middle-income countries, where mental health professionals are not readily available.

In primary care facilities, psychological distress is often a common occurrence, although it is not always recognized as such. There are instances where patients present with physical complaints such as headaches, fatigue, sleep problems, or gastrointestinal problems that could be linked to psychological distress. In such cases, the general physician is the first point of contact for individuals with psychological issues.In recognition of the gap that currently exists in the provision of care to individuals with psychological issues, several global health bodies have recognized the importance of the integration of mental health care into primary care facilities. According to the World Health Organization, the integration of mental health care into primary care facilities is crucial in the reduction of the treatment gap. In this regard, the organization advocates for the use of task-sharing methods in the provision of care to individuals with psychological issues in community settings.

The following case presents an example of the manner in which psychological distress is presented in primary care facilities and the manner in which it is possible to intervene with individuals in resource-limited settings.

Case Vignette

Lakshmi, a 34-year-old woman from a semi-rural area, presents herself at a government-funded primary healthcare facility complaining of headaches, tiredness, and difficulty sleeping. She states that she feels overwhelmed by her financial and family responsibilities since her husband lost his job recently. She is also concerned about her children's education and their family's financial security. Following a basic medical examination, which does not reveal any underlying physical illness, she is referred to a trained community health worker who provides her with brief psychosocial support. In four brief sessions, she is educated about stress, taught simple relaxation techniques, and helped to think about how she might cope with her circumstances. She begins to feel more positive and is able to cope with her circumstances.

This is an example of how brief psychological interventions can be incorporated into primary healthcare settings to deal with mental health issues faced by people in resource-scarce settings.

This chapter will explore how psychotherapy is integrated into primary health care settings in resource-scarce settings, what mental health issues are commonly faced by people, what the practical issues are, and how brief psychotherapy can be made available by non-specialized health workers.

Common Mental Health Issues in this context

Primary care settings often deal with people who have mild to moderate psychological problems rather than severe psychiatric disorders. Some of the most frequently encountered psychological problems include depression, anxiety disorders, and stress-related adjustment problems.

Depression

Depression is one of the most frequently occurring mental health disorders worldwide, which is commonly encountered in primary care settings (Patel et al., 2018). People who have depression may complain of persistent sadness, lack of interest in daily activities, fatigue, sleep disturbances, and difficulties in concentrating. However, in other cultures, psychological distress may often manifest as physical complaints, such as headaches, body pain, or gastrointestinal upsets. According to the National Mental Health Survey conducted in India, the results revealed that a significant number of people have common mental disorders, for whom the general medical facilities have become the mode of accessing mental health care, rather than specialized mental health facilities (Gururaj et al., 2016). Depression, if identified early, can significantly improve the health outcomes of the population.

Anxiety Disorders

Anxiety disorders are also commonly observed in the context of primary care (Patel et al., 2018). The symptoms of anxiety disorders may include excessive worrying, restlessness, irritability, muscle tension, and sleep problems. Individuals who are experiencing anxiety disorders may also experience physical symptoms like palpitations, dizziness, and gastrointestinal problems. These symptoms are more related to physical health problems, and hence individuals experiencing anxiety disorders may consult general physicians rather than mental health professionals.

If anxiety disorders are left untreated, they may significantly affect the daily functioning of the individual, their relationships, and their performance in the workplace. The identification of anxiety disorders in the context of primary care is essential for providing psychological support to the individuals experiencing anxiety disorders.

Stress and Adjustment Difficulties

Stress-related problems are commonly observed in individuals who are facing financial problems, family problems, caregiving responsibilities, and health problems. Stress-related problems may lead to emotional problems like anxiety, irritability, fatigue, and difficulties in concentrating.

In the context of primary care, individuals who are experiencing stress-related problems may not realize their problems as mental health problems. They may report that they feel 'tired,' 'overwhelmed,' or 'physically ill.' Psychological intervention at the primary care level can assist people in learning better coping skills, which can prevent the progression of mental health problems.

Limitations

Even though there are a number of benefits that can be derived from integrating psychotherapy into primary care settings, there are some factors that have to be taken into consideration.

High Patient Load and Limited Consultation Time

In primary care settings, physicians have to deal with a large number of patients per day. In government clinics, for instance, it is possible for each consultation session to last only a few minutes.

Limited Training

In some instances, primary care physicians have limited training regarding how to deal with mental health issues. In some cases, psychological issues have been known to be ignored, especially when they do not have medication as a cure.

Lack of Privacy

In PHC settings, it is possible for there to be a lack of privacy, especially since there is no dedicated area for psychological counseling. In some instances, it is possible for patients to be uncomfortable discussing their psychological issues in front of other people.

Stigma and Cultural Beliefs

There is still considerable stigma associated with mental illness, which is considered a major impediment to seeking psychological assistance. There is also a possibility that cultural beliefs might impact how people perceive mental illness, which might be related to spiritual or moral issues.

Shortage of Mental Health Professionals

In resource-poor settings, there is usually a scarcity of mental health professionals. Systematic reviews have recognized this workforce deficit as a major impediment to integrating mental health services into primary care systems, which is considered a major issue (Wakida et al., 2018). Task-sharing, which includes training other health workers to provide basic mental health care, has been recommended as an important solution to this problem (Gureje et al., 2015).

Low-Resource Psychotherapy Plan

The psychotherapy provided within the primary care setting needs to be brief, simple, and flexible to suit the needs of the setting (World Health Organization, 2016).

Therapy Approach

The brief cognitive behavioural therapy (CBT) model of supportive counseling is applicable within the primary care setting. CBT is a model of counseling that helps individuals understand the relationship between thoughts, emotions, and actions, and how this helps individuals cope with their problems effectively.The research suggests that psychological interventions provided by trained health workers in low- and middle-income countries can reduce symptoms of depression and anxiety effectively (van Ginneken et al., 2021).

Low-Resource Psychotherapy Pathway in Primary Health Care Settings

Patient presents to primary health centre with physical complaints
Initial medical evaluation by primary care physician

↓

Psychological distress is indicated (e.g., headaches, sleep disturbances, stress)

↓

Patient is referred to trained community health worker

↓

Psychological intervention is provided in four sessions

1.Psychoeducation

2.Relaxation techniques

3.Cognitive strategies

4.Problem-solving

↓

Follow-up assessment

Outcome pathways

Improvement-Continued use of coping strategies and routine PHC follow-up

Persistent or severe symptoms- Referral to specialized mental health services

Key Techniques

Psychoeducation

Patients are provided with basic information about the ways in which stress, thoughts, and emotions affect their overall well-being, both mentally and physically.

Relaxation and Grounding Techniques

Techniques such as breathing exercises and grounding techniques help control the physical reactions to anxiety and stress.

Problem-Solving Therapy

Patients learn to identify the problems in their lives, think of ways to solve the problems, and make plans to solve the problems.

Behavioural Activation

Patients are encouraged to participate in activities that have significance in their lives, helping to boost their mood and energy levels.

Supportive Counselling

The client is provided with emotional support and encouragement to strengthen the client-counsellor relationship.

Session Structure

Psychotherapy can be delivered in four short sessions, which are approximately 20-30 minutes.

Session	Focus	Key Techniques
Session 1	Assessment and Psychoeducation	Understanding stress, depression, and anxiety
Session 2	Stress Management	Breathing exercises and grounding techniques
Session 3	Cognitive Strategies	Identifying and understanding negative thoughts and alternative perspectives
Session 4	Problem-Solving and Relapse Prevention	Developing coping strategies for future stress

Ethical and Cultural Considerations

Ethical practice is essential when providing psychological support in primary care settings.

Confidentiality

Confidentiality is a critical issue in the delivery of mental health care services. In the absence of private spaces, efforts should be made to ensure confidentiality in the delivery of services.

Informed Consent

Patients should be made aware of the purpose, nature, and duration of the services provided. Informed consent is a critical issue in the delivery of mental health care services.

Professional Boundaries

Professional boundaries are critical, especially in the delivery of psychosocial care services by community health workers in the community, where dual relationships are likely to exist.

Cultural Sensitivity

Mental health care interventions should be sensitive to the cultural practices of the community. For example, the language used in the delivery of mental health care services should be sensitive to the community.

Referral for Severe Cases

Patients with severe mental health problems, such as suicidal ideation, psychosis, and depression, should be referred to mental health care services.

Conclusion

The development of psychotherapy interventions in resource-poor primary care settings emphasizes the need to adapt evidence-based practices to real-life situations. Most models of psychotherapy assume that individuals have access to professionals, dedicated facilities for psychotherapy, and time for long sessions, which is not the case in most communities. The use of short, structured psychotherapy models allows for the provision of psychological support in resource-poor settings.The integration of psychotherapy into primary care also promotes the normalization of mental health care as an integral part of primary healthcare. This will help in the reduction of the treatment gap in underserved communities. The strengthening of the integration of mental health care in primary health care systems is an essential strategy in the expansion of psychological support to the community.

References

Gureje, O., Abdulmalik, J., Kola, L., Musa, E., Yasamy, M. T., & Adebayo, K. (2015). Integrating mental health into primary care using the mhGAP intervention guide: A pilot study. *BMC Health Services Research, 15*, 242.

Gururaj, G., Varghese, M., Benegal, V., Rao, G. N., Pathak, K., Singh, L. K., & National Mental Health Survey Collaborators. (2016). *National Mental Health Survey of India, 2015–2016: Summary.* National Institute of Mental Health and Neurosciences.

Patel, V., Saxena, S., Lund, C., Thornicroft, G., Baingana, F., Bolton, P., Chisholm, D., Collins, P. Y., Cooper, J. L., Eaton, J., Herrman, H., Herzallah, M. M., Huang, Y., Jordans, M. J. D., Kleinman, A., Medina-Mora, M. E., Morgan, E., Niaz, U., Omigbodun, O., ... Unützer, J. (2018). The Lancet Commission on global mental health and sustainable development. *The Lancet, 392*(**10157), 1553-1598.**

van Ginneken, N., Chin, W. Y., Lim, Y. W., Ussher, M., Singh, R., Shahmalak, U., Tang, W., Zhou, W., Pendse, R., & Patel, V. (2021). Primary-level worker interventions for the care of people living with mental disorders and distress in low- and middle-income countries. *Cochrane Database of Systematic Reviews, 2021*(8), CD009149.

Wakida, E. K., Talib, Z. M., Akena, D., Okello, E. S., Kinengyere, A., Mindra, A., & Obua, C. (2018). Barriers and facilitators to the integration of mental health services into primary health care: A systematic review. *Systematic Reviews, 7*, 211.

World Health Organization. (2016). *mhGAP intervention guide for mental, neurological and substance use disorders in non-specialized health settings (Version 2.0).* World Health Organization.

Chapter 22

Brief Psychological Interventions in Government Hospitals

– Jenice Chandrashekhar Nipane

Introduction

The role of government hospitals in Indian mental health care is a distinctive and highly significant one. To the overwhelming majority of the population, especially those of low-income groups, in small communities and socially marginalized groups in society, these hospitals are not an option, they are sometimes the only choice. Most people still cannot afford private mental health care, and mental health infrastructure based in the community is still underdeveloped in most states. Consequently, the psychiatric outpatient departments (OPDs) of the district and tertiary government hospitals end up to receive massive amounts of psychological distress which in a better-endowed system would have been shared out across several levels of care.

The client population that visits a government hospital OPD is very diverse. A middle aged farmer may be telling of chronic exhaustion and work disinterest, a young female patient that her family took her to see because of what they term as strange behaviour, an old man trying to control both diabetes and depressive symptoms, or a construction worker suffering panic attacks an event that he believes is being caused by some strange power. The similarities between this population is not a diagnostic category but rather a common social reality that is comprised of low financial means, intense chronic life stress, poor mental health literacy, and a prevalent health system not initially configured with their psychological needs in the centre. It is against this background that clinical psychologists are also being posted especially after expansions of District Mental Health Programme (DMHP) under the National Mental Health Programme of India. Nevertheless, the organizational circumstances in which these professionals operate are very problematic. In a government hospital, a clinical psychologist can be required to attend between eight and twelve patients in one morning shift with only about fifteen to twenty minutes per patient. Special treatment rooms are not common and treatment often occurs in an open cubicle or common hallways or with waiting patients. They are not the perfect therapeutic conditions by any measure, but they are therapeutic conditions in which essential psychological work needs to be done (Garg et al., 2019). It is this context, with all of its pressures, its population, and its possibilities, that requires a complete understanding in order to design any intervention that may be aimed to operate in it.

Common Mental Health Issues in This Context

Although the scope of presentations in a government hospital OPD is rather extensive, some psychological challenges are present at specific frequencies and must be prioritized due to their particularity when creating a concise intervention model. Perhaps the most widespread and most often overlooked problem in this setting is Depression with Somatic Presentation. Patients do not often come with the complaint of sadness or hopelessness. Rather, they report on chronic physical complaints like chronic fatigue, unexplainable body pains, chest heaviness, lack of appetite, sleep disturbances which have taken them through numerous sessions of general medicine consultations before a psychiatric referral is involved. This psychological distress is not expressed somatically in vain. It represents a culturally influenced pattern of expression of inner anguish which is well-recorded in South Asian communities, emotional weakness can be subject to social stigma yet a physical disease is seen as a valid cause to seek assistance (Bhui and Bhugra, 2004). The ability to identify depression under its somatic manifestation is a clinical as well as a cultural competence in this regard.

The second major cluster of presentations is Anxiety Disorders and Health Anxiety. Generalised anxiety, panic attacks and health anxiety are common and usually among patients who are also dealing with chronic physical diseases like high blood pressure or diabetes. The two conditions (anxiety and physical illness) form a vicious cycle where physical symptoms exacerbate anxiety and anxiety exacerbates physical symptoms and thus it is a hard nut to crack and one should look at physical symptoms alongside anxiety. Most of such patients have gone through a series of tests which have come up clear, and have ended up at the psychology unit confused and dismissed and with more and more beliefs that something is wrong has been left unattended.

The third important category is Adjustment Disorders and Situational Stress. Financial crisis, domestic violence, bereavement, unexpected job loss, migration, and stress-related to migration all lead to the adjustment problems, which with the lack of treatment may evolve into more firmly rooted psychological disorders with time. Such presentations are typically acute and reactive, and this also implies that they are very prone to short and intensive interventions. In most aspects, individuals caught in the middle of a challenging yet specific life circumstance are one of the most receptive to temporary psychological assistance.

Limitations

The truthful description of psychological practice in government hospitals should pay due weight to the structural limitations which frame the possibilities. These are not the background information but the primary reality through which all clinical decisions are taken. The most timely and ubiquitous challenge is time constraints. There is a low ratio of time per patient to be spent on thorough assessment and structured therapeutic work due to the patient load that is often high with the limited working window, that is, within the same appointment. Each session should thus be carried out with a lot of deliberateness and with a preference of what is going to be of the most significant help in the immediate response than what would be clinically ideal. This is not only a logistical issue but also an ethical one of lack of privacy. In the cases where consultations occur in open or semi-open areas where family members, other patients, or hospital personnel feel free to view and overhear the conversation, the conditions of authentic therapeutic disclosure are severely undermined. Patients who have delicate issues like domestic violence, sexual problems, suicidal thoughts, or who have suffered abuse tend to hide in such settings and it is hard to establish the safety that more profound therapeutic treatment demands.

There is the issue of stigma and family dynamics that further complicate the issue. Most patients who visit government OPDs have their family members with them who can overshadow the session, distort information or even actively oppose the psychological explanations to why the patient is in anguish. Patients who address help on their own can also downplay their symptoms in front of family due to the social stigma of a mental health diagnosis (Garg et al., 2019).

Language and health literacy barriers imply that psychoeducation and therapeutic explanations have to be more adapted to the norms.

Patients in multilingual states are likely to use regional dialects which the clinician himself is not quite at ease with, and the low educational level will make abstract clinical concepts of less communicative interest. It is important that everything should be transferred into concrete, familiar, and ordinary language.

This is a clinical issue of high dropout rates. A large number of patients come to one or two sessions and fail to attend any more because of distance, cost, work commitment or under the notion that a slight improvement is the end of the treatment. This implies that interventions have to be designed in such a way that something that matters clinically can be obtained even in a single session.

Low-Resource Psychotherapy Plan

The intervention model which is detailed in this chapter is based on three complementary interventions, i.e., Brief Problem-Solving Therapy (PST), Supportive Counselling, and Psychoeducation. The choice of this combination was based on the evidence-based basis, flexibility to various presenting problems, lack of prolonged session time, and explicit recommendation of the World Health Organization (2016) in the mhGAP Intervention Guide as the suitable intervention in non-specialist and resource-limited health settings. The model is not presented as a strict protocol but a loose guide to the clinical practice that may be modified based on the presenting issue of the patient, the distress level, and the time at hand.

Strategies and Techniques of the Session

The intervention will be organized in three sessions of about twenty minutes long, however, the model is in a manner that allows clinically meaningful contact even when the patient participates in one or two sessions.

The initial session is focused on rapport-building and psychoeducation. In an environment of a government OPD, most patients have reported being perplexed on why they have been referred to a psychologist instead of a medical prescription. The initial and the greatest activity is hence to make the patient appreciate the relationship between his or her psychological condition and his or her physical and functional challenges in a language that is easy to comprehend and non-stigmatising. As an illustration, in the case of a patient presenting with somatic symptoms of depression, the concept may be reported through the explanation that does not distinguish between the mind and the body but instead that emotional stress and unspoken distress will be reflected in the body eventually in the form of fatigue, pain, or physical tension. This type of exposition is of significance in clinical practice in that it confirms to the patient their physical pain, normalises their psychological experience and generates the fundamental shared ground upon which their further intervention can be done. A temporary grounding method like the diaphragmatic breathing method is also presented and tested during the session so that the patient could walk away having a practical and concrete tool.

The second meeting presents the problem-solving model. The patient is led in recognizing the current stressor that is of utmost concern to him and then breaking it down into smaller and manageable parts. It is maintained to be focused on what current resources and capacities the patient has and not on what solutions would involve external support which the patient may not be provided. In conjunction to this, there is an element of behavioural activation achieved by urging the patient to re-participate in one small, pleasurable or meaningful activity that he/she is avoidant of or no longer does since his/her mood deteriorated. Studies held in low-resource and underprivileged contexts have continued to discover that even the relatively small behavioural re-engagement brings significant depressive symptom reductions in the brief durations of time (Ekers et al., 2014).

The third session is reviewed, consolidated and forward planned. Gain made since the last session is addressed, coping made is reinforced and the focus of the conversation is skewed towards the ability of the patient to cope on his/her own in the future. There is a short relapse prevention module, which assists the patient in determining the early warning signs that he or she is becoming more and more distressed and what they can do about it. This type of anticipatory planning has been demonstrated to enhance long-term outcomes even in the group of patients who have limited access to further care when provided in short-term form (Patel et al., 2011).

Ethical and Cultural Considerations

Practicing ethics in a governmental hospital OPD cannot be done without knowledge of the general principles. It involves the implementation of those concepts in a manner that is considerate in a situation that is not necessarily easily implementable.

The first of the ethical responsibilities is informed consent, which is occasionally unwittingly circumvented in a health care environment when the patient comes to have himself checked and provide instructions. The psychologist ought to be clear on what psychological consultation entails, what it does not entail and the fact that the patient has a real and significant option in terms of whether to participate. This should be presented in language understandable to the masses and should be seen as a real discussion and not a procedural ceremony.

The ethics and structure of shared OPD spaces are challenged because of the necessity of confidentiality. The psychologist should make this fact clear to the patient over the initial session and should take whatever is practically achievable to reduce the possibility of being overheard and make the patient aware of what are the definite and limited conditions like severe and immediate danger to life that would necessitate breach of confidentiality.

The cultural sensitivity of family involvement is an issue. In an Indian family setting, the personal space of confidentiality is not necessarily realized in the same sense as it would become in an individualistic cultural background. Patients usually anticipate and occasionally desire to have family members in the process of treatment and in some situations the use of a close family member can actually be a better support and outcome for the patient. However the psychologist should not disregard defending the individual voice and agency of the patient especially where the family relationship itself is a component of the presented issue as in the case of domestic conflict or gender stress (Bhui and Bhugra, 2004).

The most significant general principle here is possibly cultural humility. It demands the clinician to actively resist the imposition of Western explanatory frameworks of distress on the patient but rather to be truly involved in the explanation provided by the patient, the explanatory model of the patient that is either medical, familial, spiritual, or any combination of the above. The successful brief intervention in this case does not consist in providing a standardised protocol but rather in identifying a common language of suffering that will make sense to the individual facing you.

Conclusion

Designing a psychological intervention for a government hospital setting was, in a genuinely important sense, a humbling exercise. It required confronting the gap between how therapy is taught and how it must be practiced under conditions of real scarcity. What became clear through this process is that working within severe constraints of time, space, and resources does not diminish the possibility of meaningful therapeutic contact. It changes what that contact looks like and demands that the clinician be more focused, more creative, and more present than standardised training models typically prepare us to be. Perhaps the most important insight was that in settings like these, the therapeutic relationship itself, meaning the experience of being heard without judgment, perhaps for the very first time, can carry significant healing value independent of any specific technique applied. Designing for constraint ultimately teaches something that comfortable clinical settings rarely can: that depth in therapy is not a function of duration or resources but of genuine human attention.

References

Bhui, K., & Bhugra, D. (2004). Explanatory models for mental distress: Implications for clinical practice and research. *The British Journal of Psychiatry, 185*(1), 6–7.

Ekers, D., Webster, L., Van Straten, A., Cuijpers, P., Richards, D., & Gilbody, S. (2014). Behavioural activation for depression: An update of meta-analysis of effectiveness and sub group analysis. *PLOS ONE, 9*(6), e100100.

Garg, R., Chavan, B. S., & Bhargava, D. (2019). Assessment of psychiatric morbidity and burden on caregivers of patients attending psychiatric OPD at a government hospital in North India. *Asian Journal of Psychiatry, 39*, 35–40.

Patel, V., Chowdhary, N., Rahman, A., & Verdeli, H. (2011). Improving access to psychological treatments: Lessons from developing countries. *Behaviour Research and Therapy, 49*(9), 523–528.

World Health Organization. (2016). *mhGAP intervention guide for mental, neurological and substance use disorders in non-specialized health settings* (Version 2.0). WHO Press.

Chapter 23

Crisis Counselling in Emergency Departments

– Sake Nutan Anudeep

Introduction

The Emergency Departments in the hospitals are the first point of contact for people in acute medical and psychological crises. These places are usually highly pressurized environments with a focus on immediate medical care, not long-term psychological care. In the case of public hospitals in India, the Emergency Department is usually highly populated with people of different socioeconomic classes, including people with trauma, accidents, suicide attempts, substance abuse, or extreme emotional distress. The population in the Emergency Departments is diverse in nature, ranging from young people to elderly patients. The patients are usually from disadvantaged backgrounds with poor awareness of mental health care. Family members are usually present with the patients, who are also in a state of crisis. Mental health experts may not always be permanently attached to the emergency department, especially in low-resource facilities in the public sector. Psychological support may be offered by psychiatry residents, psychologists, social workers, and other mental health trainees who may be summoned as needed. The objectives of crisis counseling in the emergency department are not psychotherapy but immediate psychological stability, reduction of immediate distress, and prevention of further harm. Crisis counseling in the emergency department aims to assist the individual in achieving emotional control, understanding the immediate situation, and developing short-term coping strategies. Crisis counseling is brief and structured because the individual may only be in the emergency department for a short time before being discharged.

Common Mental Health Issues in This Context

Several psychological concerns commonly appear in emergency department settings. These issues often emerge suddenly and require rapid psychological intervention.

Suicidal Ideation and Suicide Attempts

The most common mental health emergency treated in emergency rooms is suicide attempts or suicidal ideas. People may come into the emergency department as a result of overdosing, self-injury, or other self-destructive behaviors. These persons may be experiencing extreme emotional pain, hopelessness, relationship problems, or financial issues. Assessment of suicide risk and emotional stabilization is of prime importance in such cases.

Acute Anxiety and Panic Reactions

In the emergency department, many patients may experience acute anxiety or panic attacks. These may include symptoms such as rapid breathing, tightness in the chest, dizziness, and intense fear. These may be the result of stressful events in life, trauma, and anxiety disorders.

Psychological Distress Following Trauma or Accidents

Patients who recently experienced accidents, violence, or loss may manifest shock, confusion, emotional numbness, or extreme emotional distress. These acute reactions might be part of a stress reaction. Psychological interventions can alleviate emotional distress and facilitate adaptive coping.

Key Constraints

Providing psychological intervention in emergency departments involves several practical challenges.

Limited Time

Emergency situations focus on medical stabilization, which does not leave room for psychological intervention. Counselling sessions may be brief, lasting only 15-30 minutes

Lack of Privacy

Emergency departments may be overcrowded, which means that there may not be special rooms for counselling. Counselling may take place in semi-private areas, which makes it hard for the patient to open up.

High Patient Load

Medical staff and mental health professionals need to deal with a number of patients at the same time. This might restrict the level of psychological intervention that could be carried out.

Emotional Intensity of Crises

Patients in a state of crisis can be extremely disturbed, disorganized, or unable to communicate effectively. This makes it difficult to carry out any psychological intervention, which calls for a lot of flexibility on the part of the counselor.

Stigma and Family Dynamics

Mental health problems are stigmatized in India, and it has been seen that sometimes the family of the patient does not take the problem seriously, thus discouraging the patient from receiving any psychological intervention.

Case Vignette

Ravi, a 27-year-old male, was referred to the emergency department of a large government hospital in Bengaluru after a suicide attempt due to extreme financial difficulties and a recent breakup in his relationship. Ravi looked extremely distressed, tearful, and hopeless. The emergency department of the hospital was overcrowded, and privacy and medical staff attention were scarce, with medical staff focusing on the medical condition of the emergency patients. A psychology trainee attached to the hospital was assigned the role of providing crisis counseling to Ravi to help him deal with his emotional issues and reduce his risk of harm to self while waiting for further psychiatric evaluation and intervention. A short-term crisis intervention approach with Ravi was planned.

Low-Resource Psychotherapy Plan

A short crisis intervention approach, along with supportive counseling, is also effective for use in emergency settings. Crisis intervention is a technique for dealing with emotional states of crisis, ensuring safety, and providing the person with a sense of control over the situation.

The approach is based on providing empathy and validating the person's feelings, and providing coping techniques rather than exploring the person's deeper psychological issues.

Session Structure

Because of the time constraints in emergency settings, the intervention may involve 1-3 brief sessions. Sometimes only one session is possible before discharge or referral.

Session	Focus	Duration
Session 1	Crisis assessment, emotional stabilization, risk assessment	20-30 minutes
Session 2	Coping strategies, problem-solving, support identification	20-30 minutes
Session 3	Safety planning and referral to follow-up care	15-20 minutes

Key Techniques Used

Psychological First Aid

The first thing the counsellor will do is provide emotional support through active listening and validation of the patient's emotions. Example:"Given everything that has happened today, it makes sense that you feel overwhelmed."

Grounding Techniques

If the patient is having severe anxiety or emotional flooding, the counsellor will help the patient through grounding exercises to calm down the physical symptoms.

Examples include: Slow breathing exercises,focusing attention on present sensory experiences and counting or naming objects in the environment

These techniques help reduce panic and bring the patient back to the present moment.

Psychoeducation

Patients are given simple explanations about the emotional reactions to the stress or trauma. Knowing that their reactions are normal reactions to crisis situations will help alleviate their fears and confusion. Example topics: Stress response,panic symptoms and emotional reactions after trauma

Problem-Solving Strategies

The patient is helped to think of practical steps he or she can take to alleviate the stress. This could involve contacting supportive family members, obtaining financial assistance, and follow-up treatment. The focus remains on short-term manageable solutions rather than complex life issues.

Safety Planning

For patients presenting with suicidal ideation or attempts, a safety plan is essential. This includes:

1. Identifying warning signs
2. Listing supportive contacts
3. Removing access to means of self-harm
4. Encouraging follow-up with mental health services

Ethical and Cultural Considerations

Confidentiality

It is not easy to maintain confidentiality in the emergency department, considering the crowded nature of the setting. The counsellor should, however, make an effort to maintain the privacy of the patients as much as possible.

Informed Consent

Patients should be advised about the purpose of the counselling and their right to refuse or withdraw from the service. In crisis situations, however, consent may not be formal or lengthy.

Professional Boundaries

The counsellor should establish professional boundaries even when providing support to the patients. This is because the patients are in a vulnerable state when they present in crisis situations.

Cultural Sensitivity

In the context of Indian culture, the role of the family is also important in the decision-making process. In this regard, the counselor has to involve the family while respecting the autonomy of the patient.

Referral and Continuity of Care

In emergency counseling, the time is short, and it is ethically important to ensure that the patient receives appropriate follow-up care. For this purpose, the patient needs to be referred to a mental health service, a psychiatric service, or a counseling center.

Conclusion

The design of a low-resource counseling plan in emergency departments underscores the significance of the emergency context in the application of a practical approach in psychological interventions. In the emergency context, unlike other traditional therapy contexts, the counselor has to give priority to the immediate needs of the patient and not the future needs of the patient. However, the exercise underscores the significance of the therapeutic skills of the counselor in addressing the needs of the patient, despite the severe time and resource constraints. It also underscores the significance of collaboration between medical and mental health practitioners in addressing the needs of the patient in a mental crisis.

References

Everly, G. S., & Mitchell, J. T. (2008). *Critical incident stress management (CISM): A new era and standard of care in crisis intervention.* Chevron Publishing.

James, R. K., & Gilliland, B. E. (2017). *Crisis intervention strategies* (8th ed.). Cengage Learning.

Roberts, A. R. (2005). Crisis intervention handbook: Assessment, treatment, and research (3rd ed.). Oxford University Press.

World Health Organization. (2011). *Psychological first aid: Guide for field workers.* WHO.

World Health Organization. (2022). *Mental health care in emergency settings.* WHO.

Chapter 24

Grief Counselling after Sudden Loss in Low-Resource Settings

– Manasa GS

Introduction

Sudden loss, stemming from events like accidents, violence, suicide, acute medical crises, or natural disasters, profoundly disrupts the psychological well-being of individuals, families, and entire communities.The removal of any time for planning or anticipatory grieving is the primary difference from expected death. As a result, shock, severe emotional distress, and a weight of unresolved questions often overwhelm survivors. The psychological effects of unexpected loss frequently affect social structures, community cohesiveness, and a shared sense of identity in addition to the immediate victims.

In low-resource environments, the difficulties of coping with sudden loss are significantly higher. The grieving process is complicated by several factors, including restricted availability of qualified mental health experts, financial instability, the social disapproval of seeking psychological help, and extensive communal exposure to trauma. Grief counselling in these settings should shift from conventional individual therapy. Instead, a shift toward a community psychology perspective is essential. This approach emphasizes prioritizing environmental understanding, maximizing shared resources, and incorporating healing practices derived from the local culture.

This chapter examines grief counselling after sudden loss through a community psychology lens. It integrates theoretical foundations from grief research with practical strategies for intervention in settings where resources, infrastructure, and specialized services may be limited.

Understanding Sudden Loss and Its Psychological Impact

Sudden loss differs significantly from expected death in its psychological profile. Individuals often experience intense emotional reactions such as shock, disbelief, anger, guilt, and confusion. The abrupt nature of the loss disrupts the individual's assumptions about safety, predictability, and control.

Research suggests that sudden bereavement is associated with higher rates of trauma-related symptoms, including intrusive memories, hyperarousal, and avoidance behaviours (Kristensen, Weisæth, & Heir, 2012). In many cases, grief and trauma responses coexist, producing what has been described as 'traumatic grief.' The sudden loss of an attachment figure intensely activates

the attachment system. Bowlby's attachment theory posits that this abrupt disappearance triggers a struggle to regain emotional security, which unfolds in distinct phases: protest, despair, and disorganization (Bowlby, 1980).

In community contexts, the effects extend beyond the individual. Families may face role reorganization, children may lose caregivers, and communities may experience collective distress, particularly when deaths occur due to disasters or violence.

Theoretical Frameworks Relevant to Community-Based Grief Counselling

Several theoretical perspectives inform grief counselling after sudden loss.

The Dual Process Model of Coping with Bereavement

The Dual Process Model, as proposed by Stroebe and Schut (1999), suggests that bereaved individuals navigate grief by moving back and forth between two distinct coping mechanisms: Loss-oriented coping: This involves actively engaging with feelings of grief and recalling memories of the person who passed away. Restoration-oriented coping: This focuses on adapting to life after the loss, including taking on new roles and adjusting to significant life changes.In low-resource environments, restoration-oriented coping often becomes particularly salient because bereaved individuals must quickly address practical challenges such as financial survival or caregiving responsibilities.

Meaning Reconstruction

Grief often involves efforts to re-establish disrupted systems of meaning. According to meaning reconstruction theory (Neimeyer, 2001), coping with loss is achieved by integrating the loss into one's personal narrative and forming a new sense of purpose and identity. Across various cultures, this process is often supported by community rituals, storytelling traditions, and spiritual practices.

Ecological Perspectives in Community Psychology

The ecological model sees grief through the prism of nested environmental systems, implying that a variety of factors influence mental health outcomes, as community psychology highlights. These influential layers include family dynamics, cultural expectations, community support networks, and larger social structures (Bronfenbrenner, 1979).

Effective grief counselling must therefore address not only the individual's emotional distress but also the impact of contextual stressors, including poverty, social stigma, and inadequate institutional support.

Structural Challenges in Low-Resource Settings

Low and middle-income regions often face a severe scarcity of mental health services. Therefore, the treatment gap for mental health disorders in these settings is alarmingly high, estimated at 75-90% (Patel et al., 2018). This significant gap means that bereavement-related mental health needs frequently remain unmet.

Key challenges include the following:

1. Limited availability of trained psychologists or counsellors
2. High patient-to-clinician ratios
3. Lack of private counselling spaces
4. Financial instability among bereaved families
5. Cultural stigma toward seeking psychological support
6. Strong community norms governing emotional expression

These realities require mental health practitioners to adopt flexible, community-based approaches. Task-sharing models, where trained community workers deliver basic psychological support, have shown promise in expanding access to care in resource-constrained settings.

Immediate Response: Psychological First Aid

In the immediate aftermath of sudden loss, individuals may experience acute distress that interferes with basic functioning. In environments with few resources, Psychological First Aid (PFA) often serves as the most practical early intervention. PFA focuses on stabilizing individuals rather than conducting formal therapy.

Core components include

1. Ensuring safety and addressing immediate needs
2. Providing emotional stabilization
3. Offering practical support and information
4. Connecting individuals with social supports
5. Encouraging adaptive coping strategies

Importantly, PFA emphasizes non-intrusive support. Practitioners should avoid pressuring individuals to recount traumatic details immediately after the loss, as forced emotional disclosure may increase distress. Community workers, teachers, religious leaders, and volunteers can be trained in PFA, allowing communities to respond more effectively to sudden bereavement events.

Assessment in Community Settings

In settings with limited resources, assessments must be efficient and focused on functional outcomes rather than lengthy diagnostic procedures.Clinicians should evaluate several key domains such as:

1. Severity of emotional distress
2. Presence of trauma symptoms

3. Suicidal ideation or self-harm risk
4. Substance misuse
5. Caregiving responsibilities
6. Availability of social support

Several factors heighten the risk of complicated grief. These include experiencing a violent or unexpected death, a high degree of dependency on the deceased, prior exposure to trauma, and a lack of social connection (Shear, 2015).And it is crucial for assessment to be culturally sensitive. Grief is expressed in vastly different ways across cultures, meaning that behaviors considered abnormal in one cultural setting may simply be standard mourning practices in another.

Intervention Strategies in Low-Resource Contexts

Stabilization and Emotional Regulation

The initial phase of grief counselling should focus on reducing overwhelming emotional distress. Simple techniques can be highly effective:

1. Slow breathing exercises
2. Grounding through sensory awareness
3. Encouraging structured daily routines
4. Facilitating family communication

These strategies help individuals regain a sense of control during a period of emotional chaos.

Narrative and Meaning-Making Approaches

As people start to deal with loss, using narrative techniques can assist in weaving the experience into a meaningful life story. Therapists can facilitate this by inviting clients to recount memories of the person who died and contemplate the importance of their bond.Narrative work should proceed gradually, particularly when the death involves traumatic circumstances. Structured storytelling or memory-sharing activities can be effective in both individual and group settings.

Supporting Continuing Bonds

While older models of grief focused on the necessity of detaching from the deceased, contemporary research highlights the adaptive significance of maintaining continuing bonds. These bonds involve sustaining symbolic or emotional connections with the deceased (Klass, Silverman, & Nickman, 1996).

Examples include:

a. Maintaining photographs or memory objects
b. Observing anniversaries or rituals
c. Sharing stories about the deceased with children

Such practices often align with cultural mourning traditions and can promote psychological adjustment.

Community-Based Group Interventions

Because mental health professionals are often scarce, group-based grief interventions provide an efficient and supportive model for care. Group settings offer several benefits such as

1. Normalisation of grief experiences
2. Reduction of social isolation
3. Opportunities for mutual support
4. Efficient use of limited professional resources

Community grief groups may involve psychoeducation, coping skill training, storytelling, and collective remembrance activities. Careful facilitation is essential to ensure that participants feel safe and respected.

Cultural and Spiritual Dimensions of Grief

Cultural beliefs and spiritual traditions significantly influence how grief is expressed. Often, religious rituals offer communities a framework of structure and meaning to navigate the aftermath of death.Community psychologists often seek to strengthen community trust and provide more culturally relevant support by collaborating with spiritual leaders, elders, and traditional healers. This approach is rooted in the belief that these practices should not be viewed as separate from psychological care. Research in global mental health supports this integration, indicating that incorporating culturally meaningful practices into psychological interventions enhances both engagement and outcomes.

Supporting Bereaved Children and Adolescents

Children process grief differently from adults and may express distress through behavioral changes rather than verbal expression. Effective support strategies include:

1. Providing clear, age-appropriate explanations about death
2. Maintaining consistent routines
3. Encouraging emotional expression through play or drawing
4. Ensuring continued caregiving stability

Schools are often crucial in supporting children experiencing grief. By training teachers to recognize behavioral changes linked to grief, schools can more effectively identify students who need extra help.

Socioeconomic Dimensions of Bereavement

The death of a family member can cause major economic strain in many low-resource areas.Families may face financial hardship, housing insecurity, or educational disruption for children, particularly with the loss of a main earner.

To address these structural stressors and promote psychological recovery, community psychologists commonly practice resource linkage. This involves connecting affected families with crucial support, such as social welfare programs, community aid networks, and local organizations.

Ethical and Professional Considerations

Practitioners working in small communities must navigate unique ethical challenges, including maintaining confidentiality when social networks are closely interconnected.Other ethical considerations include:

1. Managing dual relationships
2. Respecting cultural mourning practices
3. Avoiding pathologization of normative grief responses
4. Recognizing personal limits and referring when necessary

Supervision and peer support are crucial for maintaining ethical practice and preventing burnout.

Practitioner Wellbeing and Burnout Prevention

Community practitioners frequently encounter repeated exposure to loss and trauma. Without adequate support, this can lead to vicarious trauma or compassion fatigue.Strategies for maintaining professional wellbeing include:

1. Regular supervision or peer consultation
2. Structured debriefing after crisis situations
3. Establishing clear work boundaries
4. Engaging in personal self-care practices

Sustainable mental health services depend on supporting the well-being of those providing care.

Conclusion

Effective grief counselling following sudden loss in low-resource settings demands a multidimensional strategy. This approach must seamlessly combine psychological theories, deep cultural understanding, and active community involvement. Grounded in the principles of community psychology, bereavement is recognized as more than just an individual emotional journey; it is fundamentally a social and ecological experience, heavily influenced by cultural standards, established family structures, and underlying structural realities.Effective interventions prioritize stabilization, social connection, and meaning reconstruction while acknowledging the socioeconomic realities faced by bereaved individuals.Mental health professionals are able to expand the reach of their support, even when formal services are scarce, by fostering strong collaborations with community networks, religious organizations, and readily available local resources.Ultimately, grief counselling in areas with limited resources highlights a central principle of community psychology: healing occurs not only through professional expertise but also through the strength and resilience of communities themselves.

References

Bowlby, J. (1980). *Attachment and loss: Vol. 3. Loss, sadness and depression.* Basic Books. Bronfenbrenner, U. (1979). *The ecology of human development.* Harvard University Press.

Klass, D., Silverman, P. R., & Nickman, S. L. (1996). *Continuing bonds: New.understandings of grief.* Taylor & Francis.

Kohrt, B. A., Jordans, M. J. D., Tol, W. A., et al. (2014). Cultural concepts of distress and psychiatric disorders. *Lancet Psychiatry*, 1(4), 286-295.

Kristensen, P., Weisæth, L., & Heir, T. (2012). Bereavement and mental health after sudden and violent losses. *Psychiatry*, 75(1), 76-97.

Neimeyer, R. A. (2001). *Meaning reconstruction and the experience of loss.* American Psychological Association.

Patel, V., Saxena, S., Lund, C., et al. (2018). The Lancet Commission on global mental health and sustainable development. *The Lancet*, 392(10157), 1553-1598.

Shear, M. K. (2015). Complicated grief. *New England Journal of Medicine*, 372, 153-160.

Stroebe, M., & Schut, H. (1999). The dual process model of coping with bereavement. *Death Studies*, 23(3), 197-224.

World Health Organization. (2011). *Psychological first aid: Guide for field workers.*

World Health Organization. (2013). *Building back better: Sustainable mental health care after emergencies.*

Chapter 25

Supporting Families of Patients in Public Hospitals

– Sai Kumar Palli

Introduction

Public hospitals in crowded urban areas are the main healthcare resource for thousands of people every day. These facilities often have overcrowded wards, long waiting times, and high-stress environments where medical staff frequently face overwhelming demands. Families in these situations often take on the role of primary caregivers, moving through the hospital with little guidance while handling the practical needs of medication and bedside care. Unlike in private healthcare, these families usually don't have access to private resting areas. They must remain close to the patient in noisy, busy hallways to respond to any urgent medical needs or tests. Many of these families come from low-income backgrounds, such as daily wage workers or migrant groups, adding financial strain to the emotional challenges of illness. This volume collects student-designed therapy interventions for real-world situations where resources are scarce but the need for help is urgent.

Challenges

Families in these settings often deal with significant mental health challenges, including:

Caregiver Burnout

The constant physical and emotional demands of around-the-clock care can lead to chronic exhaustion and emotional fatigue.

Acute Stress and Anxiety

Uncertainty about medical outcomes, combined with the "information gap" prevalent in busy public wards, leads to ongoing states of heightened alertness.

Anticipatory Grief

Family members face the burden of expected loss while managing daily hospital responsibilities in cases of chronic or terminal illness.

Secondary Trauma

Observing the suffering of loved ones and other patients in open wards may cause signs of trauma and feelings of helplessness.

Financial Distress

A sudden loss of income during hospital stays creates an additional survival crisis for families.

Key Constraints

Creating an intervention in a public hospital involves navigating several real challenges:

Lack of Privacy

Dedicated therapy rooms are often unavailable, forcing conversations to take place in noisy hallways, waiting areas, or at the patient's bedside.

Time Constraints

Caregivers are often pulled away for administrative duties, diagnostic tests, or medical updates, making traditional 50-minute sessions impractical.

High Client Load

The number of families needing help far exceeds the available mental health professionals in public settings.

Stigma and Language Barriers

Families might hesitate to seek support due to societal stigma or communication difficulties in multilingual, high-volume clinics.

Environmental Stressors

Constant noise, poor sanitation, and a lack of comfortable seating or sleeping areas for caregivers contribute to mental distress.

Resource Scarcity

Limited physical resources mean that interventions must depend on low-tech or verbal methods. To respond to these needs effectively, a brief, low-tech intervention model is used, focusing on practicality and immediate relief.

Low-Resource Psychotherapy Plan

A mix of Psychological First Aid (PFA) and Brief Supportive Therapy.

Session Structure

A "micro-session" model with 2-3 sessions, each lasting around 15-20 minutes, held in available hospital spaces.

Key Techniques

1. ***Psychoeducation*:** Explaining how stress affects the body and confirming that the caregiver's emotional reactions are normal responses to an abnormal situation.
2. ***Grounding and Relaxation*:** Teaching simple techniques, such as deep breathing or the "5-4-3-2-1" grounding exercise, which can be done discreetly in a busy ward.
3. ***Problem-Solving*:** Identifying immediate, small actions to share care duties and allow for necessary rest or nutrition.
4. ***Task-Shifting*:** Using trained community volunteers or peer-support models to provide basic emotional support when professional staff are unavailable. -
5. ***Mobile Delivery*:** Leveraging accessible technology like WhatsApp for psychoeducation and follow-up when in-person time is limited.

Case Vignette

Sunita, a 42-year-old woman, has been at a public hospital for ten days caring for her husband. She looks visibly shaken and reports trouble sleeping and a constant feeling of heaviness in her chest. With no private area available, the therapist approached Sunita during a quieter moment at her bedside. A short, three-session intervention was planned to provide information about anxiety and teach her simple breathing exercises to help manage her stress while navigating the hospital system. This vignette illustrates the application of theory into practice within significant limitations.

Ethical and Cultural Considerations

Confidentiality poses a significant challenge in open wards; the therapist must speak quietly and ensure the caregiver feels safe talking. Clear informed consent is necessary, explaining that this "emotional care" is distinct from the patient's medical treatment. Culturally, the therapist should honor the family's hierarchy and incorporate existing spiritual or religious coping strategies instead of imposing Western psychological models. Attention must also be given to the gender dynamics in caregiving, ensuring support for women dealing with domestic challenges within the hospital context. Building a therapeutic relationship in busy settings requires quick rapport and sensitivity to the patient's immediate situation.

Conclusion

Designing therapy for low-resource environments shows the importance of meeting clients where they are. I discovered that in high-pressure settings like public hospitals, effective psychotherapy is often a brief intervention that provides immediate tools for coping under tough conditions. This experience highlights that mental health professionals need to be flexible, culturally aware, and ethically sound, even when resources are limited and the need for help is pressing. Adapting therapeutic principles to under-resourced settings is crucial for delivering feasible mental health care.

References

American Psychological Association. (2020). *Publication manual of the American Psychological Association* (7th ed.).

Chadda, R. K. (2014). Caring for the family caregivers of persons with mental illness. *Indian Journal of Psychiatry, 56*(3), 221–227.

World Health Organization. (2011). *Psychological first aid: Guide for field workers.*

Patel, V., & Hanlon, C. (2018). *Where there is no psychiatrist: A mental health care manual.* RCPsych Publications

Chapter 26

Short-Term Interventions for Caregiver Burnout

– Saikeerthana

Introduction

India is experiencing rapid population growth in the age groups of 60 and above. Among them, approximately 24% of the population have reported experiencing at least one limitation in Activities of Daily Living (ADL), and almost half, that is, 48% reporting limitations in Instrumental Activities of Daily Living (IADL) (Arokiasamy et al., 2022). In the Indian cultural setting, family members serve as the informal, primary caregivers to the elderly. Their responsibilities include caring for the elder family members falling primarily on them owing to cultural norms and a lack of formal long-term care facilities. (Ajay et al., 2017) This intervention of the younger family members providing care for the older ones is designed for implementation in low-resource settings such as community health centers and primary health care (PHC) facilities in semi-urban and rural areas. The target population consists of adult family caregivers providing unpaid care to elderly relatives with significant ADL dependencies.

Common Mental Health Issues in the caregiving context

Caregiving for others can be very demanding, especially for individuals with chronic illness, disability, or age-related conditions. It is associated with significant psychological stress. Although caregiving can provide meaning and a sense of purpose for the caregiver, it frequently exposes them to prolonged emotional, physical, and social stressors. These demands increase the risk of several mental health problems, including depression, anxiety, stress, burnout, and social isolation. Over time, these pressures may accumulate, leading to multiple mental health difficulties that affect both caregivers and the quality of care they provide.(Chakraborty et al., 2023).

Depression

Research indicates that depressive symptoms are significantly more common among caregivers than among non-caregivers. Caregivers frequently experience symptoms of

depression due to chronic stress, emotional strain, and the gradual decline of the person whom they care for. Approximately 29% of caregivers experienced depressive symptoms. This highlights the psychological burden that is associated with caregiving roles. Depression among caregivers may worsen when caregiving demands increase, more often with the care recipient experiencing cognitive decline, severe disability, or behavioral disturbances. (Chakraborty et al., 2023).

Anxiety Disorders

Anxiety is another common mental health concern among caregivers. Caregivers often worry about the health and safety of the care recipient, the progression of illness and severity, and their own ability to provide adequate care. The uncertainty of the future can lead to chronic anxiety symptoms such as restlessness, irritability, sleep problems, and difficulty concentrating. The prevalence of anxiety exceeded 49%, demonstrating the widespread nature of anxiety in caregiving populations. (Chen et al., 2025) Anxiety is shown to be intense, particularly when caregiving demands are intense or long-term. (Chen et al., 2025)

Burnout and Emotional Exhaustion

Caregiver burnout typically develops gradually and is characterized by feelings of helplessness, fatigue, cynicism, and reduced motivation. Long-term caregiving responsibilities can often lead to emotional exhaustion, especially when caregivers must manage challenging patient behaviors, sleep disruptions, and demanding medical routines. Burnout not only affects caregivers' mental health but may also reduce their ability to provide effective care.(Sołtys & Tyburski, 2020)

Social Isolation and Loneliness

Caregiving responsibilities may often make the caregivers feel cut off from their social life. Their opportunities for social interaction, leisure activities, and personal time is reduced considerably. Many caregivers withdraw from social activities due to time constraints or fatigue. This eventually leads to loneliness and isolation. Social isolation can exacerbate other mental health issues such as depression and anxiety, creating a cycle of psychological distress. (Oikonomou et al., 2024)

Compassion Fatigue

Compassion fatigue refers to emotional exhaustion that a caregiver experiences resulting from prolonged exposure to another person's suffering. Caregivers who continuously witness the pain, decline, or distress of the care recipient may gradually become emotionally drained. Although compassion fatigue is commonly studied in healthcare professionals, family caregivers may also experience it due to the emotional proximity that they share with care recipients. Without adequate coping mechanisms or support systems, compassion fatigue can progress into burnout or clinical depression. (Liao et al., 2022)

Guilt and Role Conflict

Caregivers may struggle to balance multiple responsibilities such as employment, family obligations, and the additional caregiving duties. Most caregivers experience feelings of guilt, particularly when they believe they are not doing enough in their capacity for the care recipient. Role conflict occurs when caregiving interferes with other aspects of life, including personal relationships and professional responsibilities. This conflict can contribute to stress, anxiety, and emotional exhaustion. (Prunty & Foli, 2019) Recognizing these mental health issues is essential for developing effective interventions and support systems for caregivers. Psychological counseling, social support networks, respite care, and psychoeducational programs are important strategies for improving caregivers' wellbeing and sustaining their caregiving capacity. (Nasreen et al., 2024)

Limitations

Caregivers face several real-world challenges in low-resource settings. Time constraints are severe due to full time caregiving responsibilities. In community health centers and rural Primary Health Center settings, private counseling rooms are rarely available, compromising confidentiality. Significant stigma surrounds mental health problems in Indian communities. Caregivers fear being labeled "weak" or "ungrateful" for expressing distress while performing their responsibilities.(Chakraborty et al., 2023). Most caregivers cannot afford private mental health services, and qualified mental health professionals are scarce in rural and semi-urban India, necessitating delivery by trained lay counselors or community health workers.

Low-Resource Psychotherapy Plan

Therapy Approach

Considering the main constraint to be a low resource plan, Group based Cognitive-Behavioral Therapy (CBT) would be the best approach. This intervention employs a brief, group-based Cognitive-Behavioral Therapy (CBT) stress management program. CBT is widely recognized as one of the most effective approaches for caregiver mental health, though traditional CBT is often limited by time and geographical constraints. Group CBT provides small but significant benefits to caregivers' depression and stress, and therapy cost-effectiveness may be improved by limiting therapy to group formats and eight sessions

Session Structure

The intervention consists of six to eight weekly group sessions (60-75 minutes each) delivered to groups of 6-8 caregivers. Recent years have seen the development of brief group CBT interventions which aim to deliver effective treatment in shorter time frames, with even very brief group CBT therapies showing significant and relatively stable efficacy on mental health benefits. (Schaffer, 2022)

Session Number	Aim of Session	Homework for Following Week	Outcome
1	Introduction to group therapy, orientation to group rules, and psychoeducation on caregiver stress	Identify and note stressful caregiving situations during the week.	Participants understand group structure and develop awareness of caregiver stress.
2	Introduction to relaxation strategies such as deep breathing and muscle relaxation.	Practice relaxation techniques daily.	Participants learn basic stress-management skills.
3	Introduction to mindfulness and present-moment awareness.	Practice short mindfulness exercises daily.	Participants improve emotional awareness and regulation.
4	Behavioral activation through pleasant and meaningful activities.	Schedule and engage in at least two enjoyable activities.	Increased positive engagement and improved mood.
5	Identifying negative automatic thoughts.	Record stressful situations and related thoughts.	Participants recognize unhelpful thinking patterns.
6	Challenging and reframing negative automatic thoughts.	Practice replacing negative thoughts with balanced ones.	Improved cognitive coping skills.
7	Group discussion and problem-solving around challenging care-recipient behaviors.	Apply problem-solving strategies to a caregiving challenge.	Peer support and improved problem-solving skills.
8	Review of CBT skills and reflection on progress.	Continue using CBT strategies in daily life.	Consolidation of learning and improved coping.

Key Techniques

Psychoeducation

Providing clear and culturally relevant information about burnout helps normalize experiences and reduces self-blame. The content of the intervention typically includes treatment initiation and brief introduction to caregiver stress and burnout.

Cognitive Restructuring

CBT teaches caregivers to recognize and change negative thought patterns, such as "I'm a terrible caregiver," and replace them with more realistic thoughts like "I'm doing my best in a difficult situation". Caregivers are taught to recognize these automatic thoughts and common cognitive distortions. Through guided exercises, they practice challenging unhelpful beliefs to cultivate healthier cognitive patterns.

Behavioral Activation and Training

The most frequently implemented component involves skill-building through evidence-based techniques. These include progressive muscle relaxation (PMR), diaphragmatic breathing, and guided imagery.

Problem-Solving Techniques

Participants learn to rework around the challenges that they face, identify the barriers that they encounter on a daily basis, evaluate coping strategies, and implement appropriate solutions. The most efficient individual therapy modality for caregiver wellbeing and mental health could be said as Problem SolvingTherapy

Social Support Enhancement

Support groups help the caregivers connect with others who understand their experience. It helps them solve problems and provides a place to make new friends and acquaintances (Mayo Clinic, 2023).

Self-Care Strategies

Practices like mindfulness, deep breathing, light exercise, and journaling promote emotional balance and physical health for caregivers (CareLink, 2025).

Ethical and Cultural Considerations

One of the most common limitations in a low resource setting is lack of private spaces. This questions the ethical aspect, that is, confidentiality principle in particular. Considering the strong Eastern values that India worships, it is important for the counselor community to integrate it to their practice. Concepts like family interdependence and filial respect are highly regarded in families. The interventions must respect these values while simultaneously validating caregivers' distress. Rather than promoting the individualistic concepts of the West, counselors should frame self-care within culturally appropriate narratives: "Taking care of yourself allows you to take better care of your loved one." Gender dynamics also play a huge role here. It requires sensitivity, as female caregivers often face additional pressures from patriarchal family structures in terms of caregiving. Religious and spiritual beliefs should be integrated rather than dismissed. Counselors must address stigma by countering irrational beliefs. For example, admitting burnout means being a "bad" caregiver. This could be reframed as burnout being a natural human response to chronic stress.

Case Vignette

Ms.LP is a 48-year-old woman from semi-urban Karnataka. She has been caring for her 78-year-old mother-in-law with advanced dementia for the past three years. Her mother-in-law requires complete assistance with bathing, dressing, toileting, and feeding. Over the past six months, Lakshmi has developed chronic insomnia, persistent feelings of exhaustion, and has withdrawn from her social networks. A community health worker recognizes signs of caregiver burnout and refers her to a six-week group intervention at the local PHC. During the intervention, Lakshmi learns that burnout is a recognized condition affecting caregivers worldwide, reducing her isolation and shame. Through cognitive restructuring, she identifies unhelpful thoughts and replaces them with balanced alternatives. Problem-solving exercises help her brainstorm solutions for nighttime caregiving and lack of respite. By the final session, Lakshmi reports significant reduction in exhaustion and renewed sense of competence.

Conclusion

The development of short-term therapies for caregiver burnout in low-resource Indian settings highlights the critical importance of contextual adaptability in the delivery of mental health services. Evidence-based therapies such as cognitive behavioral therapy (CBT) may require substantial adaptation to enable access for disadvantaged populations. These changes include, but are not limited to, shortening the intervention's duration, holding sessions in groups, and adding culturally relevant attitudes and behaviors. Achieving a balance between addressing individual distress and preserving cultural norms is essential for effective intervention in collectivistic cultural environments. If self-care is presented as a means of preserving caring ability rather than as a manifestation of individualistic priorities, psychological therapies may be more consistent with prevalent cultural values.

References

Ajay, S., Kasthuri, A., Kiran, P., & Malhotra, R. (2017). Association of impairments of older persons with caregiver burden among family caregivers: Findings from rural South India. *Archives of Gerontology and Geriatrics, 68*, 143-148.

Arokiasamy, P., Bloom, D., Lee, J., Parasuraman, S., Sekher, T. V., Mohanty, S. K., Chattopadhyay, A., Govil, D., Pedgaonkar, S., Gupta, S., Agarwal, A., Posture, A., Weerman, A., & Pramanik, S. (2022). Cohort profile: The Longitudinal Ageing Study in India (LASI). *International Journal of Epidemiology, 51*(4), e167-e176.

CareLink. (2024). *Coping strategies for caregiver stress: What works best?*

Chakraborty, R., Jana, A., & Vibhute, V. M. (2023). Caregiving: A risk factor of poor health and depression among informal caregivers in India-A comparative analysis. *BMC Public Health, 23*, 42.

Chen, H., Zou, T., Teng, Z., et al. (2025). A systematic review and meta-analysis of psychological burden in family caregivers of patients with brain tumors. *Scientific Reports, 15*, 39694. Chen, Y., Zhang, L., Zhang, S., Zhang, J., Yu, H., Li, Q., & Zhou, Y. (2025). Prevalence and sociodemographic configurations of anxiety and depression among caregivers of individuals with mental illness: A meta-analysis and qualitative comparative analysis. *Journal of Affective Disorders, 375*, 486-495.

Liao, X., Wang, J., Zhang, F., Luo, Z., Zeng, Y., & Wang, G. (2022). The levels and related factors of compassion fatigue and compassion satisfaction among family caregivers: A systematic review and meta-analysis of observational studies. *Geriatric Nursing, 45*, 1-8.

Mayo Clinic Staff. (2023, August 9). *Caregiver stress: Tips for taking care of yourself.* Mayo Clinic. Nasreen, H. E., Tyrrell, M., Vikström,

S., et al. (2024). Caregiver burden, mental health, quality of life and self-efficacy of family caregivers of persons with dementia in Malaysia: Baseline results of a psychoeducational intervention study. *BMC Geriatrics, 24*, 656.

Oikonomou, V., Gkintoni, E., Halkiopoulos, C., & Karademas, E. C. (2024). Quality of life and incidence of clinical signs and symptoms among caregivers of persons with mental disorders: A cross-sectional study. *Healthcare, 12*(2), 269.

Prunty, M. M., & Foli, K. J. (2019). Guilt experienced by caregivers to individuals with dementia: A concept analysis. *International Journal of Older People Nursing, 14*(2), e12227.

Schaffer, D. R. (2022). *Implementing an online, integrative, multi-component, group-based cognitive behavior therapy (CBT) for the reduction of caregiver burden in primary familial caregivers of persons with dementia: A preliminary test of feasibility* (Doctoral dissertation). Old Dominion University.

Shen, C. T., Shi, J., Liu, F. X., & Lu, X. M. (2025). Internet-based cognitive behavioral therapy interventions for caregivers of patients with cancer: Scoping review. *JMIR Cancer, 11*, e67131.

Sołtys, A., & Tyburski, E. (2020). Predictors of mental health problems in formal and informal caregivers of patients with Alzheimer's disease. *BMC Psychiatry, 20*, 435.

Chapter 27

Low-Resource Counselling for Perinatal Mental Health in Community Clinics

– Safeera A

Introduction

Perinatal mental health refers to the psychological well-being of women during pregnancy and up to one year after childbirth. This period is characterized by significant biological, emotional, and social changes that can influence mental health. In many low- and middle-income countries, including India, a large proportion of pregnant women receive care through community clinics, primary health centres (PHCs), and maternal health outreach programs rather than specialized mental health facilities. Community clinics typically provide essential maternal and child health services such as antenatal check-ups, immunizations, and nutritional counselling. These clinics often serve low-income women, first-time mothers, migrant populations, and women from rural or semi-urban areas. Mental health services, however, are rarely integrated into routine maternal care despite growing evidence that psychological difficulties during pregnancy and postpartum can affect both the mother and infant. Healthcare providers in such settings commonly include nurses, midwives, community health workers (such as

ASHA workers in India), and general physicians rather than trained psychotherapists. Consultation times are usually brief due to high patient loads. In addition, infrastructure limitations such as lack of private counselling rooms, limited screening tools, and shortage of trained mental health professionals create barriers to providing formal psychotherapy. Despite these challenges, community clinics represent an important access point for early identification and support for perinatal mental health problems. Low-resource counselling approaches that are brief, culturally sensitive, and feasible for non-specialist providers can significantly improve maternal well-being and child outcomes.

Case Vignette

Asha, a 24-year-old woman in her third trimester of pregnancy, attends a community clinic for a routine antenatal check-up. She reports feeling constantly worried about childbirth and finances. She has difficulty sleeping and often feels overwhelmed. Her husband works long hours and she has limited family support in the city where she recently migrated. The clinic has a heavy patient load and no dedicated mental health professional. A brief counselling intervention involving psychoeducation, emotional support, and simple coping strategies is planned over several short sessions integrated into her antenatal visits.

Common Mental Health Issues

Perinatal mental health problems are common but frequently under-recognized in low-resource healthcare settings. Several psychological conditions may emerge during pregnancy or after childbirth due to hormonal changes, psychosocial stressors, and limited support systems.

Perinatal Depression

Perinatal depression includes depressive symptoms that occur during pregnancy (antenatal depression) or after childbirth (postpartum depression). Symptoms may include persistent sadness, loss of interest in activities, fatigue, feelings of guilt or worthlessness, and difficulty bonding with the infant. In low-income settings, additional stressors such as financial hardship, gender discrimination, and limited social support may increase vulnerability.

Untreated perinatal depression can affect maternal functioning and infant development, including difficulties with breastfeeding, attachment, and child cognitive development.

Anxiety and Excessive Worry

Pregnancy often involves uncertainty about childbirth, parenting responsibilities, and health outcomes. Many women experience anxiety related to labour complications, financial pressures, or family expectations. In community clinics, women may report sleep disturbances, irritability, excessive worrying, and physical symptoms such as headaches or stomach discomfort.

Without adequate psychological support, anxiety can escalate and interfere with daily functioning and maternal self-care.

Stress Related to Social and Family Pressures

Women in low-resource communities may face multiple stressors including marital conflict, domestic responsibilities, limited autonomy, and cultural expectations regarding motherhood. Some women may also experience gender preference pressures, stigma related to mental health, or lack of emotional support from family members.

Chronic stress during the perinatal period can contribute to both depressive and anxiety symptoms, highlighting the need for accessible psychosocial support.

Limitations

Providing mental health care in community clinics presents several practical challenges that influence how psychotherapy must be adapted.

High Patient Load and Limited Time

Healthcare providers in public community clinics often manage large numbers of patients each day. As a result, counselling sessions must be brief and integrated into routine maternal health appointments.

Lack of Trained Mental Health Professionals

Many clinics do not employ psychologists or psychiatrists. Counselling responsibilities may fall on nurses, midwives, or community health workers who have limited formal training in psychotherapy.

Limited Privacy

Community clinics may lack private counselling rooms, making confidential conversations difficult. This can discourage women from discussing emotional concerns openly.

Stigma Around Mental Health

Mental health difficulties during pregnancy may be misunderstood or minimized within families and communities. Women may hesitate to disclose emotional distress due to fear of judgement.

Language and Cultural Barriers

Community clinics often serve diverse populations speaking different languages or dialects. Counselling approaches must therefore be culturally sensitive and easy to understand.

Given these constraints, mental health interventions must be simple, brief, flexible, and deliverable by non-specialist providers.

Low-Resource Psychotherapy Plan

The intervention uses a brief supportive counselling approach combined with elements of cognitive-behavioural therapy (CBT) and psychoeducation. This model focuses on emotional support, problem-solving, and coping strategies that can be delivered by trained primary healthcare workers.

The goal is not intensive psychotherapy but early emotional support, stress management, and strengthening social support networks.

Session Structure

The intervention may be delivered across three brief sessions integrated with routine antenatal or postnatal visits.

Session	**Focus**	**Duration**
Session 1	Rapport building, screening, psychoeducation	20 minutes
Session 2	Coping strategies and problem-solving	20 minutes
Session 3	Strengthening support systems and relapse prevention	20 minutes

Key Techniques

1. ***Psychoeducation***: The counsellor explains that emotional changes during pregnancy are common and treatable. Women are informed about symptoms of stress, anxiety, and depression to normalize their experiences and reduce stigma.

2. ***Emotional Validation and Support***: Active listening and empathetic responses help women feel heard and understood. Supportive counselling can reduce feelings of isolation and distress.
3. ***Simple Relaxation Techniques***: Women are taught brief relaxation exercises such as deep breathing or grounding techniques that can be practiced at home to manage anxiety.
4. ***Problem-Solving Strategies*** :The counsellor helps the client identify practical stressors and brainstorm possible solutions. For example, discussing ways to seek support from family members or community resources.
5. ***Strengthening Social Support***: Encouraging involvement of supportive family members or peer groups can improve emotional well-being. Community health workers may also connect women with maternal support groups.

Follow-Up and Referral

If symptoms are severe or persistent, the woman may be referred to a mental health specialist or higher-level healthcare facility. This brief intervention model aims to improve coping skills and reduce distress while remaining feasible within the constraints of community clinics.

Ethical and Cultural Considerations

Ethical practice is essential when providing counselling in low-resource healthcare environments.

Confidentiality

Maintaining confidentiality can be challenging in crowded clinics. Counsellors should make efforts to speak privately whenever possible and reassure clients that their information will not be shared without permission.

Informed Consent

Women should be informed about the purpose of counselling and their right to accept or decline participation. Counselling should always be voluntary.

Cultural Sensitivity

Beliefs about pregnancy, motherhood, and mental health vary across cultures. Counsellors must respect local traditions while gently addressing harmful myths or misconceptions.

Professional Boundaries

In community settings where counsellors may have ongoing relationships with clients, maintaining appropriate professional boundaries is important to ensure ethical practice.

Referral Responsibility

If a client shows signs of severe depression, suicidal thoughts, or psychosis, the counsellor has an ethical responsibility to arrange appropriate referral and ensure safety.

Conclusion

Designing a psychotherapy approach for a low-resource setting highlights the importance of flexibility and contextual awareness in mental health practice. In community clinics where time, infrastructure, and trained professionals are limited, traditional long-term therapy models may not be feasible. Instead, brief supportive interventions that focus on psychoeducation, emotional validation, and practical coping strategies can make a meaningful difference. This process also emphasizes the value of integrating mental health care into existing healthcare systems and training non-specialist providers to recognize and support psychological well-being.

Ultimately, adapting psychotherapy to real-world contexts ensures that mental health support becomes more accessible and equitable for vulnerable populations.

References

American Psychiatric Association. (2022). Diagnostic and statistical manual of mental disorders (5th ed., text rev.). APA Publishing.

Rahman, A., Surkan, P. J., Cayetano, C. E., Rwagatare, P., & Dickson, K. E. (2013). Grand challenges: Integrating maternal mental health into maternal and child health programmes. PLoS Medicine, 10(5), e1001442.

World Health Organization. (2016). Thinking healthy: A manual for psychosocial management of perinatal depression. WHO.

World Health Organization. (2022). Guide for integration of perinatal mental health in maternal and child health services. WHO.

Chapter 28

Psychotherapy for Women Facing Domestic Stress in Low-Income Settings

– Mohini Rakesh Patil

Introduction

Women living in low-income communities frequently experience multiple forms of domestic stress that affect their emotional and psychological well-being. In many developing countries, including India, women often shoulder primary responsibilities for household management, caregiving, and maintaining family relationships while simultaneously facing financial hardship and limited access to resources. These challenges are particularly visible in rural communities, urban slums, and areas served by government primary health centres (PHCs), community clinics, or non-governmental organizations (NGOs).Within such settings, psychological distress often remains underrecognized and undertreated. Mental health services are limited, and primary healthcare systems tend to prioritize physical health concerns over psychological needs. Women may visit health centres with physical complaints such as headaches, fatigue, sleep disturbances, or body pain, which are frequently linked to underlying emotional stress (Patel et al., 2018). Because mental health literacy is often low, these symptoms may not be immediately identified as indicators of psychological distress.

Domestic stress in low-income environments can arise from a range of social and interpersonal factors. These may include financial instability, marital conflicts, substance misuse within the family, caregiving burden, gender inequality, and limited autonomy in decision-making. In some cases, women may also face emotional or physical abuse within intimate relationships, which further increases vulnerability to mental health difficulties. According to the World Health Organization (2022), women are disproportionately affected by common mental disorders such as depression and anxiety due to social disadvantage, exposure to chronic stress, and unequal access to resources.

Mental health professionals working in these contexts must therefore design interventions that are practical, culturally sensitive, and feasible within limited resources. Brief psychotherapy models that can be delivered in community settings, such as supportive counselling, cognitive-behavioural strategies, and group-based interventions, are particularly useful in addressing the psychological needs of women experiencing domestic stress.

Common Mental Health Issues in This Context

Women experiencing domestic stress in low-income settings frequently present with psychological difficulties related to ongoing interpersonal and socioeconomic challenges. Among the most common concerns are depression, anxiety, and trauma-related emotional distress.

Depression

Depression is widely reported among women facing persistent domestic stress. Symptoms may include feelings of sadness, hopelessness, fatigue, irritability, and reduced interest in daily activities. The emotional strain associated with financial hardship, marital conflict, and caregiving responsibilities can contribute significantly to depressive symptoms.In many cultural contexts, depression may also be expressed through physical complaints rather than emotional language. Women may report frequent headaches, body pain, gastrointestinal discomfort, or sleep problems when experiencing emotional distress. Such somatic presentations often lead individuals to seek medical rather than psychological help (Patel et al., 2018).

Anxiety and Chronic Stress

Anxiety is another common psychological concern in low-income domestic environments. Women may experience persistent worry related to financial instability, children's future, family conflicts, or household responsibilities. Continuous exposure to such stressors can lead to chronic anxiety characterized by restlessness, irritability, difficulty concentrating, and sleep disturbances.Uncertainty regarding economic security or family relationships can further intensify anxiety. When individuals feel that they have limited control over their circumstances, stress may become a persistent psychological state.

Trauma-Related Distress

In situations where domestic stress includes exposure to emotional or physical abuse, women may develop trauma-related symptoms. These may include intrusive memories, hypervigilance, avoidance behaviors, emotional numbness, and heightened fear responses. Research indicates that intimate partner violence is strongly associated with depression, anxiety, and post-traumatic stress symptoms among women globally (Devries et al., 2013).

These mental health issues often overlap and interact with one another, creating complex psychological challenges that require sensitive and contextually appropriate therapeutic responses.

Key Constraints

Providing psychotherapy in low-resource settings involves several practical and structural challenges that influence how mental health services are delivered.

One major constraint is the lack of privacy in healthcare environments. Many counselling services in government clinics or community organisations operate in shared spaces, making confidential discussions difficult. Women may therefore hesitate to disclose sensitive information related to marital conflict or domestic violence.

Another challenge is the limited time for psychological consultations. Primary health centres often serve large populations, leaving little time for extended therapy sessions. Mental health professionals may need to provide effective interventions within brief consultations lasting 20-30 minutes.

Stigma surrounding mental health is also a significant barrier. In some communities, seeking psychological help may be perceived as a sign of weakness or family failure. Women may therefore avoid formal counselling services or delay seeking support.

Language and literacy barriers may further complicate therapy. Some clients may have limited formal education, requiring therapists to explain psychological concepts using simple language and culturally relevant examples.

Finally, economic constraints and caregiving responsibilities can affect treatment continuity. Women may find it difficult to attend regular therapy sessions due to household duties, childcare responsibilities, or employment demands.

These limitations highlight the importance of designing psychotherapy interventions that are brief, flexible, and accessible within community contexts.

Low-Resource Psychotherapy Plan

In low-resource settings, psychotherapy must be adapted to practical realities while maintaining evidence-based principles. A combination of brief Cognitive Behavioral Therapy (CBT) and supportive counselling can be effective in addressing emotional distress among women experiencing domestic stress.

CBT helps individuals recognize connections between thoughts, emotions, and behaviors. By identifying unhelpful thinking patterns, clients can develop healthier ways of interpreting and responding to stressful situations. Supportive counselling complements CBT by providing emotional validation, empathy, and encouragement.In community settings where individual therapy resources are limited, group counselling sessions may also be implemented. Group settings allow participants to share experiences, learn coping strategies, and develop social support networks.

Session Structure

A brief psychotherapy program consisting of four to six sessions can be implemented in low-resource environments. Each session may last approximately 30-40 minutes.

Session 1: Engagement and Psychoeducation. The therapist establishes rapport, explores the client's concerns, and provides basic information about stress and emotional well-being.

Session 2: Identifying Stressors and Thoughts. The client is guided to recognize common stress triggers and explore how thoughts and beliefs influence emotional reactions.

Session 3: Coping and Emotional Regulation. The therapist introduces coping strategies such as relaxation exercises, breathing techniques, and grounding practices to manage stress.

Session 4: Problem-Solving and Social Support. Clients are encouraged to identify practical steps for addressing everyday challenges and strengthening supportive relationships.

Additional sessions may focus on reinforcing coping skills and developing strategies for maintaining emotional well-being.

Key Techniques Used

Several practical techniques can be applied within low-resource psychotherapy:

Psychoeducation

Providing clear information about the connection between stress, emotions, and physical symptoms helps normalize the client's experiences.

Breathing and Relaxation Exercise

Simple breathing techniques and relaxation practices help reduce physiological symptoms of anxiety and stress.

Problem-Solving Skills

Clients learn structured approaches to identifying problems, generating possible solutions, and choosing realistic steps toward improvement.

Strength-Based Approach

Therapists help clients recognize personal strengths, resilience, and existing support systems within their community or family.

Case Vignette

Kumari, a 30-year-old woman living in a low-income urban settlement, visited a community health centre complaining of persistent headaches, fatigue, and difficulty sleeping. During the consultation, she reported feeling overwhelmed by household responsibilities and ongoing conflicts with her spouse regarding financial difficulties.

The counsellor conducted a brief psychological assessment and explained how chronic stress can affect both emotional and physical health. Over four counselling sessions, Kumari was introduced to breathing exercises to manage anxiety and basic problem-solving strategies to address daily stressors. The counsellor also encouraged her to identify supportive individuals within her extended family.

By the final session, Kumari reported improved sleep and a better ability to manage stressful situations. Although her financial challenges remained unchanged, the therapy helped her develop coping strategies that reduced emotional distress and increased her sense of control.

Real-World Context: Indian and Global Examples

Mental health interventions addressing domestic stress among women have been implemented in various parts of the world, particularly in communities with limited access to professional psychological services.

Indian Context

In India, community-based mental health programs have increasingly focused on integrating psychological support within primary healthcare systems. Organisations such as the National Institute of Mental Health and Neurosciences (NIMHANS) and various NGOs have developed training programs for community health workers to provide basic psychological support and counselling.

For example, in several rural districts, Accredited Social Health Activists (ASHAs) have been trained to identify signs of depression and emotional distress among women and refer them to appropriate mental health services. These initiatives demonstrate the importance of task-sharing approaches in expanding access to mental health care in underserved communities.

Additionally, women's self-help groups operating under rural development programs often provide informal emotional support networks. These groups create spaces where women can discuss personal challenges, share coping strategies, and receive social encouragement.

Global Context

Globally, community-based psychotherapy programs have been implemented in various low-income regions affected by social and economic hardship. For example, group interpersonal therapy has been successfully implemented in rural Uganda to treat depression among women experiencing poverty and interpersonal stress. The program demonstrated significant improvements in participants' psychological well-being and social functioning (Bolton et al., 2003).

Similarly, brief psychological interventions such as Problem Management Plus have been used in communities affected by conflict, displacement, and economic adversity. These programs highlight the effectiveness of structured, culturally adapted interventions delivered by trained community members.

These examples illustrate that meaningful psychological support can be provided even in settings with limited professional mental health resources.

Ethical and Cultural Considerations

Ethical practice is essential when providing psychotherapy in low-resource settings. Confidentiality must be maintained even in environments where privacy is limited. Therapists should clearly explain the limits of confidentiality and obtain informed consent before beginning counselling sessions.

Cultural sensitivity is also important. Therapists must respect cultural norms and family structures while supporting women's psychological well-being. Interventions should be adapted to align with local values and communication styles.

Maintaining professional boundaries is another important ethical consideration. Counsellors working in community settings may encounter expectations to provide financial assistance or personal support beyond their professional role. Clear boundaries help maintain a healthy therapeutic relationship.

When clients disclose experiences of domestic violence, therapists must prioritize safety and provide appropriate referrals to social services, legal support, or community organizations that can offer protection and assistance.

Conclusion

Designing psychotherapy interventions for low-resource settings highlights the importance of adaptability, cultural awareness, and practical problem-solving in mental health practice. Unlike traditional clinical environments, therapists working in community contexts must deliver effective care within constraints such as limited time, infrastructure, and social stigma. This process demonstrates that meaningful psychological support does not always require complex interventions: empathy, culturally sensitive communication, and simple evidence-based techniques can significantly improve emotional well-being. Developing accessible and contextually relevant psychotherapy approaches is therefore essential for promoting mental health equity among women experiencing domestic stress.

References

Devries, K. M., Mak, J. Y., García-Moreno, C., Petzold, M., Child, J. C., Falder, G., & Watts, C. H. (2013). The global prevalence of intimate partner violence against women. *Science, 340*(6140), 1527-1528.

Patel, V., Saxena, S., Lund, C., Thornicroft, G., Baingana, F., Bolton, P., & Unützer, J. (2018). The Lancet Commission on global mental health and sustainable development. *The Lancet, 392*(10157), 1553-1598.

World Health Organization. (2022). *World mental health report: Transforming mental health for all.* Geneva: World Health Organization.

Krupnick, J. L., Green, B. L., Stockton, P., Goodman, L., Corcoran, C., & Petty, R. (2008). Group interpersonal psychotherapy for low-income women with posttraumatic stress disorder. *Psychotherapy Research, 18*(5), 497-507.

Chapter 29

Supporting Adolescents from Single-Parent Families in Resource-Limited Contexts

– Fathimathul Mubassira N V

Introduction

Adolescents growing up in single-parent families often experience unique developmental challenges, particularly in resource limited environments such as government schools, rural communities, and low-income urban areas. In many such contexts, one parent assumes full responsibility for financial support, caregiving, and household management. These responsibilities can create emotional, economic, and social pressures that affect adolescents' well-being. Resource limited contexts typically include settings were access to professional mental health services, private counselling spaces, and specialized educational support is restricted. Schools may have large class sizes, minimal counselling infrastructure, and teachers who are already managing heavy workloads. Adolescents in these environments may therefore rely heavily on informal support systems such as teachers, extended family members, community leaders, or peer groups. Single parent families in such settings may arise due to divorce, separation, migration for work, or the death of a parent. Although many adolescents demonstrate resilience and adaptability, the absence of one caregiver can increase emotional stress, feelings of loneliness, and practical responsibilities at home. Financial strain can also affect access to education, extracurricular opportunities, and healthcare.

Case Vignette

Anjali, a 15year old student studying in a government higher secondary school, lives with her mother and younger brother after her father migrated abroad for work several years ago. Her mother works long hours as a domestic worker and often returns home late in the evening. Teachers recently noticed that Anjali has become withdrawn in class and her academic performance has declined. During a brief meeting with the school counsellor, Anjali reports feeling overwhelmed by household responsibilities and worried about her family's financial situation. She also feels embarrassed when classmates talk about their parents attending school meetings together. Because the school counselling service has limited time and no dedicated therapy room, a short, practical counselling intervention must be designed to support Anjali.

Common Mental Health Issues in This Context

Several psychological concerns commonly emerge among adolescents living in single parent families in resource limited environments. First, emotional distress such as anxiety, sadness, and feelings of abandonment may occur following parental separation, migration, or loss. Adolescents may struggle with questions about identity, belonging, and family stability. These emotions can manifest through irritability, social withdrawal, or reduced motivation. Second, academic stress is frequently observed. Limited parental supervision, combined with economic pressures, can make it difficult for adolescents to focus on schoolwork. Some adolescents may also take on part-time work or additional household responsibilities, reducing the time and energy available for studies. Third, low self-esteem and social comparison may arise when adolescents perceive their family situation as different from peers. In certain cultural contexts, single parent households may be stigmatized, causing adolescents to feel ashamed or reluctant to discuss family issues openly. These concerns can interact with normal developmental challenges of adolescence, making timely psychosocial support essential.

Key Constraints

Providing psychological support in low resource contexts involves several practical challenges. A major constraint is the lack of privacy and infrastructure for counselling. Many schools and community centres do not have dedicated counselling rooms, meaning conversations may occur in shared offices or classrooms. This can make adolescents hesitant to speak openly about personal concerns. Time limitations are another challenge. Counsellors or teachers may only have short periods available for individual meetings due to large student populations and academic schedules. As a result, long-term psychotherapy models are often unrealistic. Stigma surrounding mental health can also reduce help seeking behaviour. Adolescents may worry that others will view them as "weak" or "problematic" if they seek counselling support. Family members may also prioritize academic performance or economic survival over emotional well being. Finally, financial and educational constraints within families may limit opportunities for extracurricular development, tutoring, or specialized therapy services. These constraints require mental health professionals to design brief, flexible, and culturally sensitive interventions.

Low Resource Psychotherapy Plan

A practical intervention plan for adolescents in this context focuses on brief, structured support that can be delivered within limited time and resources. Therapy Approach: The primary approach combines supportive counselling with elements of brief cognitive behavioural therapy (CBT). Supportive counselling emphasizes empathy, validation, and emotional expression, helping adolescents feel heard and understood. CBT techniques focus on identifying unhelpful thoughts, building coping strategies, and improving problem-solving skills. Session Structure: Because of limited time and resources, the intervention may consist of four to six short sessions delivered over six to eight weeks. Each session may last approximately 20–30 minutes and can be conducted in a school counselling space or quiet classroom area. Follow-up support may also involve brief check-ins from teachers or community workers.

Key Techniques

Psychoeducation is used to explain the relationship between stress, thoughts, and emotions. Adolescents are reassured that their emotional reactions to family circumstances are understandable and manageable. Grounding and relaxation exercises, such as slow breathing or mindfulness techniques, can help adolescents regulate anxiety and improve concentration. Problem-solving strategies are introduced to help adolescents identify manageable steps for addressing daily challenges. For example, creating a study schedule or identifying supportive adults at school. Behavioral activation may also be encouraged by helping adolescents reengage with positive activities such as sports, creative hobbies, or peer interaction. These techniques are designed to be simple, culturally appropriate, and feasible in settings with limited therapeutic resources.

Ethical and Cultural Considerations

Ethical practice in low resource contexts requires careful attention to confidentiality, informed consent, and cultural sensitivity. Confidentiality must be explained clearly to adolescents, particularly when counselling takes place in shared spaces. Counsellors should reassure students that personal information will remain private except in situations involving safety concerns. Informed consent is also important. Adolescents and, when appropriate, their caregivers should understand the purpose of counselling, the number of sessions, and the limits of confidentiality. In contexts where literacy levels vary, verbal explanations may be more appropriate than written forms. Cultural sensitivity is essential when working with families from diverse backgrounds. Practitioners should respect cultural beliefs about family roles and responsibilities while promoting the adolescent's emotional well-being. Equity and fairness must also guide interventions. Adolescents from economically disadvantaged families should have access to supportive services without discrimination or stigma.

Conclusion

Designing a psychotherapy plan for adolescents in single parent families within resource limited contexts highlight the importance of flexibility and creativity in mental health practice. Rather than relying on intensive clinical models, practitioners must adapt evidence-based principles to realistic conditions such as limited time, infrastructure, and financial resources. This process emphasizes the value of community collaboration, culturally responsive care, and strengths-based approaches that recognize adolescents' resilience and potential for growth even in challenging circumstances.

References

Amato, P. R. (2010). Research on divorce: Continuing trends and new developments. Journal of Marriage and Family, 72(3), 650–666.

Masten, A. S. (2014). Ordinary magic: Resilience in development. New York, NY: Guilford Press.

Patel, V., Saxena, S., Lund, C., et al. (2018). The Lancet Commission on global mental health and sustainable development. The Lancet, 392(10157), 1553–1598.

World Health Organization. (2014). Health for the world's adolescents: A second chance in the second decade. Geneva: WHO.

Chapter 30

Family Counselling in Low-Resource Community Centres

– Anu Sree P

Introduction

Family counselling within low-resource community centres represents a critical yet often underdeveloped area of mental health service delivery. These centres are typically embedded within economically disadvantaged settings such as urban slums, rural villages, or semi-urban neighbourhoods, where access to specialized psychological services remains limited. They may operate under government initiatives, non-governmental organizations (NGOs), or community based outreach programs. Despite their limitations, these centres often serve as the first and sometimes only point of psychological support for individuals and families experiencing distress.

The families who access these services frequently encounter multiple, overlapping stressors. Financial instability, irregular employment, overcrowded living conditions, and limited educational opportunities contribute to chronic stress within the household. In many cases, these stressors are compounded by social challenges such as gender inequality, intergenerational conflicts, and rigid cultural expectations regarding family roles and responsibilities.

Unlike structured clinical settings, low-resource community centres often function in informal or semi-formal environments. Counselling sessions may take place in multipurpose rooms, shared offices, or even open spaces, where maintaining privacy can be difficult. Mental health professionals working in such settings are usually few in number and may include trainees or volunteers who must manage a high volume of clients within limited time frames.

In this context, family counselling shifts from a purely therapeutic model to a more pragmatic and adaptive practice. The emphasis lies not only on resolving conflicts but also on strengthening everyday functioning, improving communication, and fostering resilience within the family system. Interventions must be concise, culturally grounded, and sensitive to the realities of the clients' lives.

Common Mental Health Issues

Family Conflict and Marital Strain

One of the most frequently reported concerns in community settings is ongoing conflict within the family, particularly between spouses. These conflicts often stem from financial pressures, unmet expectations, and differences in decision-making styles. In many households, traditional gender roles play a significant role in shaping interactions, sometimes leading to power imbalances and communication breakdowns.

Arguments may revolve around issues such as income management, child-rearing practices, or responsibilities within the household. Over time, unresolved disagreements can escalate into chronic tension, emotional withdrawal, or even verbal and physical aggression. However, due to stigma and normalization of conflict, families may not initially perceive these issues as requiring professional help.

Stress and Adjustment Difficulties

Families in low-resource settings are often required to adapt to rapidly changing and challenging circumstances. Migration from rural to urban areas, loss of employment, illness of a family member, or children's academic struggles can create significant emotional strain.

Individuals may present with symptoms such as irritability, fatigue, sleep disturbances, or somatic complaints like headaches and body pain. These symptoms are often understood in physical rather than psychological terms, which can delay appropriate intervention. Adjustment difficulties may also manifest as withdrawal, reduced productivity, or increased conflict within the household.

Parenting Challenges and Child Behavioural Issues

Another common area of concern involves difficulties in managing children's behaviour. Parents may report issues such as disobedience, academic underperformance, aggression, or excessive screen use. These concerns are often linked to inconsistent parenting practices, lack of awareness about child development, and limited access to educational support.

Parents themselves may experience high levels of stress, which affects their ability to respond calmly and consistently to their children's needs. In some cases, harsh disciplinary practices or neglect may arise, further complicating the child's emotional and behavioural development.

Limitations

Limited Privacy and Infrastructure

A major challenge in community centres is the lack of dedicated counselling spaces. Sessions may be interrupted or conducted in environments where others are present, making it difficult for clients to speak openly about sensitive issues. This limitation can hinder the development of trust and reduce the effectiveness of interventions.

Time Constraints and High Client Load

Counsellors often work with a large number of clients each day, leaving limited time for each session. This necessitates a shift from long-term, in-depth therapy to brief and focused interventions. While this approach can still be effective, it requires careful prioritization of issues and efficient use of available time.

Stigma and Low Mental Health Literacy

Mental health remains a stigmatized topic in many communities. Families may hesitate to seek help or may discontinue sessions prematurely due to fear of judgment. Additionally, there is often limited understanding of psychological concepts, which requires counsellors to simplify explanations and avoid technical language.

Cultural and Linguistic Diversity

Community centres serve individuals from diverse cultural and linguistic backgrounds. Differences in beliefs about family roles, parenting, and mental health can influence how problems are perceived and addressed. Counsellors must be sensitive to these variations and adapt their approach accordingly.

Limited Resources and Follow-Up

Access to assessment tools, therapeutic materials, and referral services may be restricted. Follow up sessions are not always guaranteed, as clients may be unable to return due to financial or logistical constraints. This further emphasizes the need for brief, impactful interventions.

Low-Resource Psychotherapy Plan

Given the constraints of the setting, an integrative and flexible approach is most appropriate. The intervention combines elements of supportive counselling, brief cognitive-behavioural strategies, and basic family systems principles. The goal is not to conduct intensive therapy but to facilitate meaningful changes within a short period.

Supportive counselling provides a foundation for building rapport and offering emotional validation. Cognitive-behavioural techniques help individuals identify and modify unhelpful thought patterns and behaviours. Family systems concepts are used to understand relational dynamics and promote healthier interactions.

Session Structure

The intervention is designed to be delivered over three to five sessions, each lasting approximately 20 to 30 minutes.

Session 1: Establish rapport, understand the presenting problem, and provide basic psycho education.

Session 2: Introduce communication skills and begin addressing specific conflicts.

Session 3: Focus on problem-solving and behavioural strategies.

Session 4: Reinforce skills and address remaining concerns.

Session 5: Review progress and discuss strategies for maintaining improvements. This structure allows for flexibility, as not all families may attend all sessions.

Key Techniques

Psycho-education is introduced early in the process to help families understand the connection between stress, emotions, and behaviour.

Information is presented in simple, relatable terms, often using examples from daily life. Communication training involves teaching family members how to express their thoughts and feelings clearly without blaming others. Techniques such as active listening and using "I" statements are emphasized. Problem-solving strategies are used to help families address practical issues. This involves identifying the problem, generating possible solutions, evaluating options, and selecting a course of action. Behavioral interventions focus on establishing routines, reinforcing positive behaviours, and reducing negative interactions. For parents, guidance is provided on consistent and supportive parenting practices.Relaxation techniques, such as deep breathing, are introduced to help individuals manage emotional distress in the moment. Throughout the intervention, emphasis is placed on recognizing and strengthening existing family strengths rather than focusing solely on problems.

Case Vignette

Padma, a 32-year-old mother, and her husband Suresh, a construction worker, sought help at a local community centre due to frequent arguments at home. They reported ongoing disagreements related to financial management and their son's academic performance. Their 11-year-old son had recently been skipping school and displaying irritability. During the initial session, both parents expressed frustration and blamed each other for the situation. The counsellor acknowledged their concerns and provided basic psycho-education about how stress can affect communication and parenting. In subsequent sessions, the couple was guided to practice listening to each other without interruption and to focus on specific issues rather than general accusations. Simple problem-solving strategies were introduced to help them plan their finances and create a consistent routine for their child. The counsellor also provided guidance on positive reinforcement and setting clear expectations for behaviour. By the end of four sessions, the couple reported fewer arguments and improved cooperation. While challenges remained, they expressed greater confidence in managing conflicts and supporting their child.

Ethical and Cultural Considerations

Ethical practice in low-resource settings requires careful attention to both professional standards and contextual realities. Maintaining confidentiality is particularly challenging in shared environments. Counsellors must take practical steps to ensure privacy while also being transparent about its limitations. Informed consent should be obtained in a manner that is easily understood by clients, avoiding technical terminology. Clients need to be aware of the nature and scope of the services being offered. Cultural sensitivity is essential in family counselling. Interventions must respect cultural norms and values, particularly those related to family structure, gender roles, and decision-making. At the same time, counsellors must navigate situations where certain practices may contribute to distress, doing so in a respectful and non-confrontational manner. Professional boundaries must be clearly maintained, even when working in informal community settings. Counsellors may encounter clients outside the counselling environment, requiring careful handling of such interactions.

Conclusion

Developing a counselling approach for low-resource community centres highlights the importance of adaptability in psychological practice. It challenges the assumption that effective therapy requires extensive time and resources, demonstrating instead that meaningful change can occur through brief, focused interventions. This process also underscores the value of cultural understanding and the need to align therapeutic strategies with the realities of clients' lives. It reinforces the idea that the role of a counsellor extends beyond applying techniques to include advocacy, education, and empowerment. Working within such constraints encourages creativity and prioritization, helping practitioners develop a more grounded and practical approach to mental health care.

References

Aronen, E. T. (1993). The effect of family counselling on the mental health of children in low- and high-risk families: A longitudinal approach. Journal of Child Psychology and Psychiatry, 34(2), 155–165.

Cohen, A., Eaton, J., Radtke, B., George, C., Manuel, B. V., De Silva, M., & Patel, V. (2011). Three models of community mental health services in low-income countries. International Journal of Mental Health Systems, 5(3).

Dixon, L., McFarlane, W. R., Lefley, H., Lucksted, A., Cohen, M., Falloon, I., Mueser, K., Miklowitz, D., Solomon, P., & Sondheimer, D. (2001). Evidence-based practices for services to families of people with psychiatric disabilities. Psychiatric Services,52(7),903– 910.

Goorden, M., Schawo, S. J., Bouwmans-Frijters, C. A. M., van der Schee, E., Hendriks, V. M., & Hakkaart-van Roijen, L. (2016). The cost-effectiveness of family therapy for mental health conditions: A systematic review. BMC Psychiatry, 16, 237.

Healy, E. A., Kaiser, B. N., & Puffer, E. S. (2018). Family-based youth mental health interventions delivered by non-specialist providers in low- and middle-income countries: A systematic review. Family Systems & Health, 36(2), 182–197.

Jordans, M. J. D., Komproe, I. H., Tol, W. A., Kohrt, B. A., Luitel, N. P., Macy, R. D., & de Jong, J. T. V. M. (2010). Evaluation of a classroom-based psychosocial intervention in conflict-affected Nepal: A cluster randomized controlled trial. Journal of Child Psychology and Psychiatry, 51(7), 818–826.

Morillo, H., Lowry, S., & Henderson, C. (2022). Effectiveness of family-based interventions for psychosis in low- and middle-income countries: A systematic review. Social Psychiatry and PsychiatricEpidemiology,57(9),1749–1769.

Chapter 31

Brief Interventions for Elderly Loneliness in Community Settings

– Anushiya Mary M

Introduction

The problem of loneliness among community-dwelling older adults in India and similar settings is a common concern in the context of increased risks of depression, cognitive decline, and premature death. However, in low-resource community settings in India and similar settings, psychological interventions aimed at elderly loneliness are scarce. This chapter provides a culturally informed brief psychotherapy framework aimed at addressing elderly loneliness in community settings. It focuses on primary health care centres, senior citizen associations, panchayat-based interventions, and similar settings. It provides a four-part low-resource intervention based on supportive counselling, narrative approaches, and behavioural activation techniques. It also addresses the limitations of infrastructure constraints, stigma, caregiver dependency, and linguistic diversity. It provides a hypothetical case vignette of the applicability of the model. It also highlights the importance of cultural considerations in terms of autonomy, intergenerational factors, and indigenous notions of elder identity.

It concludes with a reflection on the transformational potential of community psychotherapy for an underserved population.

The country has a population of about 140 million people who are 60 years and above, and this figure is expected to rise to 340 million in 2050 (United Nations, 2019). This growth in population is happening at a time when there is increased urbanisation, leading to an increase in nuclear families, and at the same time, there is a decrease in traditional joint families that provided companionship and a sense of purpose to elders. This has left elders in rural and semi-urban areas, who are increasingly being left behind by their children who have moved into urban areas in search of job opportunities.

The community settings that are relevant in the context of this chapter include rural and semi-urban primary healthcare centres, anganwadi programs, senior citizen groups conducted by NGOs, panchayat-level wellness programs, and religious meetings conducted at temples and mosques. These community settings have some characteristics in common, including that they are easily accessible, they have community trust, they are conducted by healthcare staff and not mental health professionals, and they are the only point of contact that can be made with the vast majority of lonely elders who will never have contact with formal psychiatry and clinical psychology. The target group for this chapter is elderly persons living within their communities who are 60 years old or older and who experience subjective loneliness as a result of widowhood, migration of family members, stigmatisation associated with illness or disability, or simply as a result of accumulated mortality among peers. Women are particularly disadvantaged owing to immobility, economic dependence, and social isolation that commonly accompany widowhood in conservative rural societies (Shiovitz-Ezra & Leitsch, 2010). The model being described is intended to be implemented by community health workers or volunteers from nongovernmental organisations or social workers at the field level who possess some facilitation skills and equipment.

Common Mental Health Issues

Among older persons in community contexts, there are three psychological conditions that are particularly common and that frequently co-occur. The first is late-life depression. Loneliness and depression have an interlocking, mutually intensifying relationship. Depression can lead to increased withdrawal from social contact, and loneliness can increase the severity of depressive symptoms. In rural Indian communities, late-life depression tends to be expressed in somatic, rather than psychological, symptoms, including fatigue, bodily pain, and decreased appetite. These are not easily categorised within cultural idioms of distress and therefore go unrecognised. Depression in older persons in community contexts remains untreated and unresolved.

The second is grief and complicated bereavement. A substantial proportion of lonely persons in community contexts are widowed, and some have experienced the loss of siblings, friends, and adult children within a compressed time frame. Complicated grief, including yearning, ruminative thinking, functional impairment, and disbelief, is common but not well recognised in community contexts, where stoic acceptance of loss is normatively expected, particularly from women who have lost their husbands.

The third is loss of purpose and role identity. Retirement from agricultural work, loss of children from the household, and loss of household roles due to illness can leave a person feeling a profound lack of purpose and identity. The feeling of uselessness or burdensomeness is a cognitive schema that has important implications for self-worth, motivation, and social re-engagement potential. The dimension of psychological distress that is most closely related to feeling useless or burdensome is Erikson's (1963) integrity versus despair stage of development.

Key Constraints

The delivery of psychological interventions for elderly loneliness in Indian community settings is a complex process, and a variety of structural, attitudinal, and interpersonal constraints must be addressed.

The constraints related to privacy and space are ubiquitous. In most PHC waiting rooms, anganwadi halls, and panchayat offices, there is a lack of a specific room for conducting a session. Conversations take place in full view and hearing of other community people, family members, and PHC staff, thus undermining the feeling of safety and security, which is a prerequisite for self-disclosure. Here, the importance of developing skills in creating psychological privacy must be underscored.

Stigma and barriers to help-seeking are particularly salient in elderly populations. In many rural settings, "admitting to emotional distress or working with a counsellor is seen as weakness, family shame, or mental illness." Older adults may take on the shame associated with being elderly and in hardship. They may believe that they should suffer in silence. Families may dismiss reports of loneliness as an inevitable aspect of ageing. The language used to present any intervention should avoid stigmatising language and use words such as "mann ki baat," or "dil ka bojh," which means "speaking what is in the heart," or "the burden on one's heart," respectively.

The existing workforce is severely challenged to address mental health needs. CHWs and ASHA workers are overburdened with high caseloads across multiple health mandates. They are unlikely to be formally trained in mental health counselling. As such, any brief intervention model must be minimally burdensome to the facilitator and not require extensive training or skill-building.

The physical and sensory limitations of older adults, including their hearing capacity, vision limitations, and mobility limitations, demand the development of therapeutic activities that are adapted. Written material and technology-based activities would be inappropriate. Oral and relational modalities and activities would be more appropriate.

The following table summarises the key constraints and proposed adaptations:

Constraint	**Impact on Intervention**	**Proposed Adaptation**
No private space	Inhibits disclosure	Conduct in garden/outdoor corner; use warm, normalising framing
Stigma around mental health	Reduces engagement	Use community language; frame as 'wellness' conversation
Low literacy	Limits written tools	Use verbal storytelling, picture cards, and oral review
Sensory/ physical limitations	Reduces participation	Speak clearly; seat face-to-face; use a larger font if needed
High CHW caseloads	Limits session time	Four structured 45-minute sessions with clear session guides
Family interference	May undermine autonomy	Sensitise family; obtain elder's individual consent

Low-Resource Psychotherapy Plan

The intervention draws on three complementary evidence-informed approaches appropriate for the community context, namely, supportive counselling, narrative therapy, and behavioural activation. Supportive counselling is the relationship container in and through which the therapeutic work is enacted, providing empathic and non-judgmental listening, validation, and unconditional regard without the need for insight-focused work. Narrative therapy principles are also employed to help the older person distinguish who they are from the experience of loneliness, identify times in the past when they were not lonely, and create a narrative of who they would like to be in the future, namely, a connected and agentive person (White & Epston, 1990). Behavioural activation, a fundamental component of low-intensity cognitive-behavioural therapy, is used to counteract loneliness and depression by scheduling activities that are enjoyable, meaningful, and social in nature (Cuijpers et al., 2007).Collectively, these strategies are deliverable by a trained CHW or NGO volunteer without professional supervision, without the use of any written materials apart from a basic session guide, and without the older person needing to take on the social role of a mental health service user.

Session Structure

The intervention has four sessions, each lasting about 45 minutes, and is provided on a weekly basis. The sessions may be conducted at the PHC, the home of the older person, or in a community setting. A fifth session may be used as a three-month follow-up.

Session	Title	Core Objectives	Key Techniques
1	Opening and Understanding	Build rapport; explore loneliness experience; assess daily routine	Active listening; open questions; life review ('Tell me about a time you felt most connected')
2	Stories of Self and Connection	Identify past sources of meaning and connection; begin narrative re-authoring	Narrative timeline; strengths identification; externalising loneliness as 'a visitor'
3	Small Steps Back to Life	Collaboratively plan 1–2 behavioural activation activities; problem-solve barriers	Activity scheduling; graded task assignment; problem-solving; role-play if needed
4	Celebrating and Anchoring	Review progress; reinforce gains; build a relapse prevention plan; connect to a community group if available	Affirmation, future-pacing, connecting to a senior citizen group or a faith community

Key Techniques

The strategy of life review and reminiscence is used in Sessions 1 and 2, tapping into the rich autobiographical memories of the older adult as a resource. There is consistent research evidence that structured reminiscence has a significant impact in reducing depression and loneliness in older adults, with significant effect sizes even for a short intervention (Pinquart & Forstmeier, 2012). The facilitator will ask the older adult to talk about a period of their life when they felt most connected, purposeful, and valued, and gently explore with them what made them feel that way.The strategy of externalising the problem involves giving a name to loneliness, such as 'the shadow' or 'the silence,' which distances it from the older adult's identity. This strategy helps the older adult distance themselves from loneliness, thereby reducing shame and enhancing self-compassion, and creates a space for them to think about times when the shadow is less prominent and what they did that made that happen (White & Epston, 1990).

The behavioural activation component in Session 3 emphasises the importance of identifying one or two meaningful activities that the older person might engage in, such as participating in a temple gathering, sitting in the shared courtyard during the evenings, helping a neighbour, or taking up a discontinued hobby. The facilitator uses a problem-solving approach to overcome any possible hurdles that might come up during the session, such as mobility issues, family resistance, and negative thoughts about oneself.

The community connection component in Session 4 goes beyond the therapeutic relationship by exploring the availability of community resources. If senior citizen groups, self-help groups, and religious community groups are available in the community, the facilitator helps the older person to take the first step to participate in any of these groups.

Case Vignette

Savitribai is a 71-year-old widow who lives in a semi-urban village in the state of Maharashtra. Her only son works in Pune and comes back once or twice a year. Since the death of her husband three years ago, Savitribai has gradually stopped participating in activities she used to enjoy, including the weekly women's meeting of bhajan singing and helping at the village anganwadi. She mostly stays at home alone during the day and complains of low mood, lack of sleep, and a sense of burden. On a visit from an ASHA worker at a health camp in her village and a gentle inquiry about her well-being, Savitribai replied: "Koni naahi aata. Roj ekachi basto" ("There is no one now. I sit alone every day").

The ASHA worker, trained in the four-session approach, conducted the first session under a tree within Savitribai's courtyard to ensure privacy from neighbours. The life review approach was employed by the ASHA worker to engage Savitribai to recall her most meaningful experiences as a member of her community. Savitribai recollected her work as coordinator of women's savings groups within the village for more than a decade. Savitribai described her recollections from those years with animation. In Session 2, Savitribai was introduced to the concept of 'the shadow of silence' that had descended upon her after her husband's loss and had gradually confined her indoors, not to who she really is. In Session 3, Savitribai and her facilitator agreed upon a single step: attending her bhajan group the following Thursday; the facilitator agreed to accompany her the first time. In Session 4, Savitribai reported that she had attended twice already and felt 'lighter.' Savitribai was linked to a meeting of senior women's groups that met once a month at the panchayat hall. Savitribai remained an active participant at three months post-intervention.

Ethical and Cultural Considerations

The process of informed consent in community settings with older adults has special considerations. This includes communication in the older person's primary language, clear and non-technical communication, and voluntary consent, not pressured by the presence of family members or perceived authority from health workers. If there is suspicion of cognitive impairment, more time should be taken to assess comprehension and, if necessary, involve a trusted family member while prioritising expressed preferences.

However, confidentiality must be maintained despite the structural challenges of the setting. The older person must be told what will be disclosed to families or health workers. The limits of confidentiality must be explained if self-harm or harm to others is a risk. The common phenomenon of passive suicidal ideation among isolated older adults must be appreciated; that is, thoughts of death as a welcome release. The facilitators must be trained in compassionate risk assessment. Cultural sensitivity is a must as India has a diverse ageing population along various parameters like caste, religion, languages spoken, and traditional practices of different regions. The importance of religion/spirituality as a source of purpose and social bonding must be appreciated while designing a behavioural activation program. The intervention must not convey that Western constructs are superior to indigenous interpersonal relationships. The attachment of older adults to their family roles and expectations of filial obligation must be carefully managed; the approach is one of respectful curiosity.

Autonomy and dignity should inform all interactions. For those from a cultural background in which older adults, especially widowed women, have had little experience of being listened to with genuine interest and without judgment, the therapeutic relationship itself can be a corrective relational experience. Facilitators should be trained in an explicit manner regarding how not to use paternalistic language and in ensuring that the goals of the intervention are set by the older adult rather than the health system.

Conclusion

Designing this intervention drove home to me just how significantly the infrastructure of belonging contributes to mental health across the life course—and just how precipitously it can fall away for older people experiencing loss, transition, and marginalisation at once. What has struck me most is that the therapeutic factor most likely to make a difference in such a setting is not a particular intervention or a particular action, but a relationship: simply being seen, named, and taken seriously by another human being. In a low-resource setting where specialist help is out of the question and time is at a premium, this is not a sad fact; it is the intervention itself. It also forced me to think carefully about the ways in which psychological concepts like 'loneliness' or 'depression' are conceptualised and communicated across cultures and languages—and to realise that effective community psychology must always begin by listening to how people name their own pain.

Therefore, loneliness in old age is neither inevitable nor hopeless. As has been shown in the chapter, brief and culturally responsive interventions, such as supportive counselling, narrative reframing, and behavioural activation, may help alleviate loneliness in elderly people, even in resource-limited community settings. Margaret's experience is a clear example of a broader research finding that the single most powerful therapeutic factor is not a specific technique, but a relationship with another person. A lonely person may find a new sense of belonging by being heard and helped back into social life by another person. However, brief interventions are just a first step. A lonely person's social and community context must be changed for a long-term solution. For practitioners in resource-limited settings, the single most important takeaway is this: therapy is not a clinic. Therapy is a person who is present, culturally responsive, and willing to meet an elderly person at exactly where they are. Therefore, four sessions may be enough to help a lonely person rediscover a sense of purpose in life and a feeling that they have not been forgotten.

References

Cacioppo, J. T., & Hawkley, L. C. (2009). Perceived social isolation and cognition. Trends in Cognitive Sciences, 13(10), 447-454.

Cuijpers, P., van Straten, A., & Warmerdam, L. (2007). Behavioural activation treatments of depression: A meta-analysis. Clinical Psychology Review, 27(3), 318-326.

Erikson, E. H. (1963). Childhood and society (2nd ed.). Norton.

Masi, C. M., Chen, H.-Y., Hawkley, L. C., & Cacioppo, J. T. (2011). A meta-analysis of interventions to reduce loneliness. Personality and Social Psychology Review, 15(3), 219-266.

Parkes, C. M. (2006). Love and loss: The roots of grief and its complications. Routledge.

Patel, V., & Prince, M. (2001). Ageing and mental health in a developing country: Who cares? Qualitative studies from Goa, India. Psychological Medicine, 31(1), 29-38.

Pinquart, M., & Forstmeier, S. (2012). Effects of reminiscence interventions on psychosocial outcomes: A meta-analysis. Aging & Mental Health, 16(5), 541-558.

Shiovitz-Ezra, S., & Leitsch, S. A. (2010). The role of social relationships in predicting loneliness: The National Social Life, Health, and Aging Project. Social Work Research, 34(3), 157-167.

United Nations. (2019). World population ageing 2019: Highlights. Department of Economic and Social Affairs, Population Division. White, M., & Epston, D. (1990). Narrative means to therapeutic ends. Norton.

World Health Organization. (2021). Social isolation and loneliness among older people: Advocacy brief. WHO.

Chapter 32

Group Support for Caregivers of Persons with Chronic Illness

– Anakha Rajeevan

Introduction

A major psychological, emotional, and physical burden is frequently experienced by caregivers of people with chronic illnesses. Family members often provide the ongoing care and monitoring needed for chronic illnesses like cancer, dementia, diabetes, stroke, and long-term neurological conditions. Professional caregiving services are either scarce or nonexistent in many low-resource settings, especially in public hospitals or community health centers. As a result, without sufficient psychological support, family members typically spouses, adult children, or parents take on the duty of providing care.

This chapter examines a government hospital's outpatient department (OPD) in an urban or semi-urban setting for patients with long-term medical conditions. Large populations are usually served by these hospitals, which also face severe resource limitations. There may be a shortage of mental health specialists, and the counseling services that are offered are frequently quick and crowded.

Waiting in hospital hallways for several hours is a common experience for caregivers who accompany patients to follow-up appointments. They may feel worn out from continuing caregiving duties, anxious about the patient's condition, and worried about the cost of treatment during this time. In this situation, setting up quick group meetings for caregivers to attend while they wait for doctor's appointments can be a low-resource group support intervention. A psychologist, counselor, or other qualified mental health professional may lead these sessions, which can offer psychoeducation, coping mechanisms, and emotional support.

Case Vignette

Every month, Lakshmi, a 45-year-old woman, goes with her husband to a public hospital to receive treatment for chronic kidney disease. She has taken on the role of primary caregiver over previous years, handling household chores, finances, hospital visits, and medication. Lakshmi says she is always exhausted, worried about her husband's health, and stressed out about money. Families expect her to be strong, so she hardly ever finds time to talk about her emotions. She is invited to take part in a brief caregiver support group held in the waiting area while she is in the hospital. The group offers possibilities for sharing experiences with caregivers who are dealing with similar issues, relaxation techniques, and psychoeducation about caregiver stress. This vignette illustrates how group support interventions can be implemented in real-world low-resource medical settings to address caregiver distress.

Common Mental Health Issues

Caring for someone with a chronic illness takes a heavy toll mentally and emotionally. Caregivers often struggle with stress, anxiety, and depression, all tangled up in the daily grind of helping someone else.

Caregiver Stress and Burnout

Stress hits hard when the demands pile up faster than a caregiver can handle. Think about the never-ending list: helping with basic tasks, sorting out meds, driving to appointments, juggling finances. After a while, this routine wears people down. Burnout creeps in.

Anxiety

Anxiety is another matter. Caregivers often worry nonstop about health setbacks, what the future holds, how to make the right choices. Those medical appointments, treatment plans, and money worries feed the anxiety. It doesn't just stay in the mind, either. Headaches, trouble sleeping, stomach upsets these are all signs of stress bubbling over.

Depressive Symptoms

Depression isn't far behind. When the days blur together and the sense of isolation grows, sadness and hopelessness can settle in. Caregivers lose touch with friends and hobbies. Money troubles and not knowing what's next make things even worse. Sometimes, balancing caregiving with work or family feels impossible, leaving people stretched to the breaking point.

Limitations

Bringing psychotherapy into low-resource healthcare settings isn't easy. Government hospitals see crowds every day, and mental health professionals rarely have enough time for one-on-one counseling with caregivers.

Limited Privacy

The environment itself isn't ideal. There's usually no private counseling room. Sessions end up happening in shared spaces,waiting rooms, community halls, wherever there's space. Without privacy, caregivers might hold back and not talk openly about what they're going through.

Time Constraints

Time's tight, too. Caregivers squeeze in what they can before or after the patient's appointment, so sessions have to be quick and to the point. Long, ongoing therapy just doesn't work in this setup.

Stigma Around Mental Health

Then there's stigma. In many places, caregivers worry about what others will think if they ask for psychological help, or they feel pressure to handle distress on their own. Sometimes, they think their feelings don't matter as much as the patient's medical issues.

Language and Cultural Diversity

And because public hospitals serve people from all kinds of backgrounds, mental health workers need to adjust how they talk and use examples that make sense to everyone. Making sure information is clear and fits the culture really matters.

All these challenges point toward one thing: group interventions that are simple, structured, and sensitive to culture are essential in these settings.

Low-Resource Psychotherapy Plan

This intervention brings together group-based supportive counseling, bits of cognitive-behavioral therapy, and psycho education.Group support works well for caregivers. It gives them a space to connect, swap stories, and lean on each other so they don't feel like they're carrying everything alone.

Session Structure

Session	Focus	Key Activities
Session 1	Understanding Caregiver Stress	Psychoeducation about caregiver burden, group sharing
Session 2	Coping Skills	Breathing exercises, grounding techniques, stress management
Session 3	Problem-Solving and Support	Identifying support networks, planning self-care

Key Techniques Used

Psychoeducation

Caregivers learn about stress, emotional exhaustion, and the psychological ups and downs that come with long-term caregiving. When they realize these feelings are common, the guilt and harsh self-judgment start to fade.

Breathing and Relaxation Techniques

Breathing and relaxation make a difference. Even a few minutes of slow, deep breathing—diaphragmatic breathing helps ease anxiety and tension.

Grounding Techniques

Grounding exercises keep caregivers anchored in the present, pulling them out of spiraling worries about what's coming next.

Problem-Solving Strategies

Problem-solving is practical here. Caregivers name the real, everyday hurdles juggling doctor's appointments, keeping up with work, finding a moment to rest. The group tackles these challenges together, trading ideas and trying out solutions.

Peer Support and Sharing

Peer support matters. When caregivers talk openly and swap stories, they realize they're not alone. These conversations chip away at isolation and build trust, turning a room full of strangers into a team.

Ethical and Cultural Considerations

When you run group interventions in low-resource settings, ethics can't be an afterthought; they're front and center.

Confidentiality

You're working with groups, so privacy can get tricky. It's important to lay out ground rules right from the start. Let everyone know: what's said in the room stays in the room. Facilitators should make it clear that sharing someone else's story outside the group isn't okay.

Informed Consent

Nobody should walk into a session unsure about what's happening. Caregivers need a clear, straightforward explanation of what the group is for, how sessions work, and that joining in is their choice. If paperwork isn't practical, a verbal agreement works. What matters is that everyone understands and agrees.

Professional Boundaries

Facilitators walk a fine line. They support and guide, but they don't take on the role of long-term therapists for each person. Caregivers should know this group isn't a substitute for individual therapy; it's a space for support, not a stand-in for more intensive care.

Cultural Sensitivity

Culture shapes how people see illness and caregiving. In many places, caring for family is more than a job, it's a duty, a core value. Mental health professionals need to respect that, while also helping caregivers see why looking after themselves matters too.

Conclusion

Putting together psychotherapy interventions for low-resource settings teaches you to value flexibility and real-world solutions. Traditional one-on-one therapy doesn't always fit in a busy hospital or clinic. Group work steps in, offering support to more people at once and building a sense of community. Even simple tools like psychoeducation, breathing exercises, basic problem-solving can make a real difference when they're easy to access and tailored for the group. Creating these interventions isn't just about logistics; it's about staying culturally sensitive and keeping ethics at the heart of mental health care.

References

American Psychological Association. (2020). *Publication manual of the American Psychological Association* (7th ed.). APA Publishing.

Northouse, L. L., Katapodi, M. C., Song, L., Zhang, L., & Mood, D. W. (2010). Interventions with family caregivers of cancer patients: Meta-analysis of randomized trials. *CA: A Cancer Journal for Clinicians, 60*(5), 317–339.

World Health Organization. (2017). *Mental health gap action programme (mhGAP): Scaling up care for mental, neurological, and substance use disorders.* WHO Press.

Zarit, S. H., & Femia, E. E. (2008). A future for family care and dementia intervention research? *Challenges and strategies. Aging & Mental Health, 12*(1), 5–13.

Schulz, R., & Sherwood, P. R. (2008). Physical and mental health effects of family caregiving. *American Journal of Nursing, 108*(9), 23–27.

Chapter 33

Psychotherapy for Persons with Disabilities in Low-Resource Settings

–Adeline Valentina C

Introduction

The chapter looks at a setting where the needs of Families, Women and Special Population with Disabilities, can realistically be addressed: an NGO-run Community Disability Rehabilitation Centre (CDRC) in a semi-urban district of Maharashtra, India. These centres exist under the Deendayal Disabled Rehabilitation Scheme (DDRS), a Government of India programme run through the Ministry of Social Justice and Empowerment, which funds NGOs to provide rehabilitation and psychosocial support to persons with disabilities at the community level (DEPwD, 2023).

The people who come to this centre are mostly women and girls with physical or locomotor disabilities. Locomotor disability is the most common form of disability recorded in India, making up 44.7% of all disabilities nationally (Awasthi et al., 2023). Many of the women here acquired their disabilities through accidents, complications of polio, chronic illness and intimate partner violence. Most are from low-income households. Most have low literacy. The counsellor visits twice a week, speaks Marathi and Hindi, and has limited time, limited space, and no dedicated room.

Women with disabilities in India experience disability inside families, inside communities, inside cultural systems that have already decided what they are worth. Researchers call this 'double discrimination',being marginalised once for being a woman, and again for being disabled (Census of India, 2011, as cited in Socio.Health, 2025), which is why this chapter is placed under the section of Family, Women and Special Population.

Common Mental Health Issues

Depression and Grief Over Lost Roles

In Maharashtra and across India, a woman's sense of self is deeply tied to her roles: as a daughter, a wife, a mother, a worker. When disability takes away or complicates those roles, the loss is not just functional; it is deeply personal. Many women in this setting have been withdrawn from school, are unable to marry or have seen marriages break down, and feel they are a financial and emotional burden on their families. Research from Mumbai found women with disabilities to be nearly ten times more likely to experience depression than non-disabled women (Dyer et al., 2022). This is a rational response to genuine and sustained loss.

Anxiety and Chronic Stress

Much of the anxiety in this population is grounded in real uncertainty of not knowing what will happen next. Will the family continue to support her? What happens if her primary caregiver falls ill? Can she access the government schemes she is entitled to? The National Mental Health Survey 2016 found that 60% of those with common mental disorders in India also reported co-occurring disability, with a treatment gap of over 80%, meaning most people with these struggles receive no support at all (Jain et al., 2022).

Internalised Stigma and Low Self-Worth

The most painful fact is the way women in this setting have come to believe the narratives told about them. In many communities in India, disability is attributed to karma, past-life sins, or family misfortune. When a woman hears this from childhood, she internalises it. She stops asking for things because she does not believe she deserves them. She minimises her pain. She apologises for her own existence. This is not a clinical symptom that exists in a vacuum, it is the psychological scar of being told, repeatedly, that you are less (Olawale et al., 2013).

Limitations

No private room

Sessions happen in a partitioned corner of a shared hall. Full confidentiality is not possible. This is especially significant for women who may want to talk about violence at home or conflicts with their husbands and who will not do so if they fear being overheard.

Family gatekeeping

Most women arrive with a male family member who often speaks on their behalf and decides whether she returns. In some cases, that same family member is the source of her distress.

Very limited counsellor time

The counsellor has six to eight hours a week, shared across a caseload of twelve to fifteen clients.

Stigma around mental health

Families bring clients here for rehabilitation physiotherapy, assistive devices. Suggesting psychological support is often met with confusion or resistance.

Low literacy and language

Standard tools and written handouts are not useful here. Everything must be communicated orally, in Marathi or Hindi, in language that is accessible and not clinical.

Irregular attendance

Transport barriers, physical fatigue, and family permission all affect whether a client returns. Flexibility is the only option when sessions might not work.

Case Vignette

Priya is a 28-year-old woman from a semi-urban village near Pune. She has a locomotor disability affecting her left leg as the result of a road accident four years ago and walks with a visible limp. She was referred to the Community Disability Rehabilitation Centre by an ASHA worker who noticed she had stopped leaving her home entirely.

When Priya first came to the centre, she was quiet and quick to say she was 'fine.' It took most of the first session just to sit with her and to not rush past it. Slowly, she shared that her husband had left after the accident, that her in-laws no longer considered her 'useful,' and that she had moved back to her parents' home where she felt she was a burden. She had stopped stitching, something she had loved and had even earned a small income from.Because she believed there was no point anymore. She was not sleeping well. She had frequent headaches. She cried often but alone, because she did not want her parents to worry. She described herself in Marathi as 'nakamachi' (worthless).

A brief, low-resource intervention was planned over six sessions: two weeks apart, 40 minutes each, conducted in Marathi in a partitioned corner of the centre's main hall. The plan focused on validating her experience without reinforcing her self-blame, slowly reintroducing stitching as a behavioural activation activity, and gently questioning the belief that her worth had left with her husband.

Low-Resource Psychotherapy Plan

The approach used here combines Brief Supportive Counselling with selected techniques from Cognitive Behavioural Therapy,particularly behavioural activation and simplified cognitive restructuring and a single family psychoeducation session. This adheres to the time limitations and does not require formal assessment tools, and works with what the client already has rather than assuming resources that are not there. NGO-based programmes in India have shown that this kind of integrated, community-grounded counselling is feasible and meaningful for clients who would otherwise receive nothing (Murthy, 2011).

Session Structure

Six sessions in total: five individual sessions of 40 minutes each, and one family session of about 30 minutes only with the client's explicit consent. Sessions are held fortnightly over three months, with a flexible follow-up session available after the cycle ends. Fortnightly spacing is realistic given the counsellor's visiting schedule and the client's attendance constraints.

Key Techniques

Culturally framed psychoeducation (Session 1)

Rather than opening with clinical language, the counsellor links emotional distress to physical symptoms the client already recognises fatigue, disturbed sleep, persistent pain. The framing is 'mann ka dard' (pain of the heart) or 'tensions ka asar' (the weight of tensions) language that is familiar, not foreign.

Validation and safety building (Sessions 1 and 2)

Many of these women have spent years being told that their suffering is their own fault. Simply being listened to without judgment, without being given advice before being heard is itself therapeutic. The counsellor does not rush to techniques. She sits with the client's experience first.

Behavioural activation (Sessions 2 and 3)

This technique involves identifying small, meaningful activities the client has withdrawn from visiting a neighbour, listening to bhajans, stitching and slowly re-engaging with them. It requires no materials, no literacy, and no special equipment. And it works because it gives the client something concrete to do between sessions, which matters when sessions are two weeks apart.

Simplified cognitive restructuring (Sessions 3 and 4)

Rather than formal thought records, the counsellor uses conversation to gently question beliefs like 'Maza kahi upayog nahi' (I am of no use to anyone. She does not argue with the belief. She asks: 'Would you say that to your daughter if she were in your situation?' This kind of narrative questioning is far more accessible than worksheets, and often more powerful.

Problem-solving for practical stressors (Session 4)

Some of what is causing distress is not psychological,it is logistical. Not knowing how to access a disability certificate. Not understanding which government schemes she is entitled to. The counsellor addresses this directly, and where needed, connects the client to the centre's rehabilitation social worker.

Family psychoeducation session (with the client's explicit consent): One session is held with the primary caregiver. The goal is not to blame the family but to help them understand that emotional support is as important as physical care. This session can open small but meaningful shifts in how much independence the woman is given, in whether she is allowed to attend sessions alone, in how her pain is talked about at home.

Ethical and Cultural Considerations

Ethics in a setting like this cannot be reduced to a checklist. It has to be something the counsellor thinks about actively, in every session, because the conditions that make ethical practice difficult are present all the time.

Confidentiality is the most immediate challenge. There is no private room. The counsellor must tell the client honestly that before the first session begins, not after trust has already been built. The client needs to know what she is agreeing to. For the family session specifically, separate consent must be sought. And if the client discloses violence at home, the counsellor must be familiar with what the Protection of Women from Domestic Violence Act, 2005 and the Rights of Persons with Disabilities Act, 2016 as required because those are not abstract legal instruments here; they are directly relevant to the lives of the women sitting in this room.

Informed consent cannot be a written form handed to someone who cannot read it. It has to be a real conversation in Marathi or Hindi, at the client's pace, with space to ask questions. For clients with cognitive difficulties, supported decision-making is used, and a trusted person of the client's own choosing can be present.

A woman who knows her husband is waiting outside will not say certain things. The counsellor has to create conditions, even within these constraints, where the client has some time to speak for herself.

This might mean asking the family member to wait for the last ten minutes rather than the first. Small adjustments matter.

Culturally, the most important thing the counsellor can do is resist the urge to argue with the client's worldview. When a woman says her disability is God's will or her karma, the counsellor does not challenge that belief. She asks instead: 'Even if this was God's will, does that mean you should not be at peace?' That question does not disrespect the belief. It opens a door inside it.

Conclusion

The chapter highlights that the most significant challenge in low-resource settings is not merely the absence of tools or time, but the tendency to view these constraints as barriers to delivering meaningful therapy. On the contrary, such limitations often compel practitioners to return to the fundamental essence of therapeutic work: one individual offering genuine, attentive presence to another. Within these contexts, the absence of a private room, extended sessions, or formalized tools necessitates a more grounded and relational approach.Evidence from practice suggests that women accessing services in such settings do not require idealized clinical environments. Rather, their needs center on being heard, having their suffering acknowledged, and engaging with a practitioner who communicates in a culturally and linguistically attuned manner, while maintaining transparency about what can realistically be offered. This approach should not be interpreted as a compromise in standards of care. Instead, it represents a rigorous and ethically grounded form of practice that prioritizes authenticity, responsiveness, and human connection at its core.

References

Department of Empowerment of Persons with Disabilities. (2023). Deendayal Disabled Rehabilitation Scheme (DDRS). Ministry of Social Justice and Empowerment, Government of India.

Jain, S., Bhatt, M., Bhavsar, P., & Joshi, A. (2022). Mental health in India: Sociocultural dimensions, policies and programs. International Review of Psychiatry, 34(1), 1-12.

Murthy, R. S. (2011). Role of non-governmental organizations in mental health in India. Indian Journal of Psychiatry, 53(Suppl 1), S389-S395.

Olkin, R. (1999). What psychotherapists should know about disability. Guilford Press. World Health Organization. (2011). World report on disability. WHO Press.

Pattnaik, S., Murmu, J., Agrawal, R., Rehman, T., Kanungo, S., & Pati, S. (2023). Prevalence, pattern and determinants of disabilities in India: Insights from NFHS-5 (2019-21). Frontiers in Public Health, 11, 1036499.

Riley, A., Daruwalla, N., Kanougiya, S., Gupta, A., Wickenden, M., & Osrin, D. (2022).Intimate partner violence against women with disability and associated mental health concerns: A cross-sectional survey in Mumbai, India. BMJ Open, 12(4), e056475.

Chapter 34

Mental Health Support for LGBTQ+ Youth in Resource-Constrained Environments

– *Aarzoo Akbarali Damani*

Introduction

LGBTQ+ youth include adolescents and young adults whose sexual orientation or gender identity differs from heterosexual and cisgender norms. This group includes individuals who may identify as lesbian, gay, bisexual, transgender, queer, questioning, or other diverse identities. Adolescence is a period marked by important developmental tasks such as identity exploration, building peer relationships, and developing a sense of autonomy. For LGBTQ+ youth, however, this process can be more complex because identity development often occurs in environments that may not always be accepting or supportive (Russell & Fish, 2016).

The focus of this chapter is on LGBTQ+ youth living in resource-constrained environments. These settings could be rural communities, small towns, or low-income urban areas with limited mental health services. In India and many other low- and middle-income countries, mental health resources are often concentrated in large cities, leaving many regions with very few trained professionals and limited infrastructure for psychological services (Patel et al., 2018).

In such settings, LGBTQ+ youth may not have access to specialized mental health services. Instead, they may rely on general healthcare providers, school counselors, or informal support systems. While these resources can be advantageous, professionals working in these contexts may not always have specific training related to LGBTQ+ mental health concerns. Cultural and social expectations also play an important role in shaping the experiences of LGBTQ+ youth. In many communities, traditional expectations around gender roles, family responsibilities, and heterosexual relationships remain strong. As a result, young people may feel pressure to conceal their identity due to fear of rejection, discrimination, or social stigma. Studies conducted in India have shown that sexual and gender minority individuals frequently experience social exclusion and limited access to supportive services, which can negatively affect their mental health (Chakrapani et al., 2017). Because of these contextual factors, mental health interventions for LGBTQ+ youth in such environments must be practical, culturally sensitive, and feasible within limited resources.

Common Mental Health Issues in This Context

Studies consistently indicate that LGBTQ+ youth endure greater psychological distress than their heterosexual and cisgender counterparts. Importantly, these mental health concerns are not related to sexual orientation or gender identity itself but are largely linked to experiences of stigma, discrimination, and lack of social support (Meyer, 2003).

One of the most commonly reported concerns is depression. Experiences such as bullying, family rejection, and social isolation can lead to persistent feelings of sadness, hopelessness, and low self-worth. In resource-constrained environments where supportive services are scarce, these emotional difficulties may remain unaddressed and continue for long periods.

Another frequently observed concern is anxiety. Many LGBTQ+ youth report constant worry about how others might react if their identity becomes known. Fear of rejection by family members, classmates, or community members can create ongoing stress. This may manifest as excessive worry, difficulty concentrating, irritability, and sleep disturbances.

A third challenge involves identity-related distress. Adolescence is a stage during which individuals begin to develop a clearer understanding of who they are. For LGBTQ+ youth, this process can be complicated by conflicting messages from family, culture, and society. Minority Stress Theory posits that individuals from stigmatized groups endure heightened stress stemming from anticipated rejection, internalized stigma, and instances of discrimination (Meyer, 2003).

Limited supportive resources can exacerbate these psychological difficulties, underscoring the importance of providing accessible and affirming mental health support.

Limitations

Providing psychological support in resource-constrained environments presents several practical challenges. One of the most significant barriers is the shortage of trained mental health professionals. Many rural and semi-urban regions have very limited access to psychologists or psychiatrists, which means that young people may not have regular opportunities to receive professional mental health care (Patel et al., 2018).

Another important limitation is the lack of LGBTQ-affirmative training among many service providers. Some professionals may have limited knowledge about issues related to sexual orientation and gender identity. These issues can make it difficult for youth to discuss identity-related concerns openly and may lead to hesitation in seeking help.

Social stigma is another major challenge. Negative attitudes toward sexual and gender diversity are still present in many communities. Young people may fear judgment or rejection if they disclose their identity. This fear can discourage help-seeking and contribute to feelings of isolation.

In addition to these social barriers, there are also practical limitations in service delivery. Counseling services in low-resource settings often operate with limited privacy, short session durations, and high client loads. Maintaining confidentiality can also be difficult in smaller communities where individuals may know each other socially. Financial constraints may further limit access to private mental health services.

Given these challenges, mental health interventions must be brief, flexible, and adaptable to the realities of the setting.

Low-Resource Psychotherapy Plan

A supportive counseling approach, combined with LGBTQ-affirmative principles, can be particularly effective in resource-constrained environments. Supportive counselling focuses on empathy, emotional validation, and helping individuals strengthen their coping resources. When integrated with affirmative principles, the approach acknowledges the impact of stigma and discrimination while supporting identity acceptance and resilience (Craig et al., 2013).

The primary goal of this intervention is to reduce emotional distress while helping youth develop practical coping strategies and identify supportive relationships in their environment.

Key Techniques

Several simple techniques can be used within this intervention. Active listening and empathic reflection help create a supportive and non-judgmental therapeutic environment. Psychoeducation can help youth understand how stigma and stress may affect mental health.

Grounding and breathing exercises provide practical tools for managing anxiety and emotional distress. Support mapping can also be helpful in identifying individuals or spaces where the youth feels safe. In addition, collaborative problem-solving can assist the client in developing strategies to manage everyday challenges related to school, family, or social relationships.These techniques are particularly useful because they can be implemented within short sessions and require minimal resources.

Session Structure

Session	**Focus**	**Key Activities**
Session 1	Building Rapport and Safety	Establish trust, explore concerns, confidentiality
Session 2	Identity Exploration	Explore discussion about identity and emotional experiences
Session 3	Coping with Stress	Introduce grounding and breathing exercises
Session 4	Support Mapping	Identity trusted individuals and safe spaces
Session 5	Consolidation	Review coping skills and develop future coping strategies

Each session can last 30-40 minutes, depending on the availability of services.

Case Vignette

Rahul, a 16-year-old student from a small town, approached the school counsellor after experiencing persistent anxiety and declining academic performance. He reported feeling increasingly isolated and worried that his classmates might discover that he is gay. Rahul described difficulty sleeping, constant worry about being judged by others, and reluctance to participate in social activities. The school counselling service had limited resources, with sessions available only once every two weeks. The counselor implemented a brief, supportive counseling approach.

During the first session, the counselor focused on building rapport and providing a safe space for Rahul to talk about his concerns. In the subsequent session, Rahul expressed his apprehension about facing rejection from peers and family members should his sexual orientation come to light. The counselor validated his feelings and helped him understand that such reactions are common when individuals face social stigma. Later sessions focused on teaching Rahul simple grounding exercises to manage anxiety and helping him identify supportive individuals within his environment, including a trusted teacher and a close friend. The final session focused on reinforcing Rahul's strengths and helping him develop strategies to cope with future stress.

Ethical and Cultural Considerations

Confidentiality is especially important when working with LGBTQ+ youth, particularly in environments where disclosure of identity may lead to social stigma or conflict within families. Therapists must clearly communicate the limits of confidentiality and take care to protect sensitive information. Another important issue is informed consent, particularly when working with minors. Often, parental consent may be required for counseling services. Clinicians must approach these situations carefully while prioritizing the safety and well-being of the young person. Cultural sensitivity is also essential. Therapists should be aware of the cultural, religious, and family values that influence how individuals understand gender and sexuality. Rather than imposing labels or assumptions, clinicians should allow youth to describe their experiences in their terms. Maintaining appropriate professional boundaries is also important. While empathy and validation are central to supportive counseling, therapists must ensure that their interactions remain professional and ethically appropriate.

Conclusion

Designing a psychotherapy intervention for a resource-constrained setting highlights the importance of adapting psychological approaches to real-world conditions. Mental health professionals must consider limitations such as time, infrastructure, and social stigma while still providing meaningful support. This process reinforces the value of brief, practical interventions that focus on empathy, validation, and strengthening coping skills. Supporting LGBTQ+ youth in such contexts requires both clinical sensitivity and an awareness of the broader social realities that influence their mental health.

References

Chakrapani, V., Newman, P. A., Shunmugam, M., McLuckie, A., & Melwin, F. (2017). Structural violence against Kothi-identified men who have sex with men in India: A qualitative investigation. *Culture, Health & Sexuality, 19*(6), 647–662.

Craig, S. L., Austin, A., & Alessi, E. (2013). Gay affirmative cognitive behavioral therapy for sexual minority youth: A clinical adaptation. *Clinical Social Work Journal, 41*(3), 258–266.

Dua, K., & Bakhru, K. M. (2025). Psychosocial needs of LGBTQ+ and gender-nonconforming juveniles in India: A data-driven perspective on inclusion, law, and mental health. *International Journal of Indian Psychology, 13*(3), 4231–4247.

Gaur, P. S., Saha, S., Goel, A., Ovseiko, P., Aggarwal, S., Agarwal, V., Haq, A. U., Danda, D., Hartle, A., & Sandhu, N. K. (2023). Mental healthcare for young and adolescent LGBTQ+ individuals in the Indian subcontinent. *Frontiers in Psychology, 14*, 1060543.

Meyer, I. H. (2003). Prejudice, social stress, and mental health in lesbian, gay, and bisexual populations: Conceptual issues and research evidence. *Psychological Bulletin, 129*(5), 674–697.

Patel, V., Saxena, S., Lund, C., Thornicroft, G., Baingana, F., Bolton, P., Chisholm, D., Collins, P. Y., Cooper, J. L., Eaton, J., Herrman, H., Herzallah, M. M., Huang, Y., Jordans, M. J. D., Kleinman, A., Medina-Mora, M. E., Morgan, E., Niaz, U., Omigbodun, O., ... Unützer, J. (2018). The Lancet Commission on global mental health and sustainable development. *The Lancet, 392*(10157), 1553–1598.

Russell, S. T., & Fish, J. N. (2016). Mental health in lesbian, gay, bisexual, and transgender youth. *Annual Review of Clinical Psychology, 12*, 465–487.

Sanil, S. (2024). Accessibility to mental healthcare and stigma experienced by the LGBTQIA+ community in India. *International Journal of Indian Psychology, 12*(2), 3711–3717.

Chapter 35

WhatsApp-Based Psychoeducation for Mental Health in Low-Resource Communities

– *Aswath Rubena R*

Introduction

Mental health services have been very inaccessible in low-resource communities, particularly in rural and disadvantaged urban communities. This is due to a lack of mental health professionals, economic issues, transport issues, and cultural issues about mental illness, which have made people in these communities hesitant to seek psychological services. In these communities, new and innovative strategies have to be developed to bridge the gap between those who access psychological services and those who do not access them. Mobile technology has been very effective, particularly in low-resource communities. The most used mobile technology is the use of WhatsApp, a free messaging application that allows people to send messages, voice notes, pictures, and videos using the internet. It is free, easy to use, and has been used by many people, particularly in low-resource communities, and is therefore a good example of a mobile technology that can be used in the delivery of psychoeducation and providing psychological services.

This chapter will be based on the application of the WhatsApp technology in providing psychoeducation to adult populations in low-resource communities that lack access to psychological treatments. In other cases, people who feel distressed do not have an opportunity to receive support through counselling sessions since they have other commitments, such as going to work, paying bills, and so on. This is an opportunity for people to receive support from mental health professionals or facilitators who can provide psycho-educational materials to people who might be distressed. This is especially important for people who include daily wage workers, homemakers, community workers, and people who live in remote areas. The main aim of this intervention is to provide support, not to replace any other form of therapy, but to provide people with mental health education, increase people's awareness regarding their psychological well-being, and provide people with coping skills that they can apply to their daily lives. By applying digital communication technologies, which people already use, mental health professionals can provide support to people who might be underserved.

Common Mental Health Issues

The people living in low-resource communities may experience a high level of psychological pressure due to various causes, including socioeconomic problems, employment insecurity, economic problems, family demands, and lack of access to medical services. The various mental health problems experienced by low-resource communities are discussed below.

Stress and Psychological Distress

Stress is one of the major mental health problems experienced by the people living in low resource communities. The people living in low-resource communities experience various levels of psychological distress, including emotional exhaustion, irritability, sleep problems, and concentration problems, resulting from the daily pressures experienced due to various causes, including employment insecurity, economic problems, and family demands.

Anxiety

The people living in low-resource communities experience anxiety, which is characterized by extreme anxiety or worry about various issues, including economic problems, family demands, health problems, and future happenings. The symptoms of anxiety include headaches, fatigue, muscle tension, and restlessness, and the causes of anxiety are not well understood in low-resource communities with low levels of awareness about mental health problems.

Depressive Symptoms

Commonly, it has been cited that feelings of sadness, hopelessness, and lack of motivation are some of the challenges that people face. Depression, for example, has also been cited as a condition that may also manifest as a lack of interest in activities, tiredness, and avoidance of social activities. Depression, in this case, is likely to remain untreated due to a lack of awareness.

The mental health challenges that have been cited seem to have some level of interconnections. For example, depression, lack of mental health literacy, and lack of opportunities to seek professional help have been cited. In this case, the provision of information through the internet would be helpful in promoting mental health.

Limitations

There are several limitations that have been cited as challenges in the implementation of mental health interventions in low-resource communities.

One limitation that has been cited is the lack of mental health professionals. For example, most communities have very few mental health professionals, such as a psychologist or a counsellor. In this case, due to the lack of professional therapy, the psychological approaches that would be used through the internet would have to be employed.

The other major problem is the stigma associated with mental health issues. In some communities, it could be perceived as a weakness to discuss mental health issues or seek psychological assistance. This could discourage some individuals from openly seeking assistance or being part of any conventional psychological program. The use of technology such as WhatsApp could help minimize this, as individuals could seek information in a private setting.

The other limitation is associated with the technology used. Although smartphone technology is dominant, some communities could be experiencing poor or lack of internet connectivity. In addition, the information must be easily understood by the participants, who could be at different levels of technology understanding.

The problem is associated with privacy, but this could be a challenge with WhatsApp, as all the information sent would be visible to all the participants who are part of the group. This could discourage some individuals from openly sharing their problems or concerns, as they could be perceived by all the people.

Finally, time constraints must be considered. Many individuals in low-resource communities work long hours and may have limited time to engage in structured mental health programs. Interventions must therefore be brief, flexible, and easy to integrate into daily routines.

Low-Resource Psychotherapy Plan

The proposed intervention model is going to be a psycho-educational and supportive counselling model, and the intervention will be conducted through the WhatsApp platform. The intervention will include some basic components of cognitive behavioural therapy, stress management, and mental health literacy. The main objective of the intervention will be to educate the target population about mental health issues, emotions, and simple coping strategies that people can practice on their own. The intervention will not be designed to provide any kind of psychotherapeutic intervention, but it will be designed to provide preventive, emotional, and cognitive components.

Session Structure

The proposed intervention will be a 4-week intervention, and it will be conducted through the WhatsApp group platform with a mental health professional or community volunteer.

- Duration: 4 weeks
- Frequency: 2-3 times a week
- Format: Text messages, voice notes, and short videos Each week, the participants learn about a new theme related to mental health, for instance:

Session 1: Understanding Mental Health: In the first session, the participants learn about the concept of mental health. They learn to understand that experiences such as stress, anxiety, and depression are normal responses to situations that occur in their lives. They learn to understand that they are not weak for experiencing such feelings. They also learn to reflect on the situations that cause stress in their daily lives. In this session, the participants learn about mental health awareness. They also learn to eliminate the stigma that exists in the community about mental illness. They learn to talk comfortably about mental illness.

Session 2: Stress and Relaxation Techniques: In the second session, the participants learn about stress. They also learn the effects of stress on their mental and emotional well-being. They learn the effects of stress on their mental well-being. They also learn about the techniques for managing stress. These techniques are communicated through voice notes. The participants learn about managing stress.

Session 3: Managing Negative Thoughts and Anxiety: In the third session, participants learn about the relationship between their thoughts, emotions, and behaviours. They learn about the effects of negative thought patterns that may contribute to anxiety and emotional problems. They learn how they can challenge their negative thoughts and replace them with more balanced ones using simple examples. The participants learn more positive thought patterns and better emotional regulation techniques.

Session 4: Building Coping Skills and Emotional Resilience: In the final session, participants learn about the importance of building their skills in coping with problems and developing positive daily habits. They learn to identify the people in their social support network who can provide emotional support, positive activities for their well being, and stress management techniques. They are encouraged to reflect on the skills they learned during the intervention and how they can continue using the skills in the future. The participants learn more about their long-term skills in coping with problems and emotional resilience to maintain their psychological well-being.

Key Techniques to Be Used

There are many simple techniques that can be taught using the WhatsApp platform for psychoeducation.

Psychoeducation

Participants receive information about common mental health issues such as stress, anxiety, and depression. Understanding these experiences helps normalize emotional reactions and reduces stigma associated with mental illness.

Breathing and Relaxation Techniques

Guided breathing exercises and relaxation techniques can also be communicated in the form of voice notes or videos.

Cognitive Awareness

Individuals learn to become aware of their negative thoughts and change them in a positive way of thinking. This is a modified version of cognitive behaviour therapy.

Problem-Solving Strategies

Individuals learn simple problem-solving techniques, which help them cope with their problems in their day-to-day lives.

Peer Support and Group Interaction

Individuals can communicate with each other through a WhatsApp group and share their experiences, which will reduce the feelings of loneliness and isolation.

Case Vignette

Anita, a homemaker aged 35, residing in a semi-urban community, was complaining of frequent stress and sleep problems due to financial issues and family demands. She was worried about the future of her children. Since the mental health clinic was located far from the residence of the client, she had never visited the clinic to seek help. Anita was part of the mental health psycho education program, which was conducted through the WhatsApp group. The program was initiated through the community health initiative program in the local community. Through the program, Anita was able to learn about the effects of stress.

Anita was able to learn and develop a sense of awareness about the effects of stress. In addition, Anita was able to learn about the support that she received from other people in the community, despite going through the same problems.

Ethical and Cultural Considerations

There are several ethical issues that must be considered while providing mental health intervention through the use of digital media. One of the major ethical issues that must be considered while providing mental health intervention through the use of the WhatsApp group is confidentiality. In this context, the people who are part of the intervention must be made aware that the messages they share through the group can be accessed by other people. Informed consent is the other ethical requirement that needs consideration. Informed consent will involve the participants being given information about the purpose of the program, the nature of the information they are about to share, and the freedom to exit the program at any time. Informed consent will also involve the seeking of the participants' consent to become part of the WhatsApp group. Cultural sensitivity is also vital in the consideration of the program. Information about mental health issues will be explained in simple terms and concepts that are easily understandable by the participants.

The other ethical requirement that needs consideration is the awareness of the limitations of digital interventions. The facilitators will also be able to identify the situations in which the participants will need to seek mental health services and refer those in need of the services to the health facilities. The WhatsApp-based psychoeducation program will be able to provide mental health services to the participants in a sensitive and ethical manner.

Conclusion

The process of developing the psychotherapy intervention for the low-resource communities highlighted the need to adapt mental health interventions to the reality of the communities. For example, the usual assumptions of the conventional approach to psychotherapy take for granted the availability of space, sessions, and qualified personnel, which may not always be the case. The experience highlighted the value of even the simplest of interventions, such as psychoeducation, relaxation, and communication, which may have beneficial psychological effects. The experience highlighted the value of technology in the delivery of mental health services. For example, WhatsApp allows mental health service providers to reach the population that would otherwise remain outside the service delivery system. Effective mental health service delivery, in the final analysis, depends on the flexibility, sensitivity, and innovativeness of the service providers.

References

Andersson, G., & Titov, N.. (2014). Advantages and limitations of internet-based interventions for common mental disorders. World Psychiatry, 13(1), 4-11.

Cuijpers, P., Karyotaki, E., Reijnders, M., & Purgato, M.. (2019). Psychological treatment of depression in primary care: A meta-analysis. World Psychiatry, 18(2), 208-219.

Kazdin, A. E., & Rabbitt, S. M.. (2013). Novel models for delivering mental health services. Clinical Psychological Science, 1(2), 170-191.

The Lancet Commission on global mental health and sustainable development. The Lancet, 392(10157), 1553-1598.

World Health Organization. (2022). *World mental health report: Transforming mental health for all.* World Health Organization.

Chapter 36

Mobile Mental Health Clinics: Psychotherapy on Wheels

– Neha SP

Introduction

Mobile Mental Health Clinics (MMHCs) purpose is to build therapeutic spaces on wheels that travel directly into the lives of people who have been systematically left behind by traditional healthcare systems. Unlike traditional clinics, which are supposed to be clean workplaces, these clinics are intended to be friendly and welcoming, with seating spaces, work tables, and natural light to remove psychological obstacles to disclosure. They are not fixed clinics, but rather mobile units dispatched along a predetermined path to target regions with high levels of need and little mental health infrastructure. They are dispatched to locations such as remote communities where mental clinics are hours distant, informal settlements within cities with significant levels of poverty and overpopulation, and shelters on the outskirts of towns.

They are also deployed in high-risk contexts such as refugee camps and disaster zones, where trauma is commonplace and mental health infrastructure has been decimated. The target group includes people who are medically underserved, marginalised, and face a range of barriers to healthcare access due to their geographic location, socioeconomic position, and immigrant status. For example, this includes elderly farmers in rural areas, homeless people in cities, and immigrants in agricultural districts.

In the context of India, this environment and population are further demonstrated by projects such as the SCARF telepsychiatry mobile bus, which goes to 156 villages in Tamil Nadu, reaching a population of 300,000. Other projects include those of IHBAS in Delhi, which traverses the streets to reach homebound and homeless mentally ill persons who are completely outside the system. All of these projects are unhealthy. Describe how this mobile setting is a specialised way to reach individuals who have been consistently left behind.

Common Mental Health Issues

Populations served by mobile mental health clinics experience a range of different psychological concerns, but researchers have found that there are some patterns of distress that are consistent across these underserved settings.

One of the most common concerns is depression and anxiety related to poverty and social isolation. In remote or resource-poor settings, economic stress and the lack of a social support system create an environment in which major depressive disorder and generalized anxiety disorder thrive. What is perhaps interesting is that these disorders often do not manifest as clearly defined mood disorders but as physical or somatic complaints such as fatigue, headaches, and sleep disturbances. This may be because the clients have not been socialized to discuss their distress in terms of psychological problems or because they may be new to professional mental health care.

Trauma and Post-Traumatic Stress Disorder (PTSD) represent perhaps the most pervasive mental health concerns encountered in these settings. The individuals reached by mobile units often carry complex trauma, which is the accumulated psychological damage resulting from prolonged and repeated experiences rather than a single event. This includes survivors of domestic violence, victims of communal or political violence, and individuals who have experienced forced displacement. A significant challenge in treating PTSD in this context is that it is often complicated by ongoing stressors, such as immediate threats to safety or housing instability, which can prevent a client from fully engaging in therapeutic work while they are still in "survival mode".

Another commonly occurring but less often discussed problem is "survival stress," which is defined as psychological exhaustion. Survival stress is present when people have to use the vast majority of their psychological resources to simply cope with the demands of living in a difficult situation. Over time, the psychological resources of the person will begin to deplete to the point where the person cannot function or feel any sense of hope for the future. For those in a constant state of exhaustion, the arrival of a mobile clinic in their neighborhood can provide them with a sense of hope for their psychological well-being.

In some cultural settings, such as in India, these mental health concerns are addressed through a spiritual or somatic model. For example, a client may not report their concerns as a "mood disorder" but as a sacred burden felt in their body. Therapists in these cultural settings must be willing to work within these cultural explanations of mental health concerns in a respectful manner. Furthermore, in a joint family system, it becomes difficult to work with an individual client because of the cultural concept of disrespecting the family unit by revealing personal psychological concerns in a Western manner.

Limitations

Working in a mobile mental health clinic introduces a unique set of real-world constraints and complications that have no direct equivalent in traditional fixed-clinic practice. These challenges range from the physical limitations of the vehicle to complex social and logistical barriers.

Physical Environment and Privacy

The most obvious restriction is a lack of physical space; a therapy session takes place in only a few square meters, with no "buffer zones" of waiting rooms or corridors like in normal clinics. This makes it tough to control a patient's anxious energy before an appointment. Furthermore, the vehicle's thin walls continuously threaten privacy by allowing exterior noise from street traffic, community activities, and weather into the consultation space. While white noise devices and cautious parking can help, they are insufficient to address a fundamental lack of soundproofing.

Stigma of Visibility

There is an "uncomfortable irony" in mobile outreach service delivery in that the act of placing a clearly identifiable mental health service in a community can actually cause the stigma it is trying to alleviate. In some communities, being seen entering or exiting a "mental health van" can cause a client to experience unwanted social stigma or social consequences that are severe. In response to this challenge, service providers often have to integrate mental health service delivery with other health care service delivery so as not to isolate psychological health as shameful.

High client load and time constraints

Mobile units often cover wide catchment areas with minimal personnel, putting enormous pressure on physicians to visit more patients in less time. Because a van may only be parked in one area for a few hours, psychologists are unable to give the same level or duration of intervention as an outpatient clinic. This needs faster evaluations, more targeted intervention strategies, and a strong dependence on novel referral mechanisms.

Disrupted therapeutic continuity

Because the clinic runs on a predetermined schedule, such as once a week or every two weeks, the mobile approach produces an inherent lack of consistency. This

implies that clients cannot be seen during an imminent crisis. According to research, follow-up rates are frequently lower in these settings because patients may heal on their own, relocate, or encounter financial obstacles to returning when the clinic is next in town.

Language, Logistics, and Cultural Barriers

Clinicians frequently negotiate exceptional linguistic variety, meeting various languages from one hamlet to the next on the same route, making effective communication difficult. Furthermore, the service is prone to operational problems that do not occur at established clinics, such as vehicle maintenance concerns, flooded roads, or inclement weather. In the Indian setting, there are further issues with joint family arrangements, where the Western idea of individual privacy may appear culturally discordant or insulting to the family.

In order to overcome these limitations of mobile clinics, various physical, clinical, and community strategies are employed by various organizations. For example, to overcome environmental challenges like noise levels and lack of space, sound-dampening materials are used, white noise machines are employed, and parking strategies are implemented to create a more private therapeutic space. To overcome the stigma of being seen accessing mental health services, these are embedded within overall health services, or they are promoted through various community outreach strategies like street plays and movies. To overcome high client volumes and time constraints, a "rolling session model" and "Brief CBT" are employed, ensuring each session is "therapeutically meaningful in itself". Interruptions in therapeutic continuity are addressed through tele-counselling services and the concept of "task shifting," where community health workers are trained to deliver continuous services. Finally, cultural and linguistic barriers are addressed through cultural humility, the use of interpreters, and the concept of documented verbal consent for those with low literacy.

Low-Resource Psychotherapy Plan

The psychotherapy plan developed for mobile clinics is deliberately made to be effective, flexible, and "complete-in-itself," which ensures that every session has some value regardless of whether subsequent sessions are interrupted. The recommended approach is an integration of brief Cognitive Behavioural Therapy and supportive counseling.

Brief CBT

This approach has been recommended because of the structured nature of CBT, which is more appropriate when continuity of sessions cannot be guaranteed. This approach is effective for treating acute and chronic PTSD.

Supportive Counseling

This approach has been recommended because supportive counseling provides the framework that allows for the building of trust with patients, which is very important because the patient may be seeking psychological services from a mental health expert for the first time.

Dual-Track Model (Indian Context)

In Indian contexts like SCARF's model, the approach has been modified to include dual tracks of counseling while the patient receives counseling, psychoeducation is provided to the caregiver by community health workers.

Session Structure

The psychotherapy delivered in mobile clinics follows a Rolling Four-to-Six Session Model, where each session is designed to be therapeutically meaningful as a standalone encounter.

Session 1: Assessment and Alliance Building: This session prioritizes earning the client's trust over immediate intervention, as many clients may be wary of professional services. The clinician conducts a brief assessment of the client's presenting problems, risks, and social context while providing simple psychoeducation on what to expect from the process.

Sessions 2-3: Psychoeducation and Skill Introduction: These sessions focus on providing self-management tools that the client can use independently. Key topics include explaining the link between thoughts, feelings, and behaviors, as well as teaching grounding techniques (like the 5-4-3-2-1 method) and breathing exercises to manage trauma or anxiety symptoms.

Sessions 4-5: Problem-Solving and Behavioural Activation: This stage moves toward concrete action to address the client's immediate reality. Problem-solving therapy helps identify manageable solutions for the practical stressors common in underserved communities, while behavioural activation encourages clients to re engage with activities that provide a sense of mastery or connection.

Session 6: Consolidation and Relapse Prevention: The final session is used to review skills and consolidate gains made during the course. A collaborative relapse prevention plan is developed to identify future warning signs and coping strategies, often using telecounselling as a bridge for support until the clinic's next scheduled visit.

The intervention follows a progressive structure that begins with assessment and alliance building, where clinicians prioritize earning the client's trust through brief structured assessments of risks and cultural context. Psychoeducation is then utilized to normalize psychological distress by providing a framework for understanding the relationship between thoughts, feelings, behaviors, and physical symptoms. To manage acute anxiety or trauma related arousal, clinicians teach grounding techniques like the 5-4-3-2-1 method, which are immediately accessible tools that require no equipment and can be used anywhere. Cognitive restructuring further assists clients in identifying and challenging maladaptive thought patterns through simple questioning techniques that highlight how interpretations drive emotional responses. For populations facing significant material stressors, problem-solving therapy offers a structured, step-by-step approach to finding manageable solutions for real world difficulties. Additionally, behavioural activation is employed to disrupt the cycle of withdrawal and depression by scheduling meaningful activities that foster a sense of mastery or connection. Finally, relapse prevention ensures that clients can manage future crises independently by collaboratively identifying personal warning signs and effective coping strategies.

Ethical and Cultural Considerations

Confidentiality

To protect privacy in a vehicle, clinicians use white noise devices, sound-dampening materials, and strategic parking away from gathering spots.

Informed Consent

In areas with low literacy, verbal consent documented by the clinician is often more appropriate and less threatening than written forms. It must be a genuine conversation in accessible language

Professional Boundaries

In close-knit communities, therapists may be recognized in public, requiring careful management of dual-role challenges to protect the therapeutic bond

Cultural Humility

Clinicians must respect and defer to the client's cultural understanding of their distress. In India, this involves navigating joint family structures where individual privacy may conflict with family involvement

Community Integration

Organizations practice cultural humility by consulting with local leaders and healers during the planning of services.

Conclusion

Designing psychotherapy for the low-resource, mobile context has been a crash course in humility and flexibility. It has taught me that mental health care is not about optimizing the ideal circumstances for therapy, but about connecting with people exactly as they are—geographically, financially, and culturally. It has required me to distill therapy to the bare bones: trust development, skill building, and respect for local models of mental health and illness. Perhaps most importantly, I have learned that the term 'brief' does not mean 'shallow'; a single therapeutic encounter can have the power to foster long-term resilience beyond the lifetime of the single session itself. This experience has reminded me that some of the greatest breakthroughs and innovations in mental health are not the result of having more, but having less resources, fewer options, and fewer excuses for not being present, consistently and with humility, in the places the system has forgotten to look.

References

Grelotti, D. J., Thérosmé, T., Belkin, G. S., Dorvil, N., Daimyo, S., Severe, J., Guerda, N., & Katz, C. L. (2018). A mobile clinic approach to the delivery of community-based mental health services in rural Haiti. *PLOS ONE, 13*(6), e0199313.

Oriol, N. E., Cote, P. J., Vavasis, A. P., Bennet, J., Donahue, S., DeLorenzo, D., & Blanc, P. (2017). The scope and impact of mobile health clinics in the United States: A literature review. *International Journal for Equity in Health, 16*(1), 77.

Schizophrenia Research Foundation. (n.d.). *Clinical services: Mobile telepsychiatry (STEP) programme.* SCARF India.

Institute of Human Behaviour and Allied Sciences. (n.d.). *Mobile mental health unit (MMHU).* Government of Delhi.

Ministry of Health and Family Welfare, Government of India. (2022). *Tele MANAS: National tele mental health programme.*

Chapter 37

Community Radio for Mental Health Awareness and Support

– Kamepally Divya Sree

Introduction

Mental health services remain limited in many rural areas of India due to shortages of trained professionals, stigma surrounding psychological problems, and limited access to healthcare infrastructure. In such contexts, community-based communication platforms can play an important role in improving awareness and access to support. One such platform is community radio, which has expanded significantly in India over the past two decades. Community radio stations are locally operated, low-cost broadcasting services that deliver programs in regional languages and address issues relevant to local communities.In rural districts, community radio stations are often run by local educational institutions, non-governmental organizations (NGOs), or community groups. These stations broadcast programs related to agriculture, education, women's empowerment, and public health. Because radio is relatively inexpensive and accessible, it reaches populations that may not have regular access to internet-based mental health resources.

In the context of mental health, community radio can serve as a platform for psychoeducation, stigma reduction, and basic psychological support. Mental health professionals or trained counselors may collaborate with radio stations to produce programs that discuss stress management, emotional wellbeing, and coping strategies. Listeners may also be encouraged to seek support from nearby Primary Health Centres (PHCs) or community counsellors if they require additional help.The target population in this context includes rural adults, farmers, homemakers, and adolescents who may experience psychological distress but have limited opportunities to access formal therapy. Community radio provides a culturally appropriate and scalable way to introduce mental health concepts in simple and relatable ways.

Common Mental Health Issues in This Context

Several mental health concerns are commonly observed in rural communities in India. These problems are often influenced by socioeconomic stressors, limited access to healthcare, and social stigma.

Stress and Anxiety

Many individuals in rural communities experience high levels of stress related to financial uncertainty, agricultural challenges, and family responsibilities. Farmers may face crop failures, debt, and unpredictable weather conditions, which can contribute to anxiety and chronic worry. Adolescents and young adults may also experience academic stress and uncertainty about employment opportunities.

Depression and Feelings of Hopelessness

Depression is another significant concern, particularly among individuals facing prolonged financial difficulties, social isolation, or family conflicts. Symptoms may include persistent sadness, lack of motivation, sleep disturbances, and reduced interest in daily activities. In many cases, these symptoms are not recognized as mental health issues but are instead viewed as personal weakness or fate.

Alcohol Misuse and Family Conflict

In some communities, alcohol use becomes a coping mechanism for stress and emotional distress. Excessive alcohol consumption can contribute to family conflict, financial strain, and emotional problems within households. Addressing underlying stress and providing healthier coping strategies is therefore important.

Community radio programs can help normalize discussions about these challenges and encourage individuals to seek support.

Limitations

While community radio offers many advantages, implementing mental health interventions in low-resource settings also involves several challenges.

One major limitation is the lack of trained mental health professionals in rural areas. Many Primary Health Centres do not have dedicated psychologists or counsellors. As a result, mental health programs often rely on brief interventions delivered by trained community workers or visiting professionals.

Another challenge is stigma associated with mental health problems. Many individuals hesitate to seek help due to fear of being judged by others in their community. Radio programs must therefore present mental health topics in a sensitive and non-stigmatizing manner.

Language and literacy barriers may also affect communication. Mental health concepts must be explained using simple language, culturally relevant examples, and storytelling formats that listeners can easily understand.

Additionally, privacy and confidentiality can be difficult to maintain in small communities where everyone knows each other. Individuals may feel uncomfortable discussing personal problems in public settings.

Finally, time and resource constraints limit the availability of long-term therapy. Interventions must therefore be brief, practical, and focused on coping strategies that individuals can use in their daily lives.

Low-Resource Psychotherapy Plan

The intervention combines brief cognitive behavioural therapy (CBT) principles, supportive counselling, and psychoeducation delivered through community radio programs. The goal is to increase awareness about mental health while providing simple coping strategies that listeners can practice independently.Listeners who identify with the issues discussed in radio programs may be encouraged to visit a nearby PHC or community counsellor for short-term support sessions.

Session Structure

The counselling component consists of three brief sessions, each lasting approximately 30-40 minutes. These sessions focus on practical coping skills rather than intensive psychotherapy.

Session	Focus	Key Activities
Session 1	Understanding stress	Psychoeducation about stress, emotional validation, identifying stress triggers
Session 2	Coping strategies	Breathing exercises, grounding techniques, problem-solving strategies
Session 3	Strengthening support	Encouraging social support, relapse prevention, reviewing coping strategies

Key Techniques Used

Several simple techniques are used within the intervention:

Psychoeducation

Listeners are provided with basic information about stress, anxiety, and depression. Radio programs explain that these experiences are common and manageable.

Breathing and Relaxation Exercises

Guided breathing exercises are introduced during radio segments so that listeners can practice relaxation at home.

Problem-Solving Skills

Individuals are encouraged to identify specific problems and generate possible solutions in manageable steps.

Encouraging Social Support

Participants are encouraged to talk with trusted family members or community members about their concerns.

Case Vignette

Sita, a 32-year-old woman living in a rural village in Maharashtra, regularly listens to a local community radio station while completing household work. Over the past several months, she has been experiencing persistent worry about her family's financial situation and her children's education. She often feels tired, has difficulty sleeping, and reports frequent headaches.

One day, Sita hears a radio program discussing stress and emotional wellbeing. The program explains how constant worrying can affect sleep and physical health, and it introduces a simple breathing exercise for relaxation. Sita finds the discussion relatable and decides to visit the local Primary Health Centre where a counsellor is available once a week.

During three brief counselling sessions, the counsellor helps Sita identify the main sources of her stress and teaches her simple coping strategies such as slow breathing, breaking problems into smaller steps, and seeking support from family members. By the end of the sessions, Sita reports improved sleep and feels more confident in managing her worries.

Example Structure of Community Radio Mental Health Program

Segment	**Content**	**Duration**
Introduction	Discussion of common emotional challenges	5 minutes
Expert Talk	Mental health professional explains coping strategies	10 minutes
Guided Exercise	Breathing or relaxation exercise for listeners	5 minutes

(condt.)

Segment	Content	Duration
Listener Story	Short fictional story illustrating coping skills	5 minutes
Resource Information	Information about local PHC or counselling services	3 minutes

Ethical and Cultural Considerations

Ethical considerations are important when delivering mental health interventions in community settings. Although radio programs are designed for public education, confidentiality must be maintained when individuals seek counselling services after hearing the broadcasts.

Clients attending counselling sessions should be informed about confidentiality, including the limits of privacy in small healthcare settings. Informed consent should be obtained before beginning any counselling process.

Cultural sensitivity is also essential. Mental health concepts should be presented in ways that respect local beliefs, traditions, and languages. Using relatable examples, stories, and culturally familiar metaphors can make psychological information more understandable and acceptable.

Another ethical consideration involves maintaining appropriate professional boundaries. Counsellors must avoid providing advice beyond their level of training and should refer individuals with severe mental health conditions to specialized services whenever possible.

Finally, radio programs must ensure that mental health information is accurate, responsible, and non-stigmatizing, so that listeners feel supported rather than judged.

Conclusion

Designing a mental health intervention for a low-resource setting highlights the importance of creativity and flexibility in psychological practice. It becomes clear that effective mental health support does not always require highly specialized infrastructure; simple, accessible tools such as community radio can play a meaningful role in promoting wellbeing. This exercise also emphasizes the importance of cultural sensitivity, community engagement, and practical coping strategies when working with populations that may have limited access to formal therapy services. Overall, integrating mental health awareness into existing community platforms can help bridge the gap between psychological knowledge and real-world needs.

References

Patel, V., Saxena, S., Lund, C., Thornicroft, G., Baingana, F., Bolton, P., ... Unützer, J. (2018). The Lancet Commission on global mental health and sustainable development. The Lancet, 392(10157), 1553-1598.

Singhal, A., & Rogers, E. M. (2003). Combating AIDS: Communication strategies in action. Sage Publications.

Thornicroft, G., Deb, T., & Henderson, C. (2016). Community mental health care worldwide: Current status and further developments. World Psychiatry, 15(3), 276-286.

World Health Organization. (2021). Guidance on community mental health services: Promoting person-centred and rights-based approaches. WHO.

Chapter 38

Brief Mindfulness and Relaxation Programs in Community Settings

– Leiyaso Khaleng

Introduction

This chapter focuses on implementing brief mindfulness and relaxation interventions as innovative approaches to mental health support when traditional mindfulness-based and relaxation programs are difficult to implement in community settings. These settings often include individuals from low-resource and underserved populations. Examples may include rural primary health centres, educational institutions, workplaces, community clinics, outreach programs, and rural communities where access to specialized mental health services is limited. In these settings, the population typically includes working adults, students, frontline workers, and other community members who experience high levels of daily stress due to demanding work conditions, financial pressures, and limited social support. Mental health services in such environments are often constrained by a shortage of trained professionals, heavy client loads, financial limitations, and limited time for extended psychotherapy sessions. As a result, healthcare systems may prioritize physical medical concerns, while psychological needs often receive less attention. Additionally, limited awareness about mental health, social stigma, and stereotyping of psychological problems may further prevent individuals from seeking professional help, increasing the need for accessible and community-based interventions. Due to these constraints, traditional long-term therapy approaches may not always be feasible. Brief psychological interventions such as mindfulness and relaxation techniques provide practical alternatives that can be delivered in shorter sessions with minimal resources. These approaches help individuals develop awareness of their thoughts, emotions, and physiological responses to stress while learning simple strategies that support emotional regulation and stress management.

What is Mindfulness?

Mindfulness has its roots in Buddhist contemplative traditions and was later adapted for use in modern psychological and healthcare settings by Jon Kabat-Zinn. He introduced mindfulness into clinical practice through the development of Mindfulness-Based Stress Reduction (MBSR). Kabat-Zinn described mindfulness as the awareness that develops when individuals intentionally focus their attention on the present moment while observing their experiences in a non-judgmental way. To elaborate mindfulness can be generally understood as the deliberate cultivation of present-moment awareness, characterised by purposeful attention and a non-judgmental stance toward ongoing experiences. It involves consciously directing attention to current internal and external events with openness, acceptance, and curiosity, rather than functioning as an "automatic pilot." The quality of non-judgment is central, as it fosters an attitude of acceptance toward thoughts, emotions, and sensations as they arise. The term mindfulness may refer to a temporary state of awareness, a dispositional tendency to be attentive in daily life, or to formal meditation practices designed to develop this capacity

What is a relaxation response?

First described by Herbert Benson in the 1970s through his research on Transcendental Meditation, the relaxation response (RR) refers to a physiological condition characterized by the dominance of the parasympathetic nervous system, meaning that parasympathetic activity is greater than sympathetic nervous system activity. (Luberto et al., 2020, pp. 2–4)

What are brief mindfulness and relaxation techniques?

Brief mindfulness and relaxation techniques are short, structured practices aimed at enhancing present-moment awareness or activating the body's relaxation response within a limited time. Brief mindfulness practices involve intentionally focusing attention on present experiences such as breathing or bodily sensations while maintaining a non-judgmental attitude. Brief relaxation techniques aim to reduce stress by activating the parasympathetic nervous system through methods like deep breathing, progressive muscle relaxation, and guided imagery. These practices are simple, accessible, and can be easily integrated into daily life.

How is it different from the traditional mindfulness based and relaxation intervention?

Aspect	Traditional Mindfulness/ Relaxation Programs	Brief Mindfulness/ Relaxation Interventions
Duration of program	Usually conducted over 8 weeks	Conducted in single sessions or short modules
Session length	Sessions typically last 2-2.5 hours per week	Session usually last a few minutes to about 30 minutes

Aspect	Traditional Mindfulness/ Relaxation Programs	Brief Mindfulness/ Relaxation Interventions
Structure	Structured and intensive training with regular guided practices and discussions	Short,focused exercises designed for quick practice.
Home practice	Requires regular and extended home practice between sessions.	May include short and flexible home practices
Training intensity	Provides in-depth mindfulness training over time	Focuses on quick and practical stress reduction techniques
Feasibility	Requires significant time commitment from clients	More feasible for individuals with limited time or resources.

Innovative approach to traditional mindfulness based intervention and relaxation technique.

Brief mindfulness-based interventions and relaxation techniques were developed to address the practical limitations of traditional mindfulness programs, which often require long sessions and extended training periods. Shorter formats were designed to improve accessibility and allow individuals in busy or low-resource environments to benefit from stress-management practices within a limited time frame (Carmody & Baer, 2009; Kabat-Zinn, 2003; Burgess et al., 2021).

Approach Type	Examples	Purpose	Evidence Status
Brief Mindfulness-Based Interventions	Brief Mindfulness-Based Stress Reduction (Brief MBSR), Brief Mindfulness-Based Cognitive Therapy (Brief MBCT), Brief Online Mindfulness Training	To increase present-moment awareness, reduce stress, and improve emotional regulation.	Strong evidence from clinical and community studies.
Relaxation Techniques	Deep Breathing Exercises, Progressive Muscle Relaxation (PMR), Body Scan Meditation, Grounding Techniques (5-4-3-2-1 method)	To reduce physiological tension, activate the relaxation response, and manage stress symptoms.	Widely supported in psychological and health research.
Emerging Adaptations	Mobile App–Based Mindfulness Programs, Telehealth Mindfulness Interventions, Culturally Adapted Mindfulness Programs	To improve accessibility and scalability, especially in low-resource or underserved communities.	Growing evidence with ongoing research.

Critical Need for Brief Interventions

The brief mindfulness and relaxation interventions are designed for community settings where individuals experience significant daily stress but have limited access to structured psychological support. Such settings may include working adults, students, frontline workers, or residents in semi-urban and rural communities where time, financial resources, and mental health services are limited. Kathi J. Kemper conducted research on the immediate impact of brief online mindfulness training among health professionals. Prior knowledge in this area indicated that burnout, also referred to as compassion fatigue, was highly prevalent among health care professionals and could negatively affect empathic communication, professional relationships, and the quality of clinical care. Mindfulness-based stress reduction had already been recognized as an effective approach for improving mindfulness, enhancing resilience, and reducing burnout among health professionals; however, most existing programs required lengthy in-person training sessions, making them difficult for busy professionals to attend. Consequently, the study focused on examining whether a shorter and more convenient form of mindfulness training could still provide benefits for health professionals experiencing work-related stress and burnout. The findings revealed that brief online mindfulness training was appealing to diverse health professionals, most clients who began the training completed the full program, and even the short intervention led to small but statistically significant improvements in mindfulness scores. Additionally, the improvements were consistent across gender, professional groups, and both trainees and practitioners, suggesting that brief online mindfulness training can be an accessible and effective strategy for promoting mindfulness and resilience among health professionals. (Kemper, 2017, pp. 77–78)

Common Mental Health Issues in This Context

Several psychological concerns are commonly observed in community populations experiencing high stress and limited psychological support like

Stress and Burnout

Chronic stress related to workload, financial pressure, academic demands, and family responsibilities is highly prevalent in many community settings. Persistent stress can lead to burnout, emotional exhaustion, and reduced coping capacity, affecting both personal functioning and productivity. Research conducted in low-resource communities has shown that individuals often experience higher levels of stress due to financial insecurity, limited access to healthcare, and fewer social support systems, which increases vulnerability to psychological distress and burnout (Lund et al., 2011; Patel et al., 2018).

Anxiety and Worry

Studies conducted in low-resource and underserved communities indicate that limited access to stable employment, healthcare services, and social protection systems can increase uncertainty and daily stress, thereby contributing to higher levels of anxiety and psychological distress among community members (Patel et al., 2018; World Health Organization, 2022).

Emotional Fatigue and Reduced Resilience

Research in low-resource settings suggests that prolonged exposure to socioeconomic challenges, limited mental health services, and ongoing environmental stressors can reduce individuals psychological resilience and increase vulnerability to emotional exhaustion and mental health difficulties (Lund et al., 2011; Patel et al., 2018)

Key Constraints and Limitations

Implementation Challenges

Although mindfulness base interventions and relaxation interventions show promise, several challenges may arise when implementing these programs, particularly in underserved settings.

Limited resources and time constraints can affect participation and program completion

Individuals may face demands related to employment, family responsibilities, or transportation, which can make regular attendance difficult (Foale et al., 2025).

Cultural relevance

Mindfulness and relaxation programs developed in Western contexts may not always reflect the cultural values or experiences of diverse populations. Without appropriate adaptation, clients may feel disconnected from the practices (Morales & Burnett-Zeigler, 2025).

Limited mental health workforce

Many low-income settings have a shortage of trained mental health professionals. This limits the availability of specialized services and requires training non-specialist providers (Mugo et al., 2025).

High workload within healthcare systems

Health facilities often have heavy patient loads and limited time to provide psychological support. Providers may prioritize medical care over mental health interventions (Mugo et al., 2025).

Real-World Problems Addressed

Brief mindfulness-based interventions (MBIs), including Mindfulness-Based Stress Reduction and relaxation interventions, are designed to address several real-world psychological and social challenges experienced by diverse populations. These interventions combine mindfulness practices with relaxation techniques to improve emotional regulation, reduce psychological distress, and strengthen resilience. Because they are flexible and relatively low cost, MBI and relaxation interventions are particularly useful for populations that may not have easy access to traditional mental health services. Some of the main problems addressed by MBI and relaxation is chronic stress, anxiety, and emotional distress, especially among individuals living in high-pressure environments or coping with health-related challenges. Many individuals lack effective strategies to manage stress or to relax during demanding situations. Mindfulness practices such as breathing exercises, body scan meditation, and present-moment awareness help individuals slow down their reactions and activate the body's relaxation response. These practices encourage individuals to observe their thoughts and emotions without judgment, which can reduce stress responses and increase emotional awareness. Research shows that mindfulness-based programs can decrease symptoms of stress, anxiety, and depression by promoting healthier coping strategies and greater self-compassion (Phan et al., 2025; Foale et al., 2025; Smith et al.,2015). Another important issue addressed by MBIs is trauma and exposure to violence. Adolescents and adults living in communities affected by structural or community violence often experience higher levels of anxiety, depression, and post-traumatic stress. Mindfulness programs adapted for these contexts help clients develop emotional regulation skills and increase awareness of internal experiences. Trauma-informed mindfulness practices allow clients to recognize emotional triggers while maintaining a sense of safety and choice during meditation exercises. These practices also support relaxation and grounding techniques that help individuals manage intense emotional reactions and build resilience in stressful environments (Elsaesser et al., 2026). MBIs also address mental health inequalities in underserved communities. Individuals from racial, ethnic, or socioeconomically disadvantaged backgrounds often face barriers to accessing mental health care. Mindfulness-based programs offer a low-cost and adaptable approach that can be implemented in community clinics, schools, and nonprofit organizations. When these programs are culturally adapted in terms of language, examples, and delivery methods, they can effectively reduce symptoms of depression, anxiety, and stress among diverse populations. Research indicates that mindfulness interventions implemented in inner-city health centers can improve health-related quality of life and reduce psychological distress in underserved groups (Morales & Burnett-Zeigler, 2025). Another real-world challenge addressed by brief MBIs is occupational stress and burnout, particularly among healthcare professionals and helping professionals. Individuals working in demanding environments often experience emotional exhaustion, high stress levels, and limited opportunities for self-care. Brief mindfulness and relaxation practices provide practical strategies for improving emotional balance, reducing anxiety, and strengthening well-being. Because these professionals often have limited time, shorter mindfulness programs offer a feasible way to support mental health while maintaining work responsibilities. Finally, mindfulness interventions are used to address psychological distress associated with chronic illness, such as cancer and other long-term health conditions. Patients experiencing serious illness often report anxiety, sleep problems, and emotional strain during treatment. Mindfulness programs delivered in community settings or through remote formats help clients practice relaxation techniques and develop coping skills for managing uncertainty and emotional distress. Evidence suggests that culturally adapted mindfulness interventions can significantly reduce anxiety among patients dealing with serious health conditions (Juarez-Reyes et al., 2024). Overall, brief mindfulness-based interventions address a wide range of real-world problems including stress, lack of relaxation skills, trauma exposure, mental health disparities ,occupational burnout, and illness-related distress. By combining mindfulness awareness with relaxation-based techniques, these interventions provide practical tools that individuals can use in daily life to improve emotional well-being and resilience across different stages of life.

Hypothetical Case Example

Case 1

To illustrate how mindfulness interventions address real-world problems, consider the hypothetical case of Luis, a 17-year-old student living in a neighborhood with high levels of community violence. Luis frequently experiences anxiety, difficulty concentrating in school, and feelings of anger after witnessing violent incidents in his community. These experiences begin to affect his academic performance and relationships with peers. Luis joins a community program that offers a six-week mindfulness-based intervention designed for youth exposed to stress and trauma. During the program, he learns several mindfulness techniques such as mindful breathing, body scan meditation, and awareness of emotions. These exercises help him notice his emotional reactions without immediately responding with anger or withdrawal. Over time, Luis begins to recognize early signs of stress and uses breathing exercises to calm himself during difficult situations. He reports feeling more focused in school and less overwhelmed by negative emotions. The program also allows him to discuss his experiences with other clients , which increases his sense of support and belonging. This hypothetical example demonstrates how mindfulness-based interventions can help individuals develop emotional regulation skills and resilience when facing real-world challenges such as stress, trauma, and environmental adversity. Programs like these provide practical tools that individuals can continue using in daily life, making them valuable for community-based mental health support.

Case 2

A hypothetical example can illustrate how mindfulness-based interventions address real-world problems. Consider Maria, a 45-year-old woman recently diagnosed with breast cancer. Along with physical treatment, Maria experiences persistent anxiety, difficulty sleeping, and fear about the future. Because her community has limited access to mental health specialists, she is referred to a six-week community-based mindfulness program delivered online. During the program, Maria learns several mindfulness practices, including mindful breathing, body scan exercises, and brief meditation techniques. These practices help her notice anxious thoughts without becoming overwhelmed by them. Over time, she begins to feel more emotionally stable and better able to cope with treatment-related stress. By the end of the program, Maria reports improved emotional control and reduced anxiety. She continues to practice mindfulness at home using short daily exercises. This example illustrates how brief mindfulness interventions can provide practical coping tools for individuals facing real-world psychological challenges, especially when traditional mental health services are limited (Juarez-Reyes et al., 2024; Morales & Burnett-Zeigler, 2025).

Low-Resource Psychotherapy Plan

The intervention follows a brief mindfulness and relaxation-based psychoeducational model that integrates elements from:

Brief Mindfulness Interventions

Brief mindfulness interventions are grounded in the broader theory of mindfulness, which emphasizes awareness of the present moment and the relationship between attention, emotions, and behavior. Mindfulness involves intentionally focusing attention on present experiences with openness and without judgment. According to this framework, individuals often respond to stressful situations through automatic patterns of thinking and emotional reactions. Mindfulness practice helps individuals become aware of these patterns by observing thoughts, emotions, and bodily sensations as they arise. Through repeated practice, individuals gradually develop the ability to respond to stress more consciously rather than reacting impulsively (Foale et al., 2025). The theoretical foundations of mindfulness-based interventions also draw from contemplative traditions that emphasize awareness, acceptance, and non-judgmental attention to experience. In contemporary psychological practice, these principles have been integrated into structured therapeutic approaches that combine meditation practices with cognitive and behavioral strategies. Programs such as mindfulness-based stress reduction apply these principles to support emotional regulation, increase self-awareness, and improve individuals' ability to manage psychological and physiological responses to stress (Foale et al., 2025).

Brief Relaxation Interventions

Brief relaxation interventions are supported by psychological and behavioral theories that explain how individuals manage stress and adopt healthy coping behaviors. One important framework is Bandura's self-efficacy theory, which suggests that individuals are more likely to practice beneficial behaviors when they believe they are capable of performing them successfully. Relaxation training helps strengthen this confidence by teaching simple and manageable techniques such as controlled breathing and muscle relaxation that individuals can practice independently to reduce stress and regulate emotional responses (Sun et al., 2025). Additional theoretical perspectives also support relaxation interventions. The Health Belief Model suggests that individuals are more likely to adopt health-promoting behaviors when they understand the risks associated with stress and recognize the benefits of relaxation strategies. Similarly, Conservation of Resources Theory proposes that people attempt to protect and restore their physical and emotional resources, which may become depleted during stressful situations. Relaxation techniques help replenish these resources and restore emotional balance. In addition, Social Support Theory highlights the value of supportive environments, suggesting that relaxation programs delivered in group settings can enhance emotional support and reduce feelings of isolation among clients (Sun et al., 2025).

Session Structure

The intervention follows a brief structured format lasting approximately four to six sessions, depending on the needs and feasibility of the community setting. Short-form mindfulness programs have demonstrated effectiveness when delivered through condensed schedules, making them appropriate for populations that may face barriers such as work demands, childcare responsibilities, or transportation limitations. In an abbreviated mindfulness-based stress reduction program, clients meet once per week for approximately 30-60minutes, guided by a trained facilitator in a safe and supportive environment. Each session typically includes an opening check-in, psychoeducation related to stress and emotional regulation, guided mindfulness exercises, and group reflection. Participants are also encouraged to engage in daily home practice for approximately 5-10 minutes, using simple guided exercises or informal mindfulness activities incorporated into everyday routines. In some community-based adaptations, four to six weekly sessions lasting approximately 30 to 60 minutes each have been successfully delivered by trained facilitators or community workers. These shorter formats demonstrate that mindfulness and relaxation interventions can be feasibly implemented in underserved populations where time, resources, and access to trained mental health professionals may be limited.

Session	Focus	Activities
Session 1	Introduction and psychoeducation	Understanding stress,introduction to mindfulness
Session 2	Mindful awareness	Breathing exercises,body scan
Session 3	Emotional awareness	Recognizing thoughts and emotions
Session 4	Stress management	Relaxation techniques,grounding
Session 5	Coping skills	Problem solving and discussion
Session 6	Integration	Review,relapse prevention,home practice

Key Techniques Used in the Intervention

The intervention incorporates several core therapeutic techniques that are both evidence-based and feasible for low-resource settings. One important component is psychoeducation, which involves providing clients with information about stress, emotional responses, and the relationship between mental and physical health. Psychoeducation also helps individuals understand how mindfulness practices influence stress responses and emotional regulation. Another key technique is the use of mindfulness practices, such as mindful breathing, body scanning, sitting meditation, and mindful movement. These practices encourage individuals to focus their attention on present-moment experiences while observing thoughts and emotions without judgment. Participants are gradually introduced to these practices so that they can develop awareness of their bodily sensations, emotions, and cognitive patterns. The intervention also incorporates grounding and relaxation techniques, including brief breathing exercises and structured short meditations that help individuals manage emotional reactivity and reduce physiological arousal during stressful situations. These strategies are particularly useful for individuals experiencing high levels of stress or anxiety. In addition, clients are encouraged to develop reflective awareness of thoughts and emotions by noticing when stress reactions arise and responding to them in a more skillful and regulated manner. This process often includes group discussions and reflection on personal experiences during the sessions, allowing clients to learn from one another's coping strategies and challenges. Finally, home practice and integration into daily activities form an essential component of the intervention. Participants are encouraged to practice mindfulness informally throughout their day, such as paying attention to breathing, bodily sensations, or routine activities. These practices help reinforce learning and support the development of long-term coping skills beyond the formal therapy sessions.

Summary

Technique	Brief Description	Time Taken
Psychoeducation about stress and emotional regulation	Explanation of how stress affects thoughts,emotions and the body	10-15 minutes
Mindful breathing	Guided breathing exercise focusing attention on the breath	5-10 minutes
Body scan meditation	Awareness of sensations in different parts of the body to release tension	10-15 minutes
Grounding techniques	Sensory awareness exercise to bring attention to the present moment	5-10 minutes
Relaxation exercises	Techniques such as slow breathing or muscle relaxation to calm the body	10 minutes
Group reflection and discussion	Participants share experiences and discuss coping strategies	15-20 minutes
Home practice assignments	Daily mindfulness or relaxation exercises practiced independently	10-15 minutes per day

Ethical and Cultural Considerations

Informed Consent

Obtaining informed consent is a fundamental ethical requirement when implementing mindfulness-based interventions. Participants should receive clear information about the purpose of the program, the activities involved, and the expected duration of the sessions so that they can make an informed decision about participation. It is also important to emphasize that participation is voluntary and that individuals have the right to withdraw from the intervention at any time without negative consequences. Providing transparent information supports participant autonomy and ethical practice in community-based psychological programs (Phan et al., 2025).

Confidentiality

Confidentiality is essential in group-based mindfulness interventions, as participants may share personal experiences related to stress and emotional difficulties. Facilitators must ensure that information discussed during sessions remains private and encourage participants to respect the confidentiality of other group members. Any data collected for evaluation purposes, such as questionnaires or feedback forms, should be stored securely and accessed only by authorized personnel. Maintaining confidentiality helps create a safe and supportive environment for open participation (Sims-Russell, 2025).

Professional Boundaries

Facilitators delivering mindfulness interventions must maintain clear professional boundaries throughout the program. This includes avoiding dual relationships or personal engagements with participants that could interfere with the therapeutic goals of the intervention. Maintaining appropriate boundaries ensures that the facilitator's role remains focused on supporting participants' well-being while preserving the integrity and safety of the intervention process (Juarez-Reyes et al., 2024).

Cultural Sensitivity

Cultural sensitivity is particularly important when implementing mindfulness interventions in diverse community settings. Although mindfulness originates from contemplative traditions, contemporary psychological programs typically present these practices in a secular and inclusive manner so they are accessible to individuals from different cultural or religious backgrounds (Phan et al., 202). Facilitators should use simple and accessible language and incorporate examples that reflect participants' everyday experiences. Research suggests that culturally adapted mindfulness interventions are more acceptable and effective because they acknowledge the social and cultural factors influencing stress and well-being (Morales & Burnett-Zeigler, 2025). Involving community members in adapting programs can further enhance cultural relevance and strengthen trust in the intervention (Elsaesser et al., 2026).

Conclusion

Designing a psychotherapy program for a low-resource setting highlights the importance of flexibility, cultural awareness, and practicality in mental health care. While evidence-based interventions are often developed in well-resourced clinical environments, adapting them to community contexts requires simplifying techniques without losing their therapeutic value. This process emphasizes the need to create accessible and sustainable psychological interventions that can reach individuals who might otherwise have little or no access to mental health service.

References

Ameli, R., Sinaii, N., West, C. P., Luna, M. J., Panahi, S., Zoosman, M., Rusch, H. L., & Berger, A. (2020). Effect of a brief mindfulness-based program on stress in health care professionals at a US biomedical research hospital: A randomized clinical trial. JAMA Network Open, 3(8), e2013424.

Burgess, E. E., Selchen, S., Diplock, B. D., & Rector, N. A. (2021). A brief mindfulness-based cognitive therapy (MBCT) intervention as a population-level strategy for anxiety and depression. International Journal of Cognitive Therapy, 14, 380–398.

Creswell, J. D. (2017). Mindfulness interventions. *Annual Review of Psychology, 68*, 491–516.

Foale, S., Seedat, S., & Heyns, T. (2025). Considerations for sociocultural adaptations of a mindfulness-based program within a low socioeconomic setting in Cape Town, South Africa. BMC Complementary Medicine and Therapies, 25, 453.

Kabat-Zinn, J. (2013). *Full catastrophe living: Using the wisdom of your body and mind to face stress, pain, and illness* (Revised ed.). Bantam Books.

Kemper, K. J. (2017). Brief online mindfulness training: Immediate impact. Journal of Evidence-Based Complementary & Alternative Medicine, 22(1), 75–80. Luberto, C. M., Hall, D. L., Park, E. R., Haramati, A., & Cotton, S. (2020). A perspective on the similarities and differences between mindfulness and relaxation. Global Advances in Health and Medicine, 9, 1–13.

Mugo, C., Njuguna, I., Maganga, V., Flaherty, B. P., Wagner, A. D., Mukumbang, F. C., Dorsey, S., Mwai, D., Mburu, C., Kumar, M., Mbwayo, A., Mathai, M., Collins, P. Y., & Wamalwa, D. (2025). Integration of a brief, transdiagnostic psychological intervention in the care of adolescents and young adults with HIV in Kenya: Protocol for a cluster randomized clinical trial. PLOS ONE, 20(6), e0325374.

Rangel, R., Brown, A. D., Galea, J. T., Rai, S., Ross, N., Raji, M., Shrestha, P., Cheng, B., Akellot, J., & Kohrt, B. A. (2025). A guide to selecting psychological interventions that can be delivered by people who are not mental health specialists in low-resource settings. PLOS Global Public Health, 5(11), e0005123

Sun, J., Li, X., Cheng, Y., Liu, H., Tian, X., Liang, P., & Wang, H. (2025). Empowering informal caregivers of patients with musculoskeletal disorders: A randomized controlled trial of a structured home-based exercise intervention in a resource-limited Chinese community. BMC Nursing, 24, 1207.

Smith, B., Metzker, K., Waite, R., & Gerrity, P. (2015). Short-form mindfulness-based stress reduction reduces anxiety and improves health-related quality of life in an inner-city population. Holistic Nursing Practice, 29(2), 70–77.

World Health Organization. (2021). *Guidance on community mental health services: Promoting person-centred and rights-based approaches.*

Chapter 39

Ethical Challenges in Low-Resource Psychotherapy Practice

– Jessmon Jayson

Case vignette

Lakshmi, a 32-year-old married woman from a nearby village, presents to the PHC with headaches, poor sleep, and "tension" following ongoing conflicts with her husband and in-laws about finances and childcare. Her mother-in-law insists on being present during consultations, and there is no dedicated counselling room; sessions occur in a curtained corner of the general OPD with frequent interruptions. The psychologist must negotiate privacy, obtain meaningful consent, and plan brief, low-intensity therapy while balancing the expectations of the family and the time pressures of a high-volume clinic day.

In semi-rural PHC settings in low- and middle-income countries, the most common presentations are depressive disorders, anxiety-related conditions, and medically unexplained somatic complaints. These difficulties often emerge in the context of chronic poverty, family conflict, intimate partner violence, alcohol misuse in a family member, or academic and employment stress.

Depressive symptoms and adjustment difficulties

Individuals present with low mood, anhedonia, fatigue, poor sleep, feelings of worthlessness, and passive death wishes, often framed as "weakness of nerves" or "tension" rather than "depression." Adolescents and young adults may show academic decline, withdrawal, and irritability rather than explicit emotional complaints, shaped by local idioms of distress.

Anxiety, trauma, and stress-related problems

Clients frequently report generalized worry about finances, health, or children, panic-like episodes, or post-traumatic symptoms following accidents, domestic violence, or disaster exposure. These symptoms may be expressed through bodily sensations (palpitations, breathlessness) and sought care for in general medicine rather than as "mental" concerns.

Somatic symptom presentations and comorbidity with physical illness

Headaches, gastrointestinal complaints, chronic pain, and fatigue often have significant psychological components, but are presented as purely physical problems. Comorbid conditions such as diabetes or hypertension are common, complicating adherence and requiring collaboration with PHC doctors to integrate psychosocial care.

Limitations

Providing psychotherapy in a semi-rural PHC involves multiple, overlapping constraints that shape what is ethically feasible and clinically realistic. These constraints create tensions between ideal ethical standards and what can be implemented without compromising access and safety.

Structural and resource constraints

Lack of dedicated counselling rooms leads to compromised privacy, with conversations audible to staff and other patients. High client load and brief consultation slots (often 15-20 minutes) limit the depth of assessment and intervention per visit. Inconsistent access to psychotropic medication and referral pathways restrict stepped-care planning and continuity of care.

Sociocultural factors and stigma

Strong family involvement means relatives frequently insist on being present, making individual confidentiality and autonomy difficult to uphold in practice.

Stigma around mental illness and therapy leads to under-reporting of psychological symptoms and reluctance to attend follow-up sessions.

Gender norms (e.g., expectations of female silence or obedience) constrain what women feel safe to disclose.

Communication and literacy barriers

Low literacy complicates the use of written consent forms, psychoeducational handouts, and standard measures; oral explanations and visual aids are required.

Differences in language and idioms of distress between the psychologist (often urban-trained) and clients can lead to misunderstanding, requiring careful use of locally meaningful terms.

Professional isolation and limited supervision

Single-handed practitioners in rural settings often have limited access to ethics consultation or regular supervision, increasing the burden of complex ethical decisions.

Task-sharing with non-specialist health workers requires ongoing training and monitoring to prevent boundary violations or inadvertent harm.

Low-Resource Psychotherapy Plan

Given these constraints, a brief, low-intensity cognitive–behavioural and supportive counselling approach, aligned with mhGAP principles, is proposed as a realistic and ethically defensible psychotherapy plan. The focus is on maximizing benefit within limited time, prioritizing safety, and integrating culturally resonant explanations and strategies.

Overall Therapy Approach

Brief CBT components

Activity scheduling, cognitive coping, exposure to avoided situations, and structured problem-solving adapted to local idioms and literacy levels.

Supportive counselling

Empathic listening, validation, normalization of distress, and strengthening of existing social supports.

Psychoeducation

Simple, culturally sensitive explanations of stress, mood, and mind-body links, involving family where appropriate and with consent.

Task-shared elements

Some psychoeducation, follow-up reinforcement, and basic monitoring can be delegated to trained nurses or community health workers using mhGAP-based tools.

Session structure

Given client load and travel constraints, a stepped, flexible structure is proposed:

Number of Sessions

4-6 sessions over 6-10 weeks, with the first session slightly longer to allow assessment and rapport-building.

Session 1: 30-40 minutes (if feasible).

Sessions 2-6: 20-25 minutes each, often timed around the PHC schedule.

Format: Individual sessions with the option of brief family involvement segments, negotiated with the client to balance privacy with social support.

Follow-up: Brief check-ins by PHC staff or via phone (where acceptable) between sessions to support adherence and safety monitoring.

Key Techniques

Psychoeducation and Normalization

Use simple metaphors (e.g., "the mind getting tired like the body") and locally relevant examples of stress.Clarify that symptoms are common and treatable, reducing shame and encouraging help-seeking.Provide brief, verbal safety planning when risk is detected (e.g., identifying trusted persons, crisis contacts at the PHC).

Grounding and emotion regulation skills

Teach basic grounding exercises (e.g., slow breathing, 5-senses grounding, "naming and noticing" feelings) that clients can practice in everyday contexts without special materials.Introduce simple behavioural activation, encouraging small, meaningful activities (e.g., social contact, routine chores, time in nature) to counter withdrawal.

Structured problem-solving

Guide clients to define a specific, manageable problem, brainstorm options, weigh pros and cons, and plan small steps within their socio-economic realities.Where appropriate, involve family in collaborative problem-solving to reduce interpersonal stressors (e.g., sharing household responsibilities, planning study time).

Cognitive coping and re-framing

Use simple questions ("Is there another way to look at this?", "What would you say to a friend in this situation?") rather than formal cognitive restructuring worksheets.Focus on identifying and gently challenging global self-blame and hopelessness, using culturally resonant strengths such as family responsibility or spiritual values, while avoiding coercive religious advice.

Group interventions where feasible

When space and scheduling allow, brief psychoeducational or skills groups (e.g., for caregivers of people with chronic illness, or adolescents with exam stress) can extend reach. Groups emphasize shared experiences, basic coping skills, and mutual support, but require careful attention to confidentiality and stigma (see Ethical Considerations).

Illustration: Applying the plan for Case Vignette (Lakshmi)

With Lakshmi, the psychologist begins with brief psychoeducation about stress and its physical effects, using examples from her daily life. Over four sessions, the focus is on behavioural activation (scheduling small pleasurable activities), grounding skills for sleep and anger, and collaborative problem-solving around household roles, with a short, negotiated family segment where expectations are clarified and her safety is assessed.

Ethical and Cultural Considerations

Ethical practice in low-resource psychotherapy is not simply the application of universal principles, but a process of balancing autonomy, beneficence, non-maleficence, and justice within contextual constraints. In semi-rural PHCs, confidentiality, consent, boundaries, and cultural sensitivity require explicit, ongoing negotiation rather than one-time decisions.

Confidentiality in constrained spaces

Physical privacy limits: Thin curtains, shared rooms, and the constant presence of other staff threaten confidentiality; the therapist must proactively select the most private available space, lower their voice, and avoid unnecessary mention of sensitive details.

Explaining limits: Clients should be informed in simple language that the therapist will try to keep information private but there may be physical limits; exceptions for risk of self-harm or harm to others, and legal mandates, need to be clearly described.

Managing family presence: When relatives insist on staying, therapists can explore the client's preference, negotiate partial time alone, or frame individual time as "routine practice" for all patients to reduce suspicion.

Informed consent and autonomy in a collectivist context

Process, not form: With low literacy, consent is best treated as a conversational, ongoing process rather than a one-time signature. The therapist explains the nature of counselling, duration, possible benefits and limits, and the voluntary nature of participation in language that fits local idioms.

Balancing individual and family autonomy: In contexts where family decision-making is central, strict individualism may be unrealistic; the therapist strives to honour the client's expressed preferences while recognizing that some decisions (e.g., discontinuing medication) are negotiated within the family. Where family wishes clearly conflict with the client's safety or rights, ethical obligations to the client's well-being take priority, within legal frameworks.

Boundaries, dual roles, and role strain

Overlapping roles: In rural communities, practitioners may know clients socially or see them in multiple settings (health camps, community events), which can complicate boundaries. Therapists should avoid discussing clinical matters outside sessions, maintain a consistent professional stance, and decline dual relationships where they pose a risk of exploitation or harm.

Gift-giving and expectations: Clients may offer small gifts or expect special favours; the therapist must respond respectfully while considering equity, avoiding situations that could be perceived as coercive or create obligations.

Cultural sensitivity and equity

Respecting local beliefs: Many clients see distress through spiritual or moral lenses; the therapist acknowledges and explores these beliefs without ridicule, and when appropriate, integrates them (e.g., incorporating prayer or rituals) in ways that do not reinforce self-blame or discrimination.

Addressing stigma and discrimination: Ethical practice includes advocacy for fair treatment of people with mental illness, as well as attention to caste, gender, disability, and poverty-based inequities in access. Brief psychoeducation with families and community health workers can reduce harmful attitudes and promote inclusion.

Data protection and digital tools

Where mobile phones or digital records are used for follow-up or documentation, sensitive mental health information must be stored securely, with minimal identifiable details and explicit client consent. Practitioners must also remain aware of the evolving data privacy frameworks in India and the unique vulnerability of mental health data to misuse and stigma.

Conclusion

Designing a psychotherapy plan for a semi-rural PHC highlights that ethical excellence in low-resource settings is less about replicating high-intensity, urban models and more about creatively upholding core values:respect, safety, and fairness within real-world constraints. Working within structural limitations demands humility, flexibility, and collaboration with non-specialist staff, clients, and families, as well as ongoing critical reflection on how power, culture, and resource scarcity shape what "good" care can look like in practice.

References

Hooper, C. R. (2010). Ethical and professional challenges in mental health care in low- and middle-income countries. *International Review of Psychiatry, 22*(3), 245-251.

Jenkins, J., & DelVecchio Good, M. J. (2014). Global mental health: Ethical challenges. *Transcultural Psychiatry, 51*(6), 803-826.

Thornicroft, G., Deb, T., & Henderson, C. (2016). Community mental health care worldwide: Current status and further developments. *World Psychiatry, 15*(3), 276-286.

World Health Organization. (2010). *mhGAP intervention guide for mental, neurological and substance use disorders in non-specialized health settings* (Version 1.0). WHO Press.

Yasamy, M. T., Maulik, P. K., Tomlinson, M., Lund, C., Van Ommeren, M., & Saxena, S. (2011). Responsible governance for mental health research in low resource countries. *PLoS Medicine, 8*(11), e1001126.

Chapter 40

Language Barriers and Therapy: Adapting Interventions in Multilingual Settings

– Sai Charitha Rangisetti

Introduction

Many aspects of mental health therapy rely on the therapist and client talking, expressing emotions, and understanding one another. However, therapy may be conducted in multilingual societies when a client and a therapist do not speak the same primary language. As a result, the language barrier could be a major barrier to psychological evaluation, diagnosis, and treatment. In countries like India, language variety is a common occurrence in medical facilities. People frequently move between regions in search of employment, education, or economic opportunities. As a result, in situations where the spoken language is not their mother tongue, individuals may seek psychological support. In these situations, clients may find it challenging to discuss personal narratives, cultural expressions of pain, or emotional experiences, which are strongly related to their language identity.

According to research, language difficulties may affect treatment outcomes, therapeutic alliances, and the standard of psychiatric care. According to a study by Bauer and Alegria (2010), patients with inadequate language skills typically experience poor satisfaction with care and misconceptions during clinical communication. Similarly, Dewaele and Costa (2013) discovered that multilingual individuals frequently refer to emotionally charged events in their native tongue, suggesting that language plays an important role in psychotherapy's emotional processing. Multilingual therapy settings include social and cultural complexities in addition to the communication difficulties. It may be difficult to translate some of these feelings, metaphors, or distressing idioms into other languages. For instance, psychological anguish is typically expressed in culturally specific ways that reflect social relationships, familial customs, or religious beliefs. The meaning of distress may be misunderstood by therapists who are unfamiliar with certain linguistic phrases.

This chapter examines the challenges of providing psychotherapy in low-resource, multilingual environments, particularly in basic healthcare settings. In addition to outlining a methodical yet adaptable psychotherapy strategy that is anticipated to help overcome a language barrier, it discusses the mental health issues that are likely to occur in this context and offers a list of practical restrictions. The chapter examines a rural government Primary Health Center (PHC) in South India that serves many nearby villages. These clinics typically provide primary care to individuals working in the agricultural, daily wage, and informal sectors.

These locations typically have a diverse linguistic environment. Due to migration and interstate labor movement, many people are able to speak Telugu, Tamil, Hindi, Kannada or even the local dialects. Additionally, patients at these facilities may speak a variety of languages, and mental health providers may not be fluent in all of these languages. There aren't many mental health services offered by these organizations. A visiting psychologist or psychiatrist may conduct consultations once or twice a week; full-time counselors are rarely available. The majority of the time, family members or community health professionals serve as informal interpreters during consultations; these services are usually unstructured. The conditions present significant treatment challenges. When an interpreter is used in therapy, communication is a three-way process that involves the client, the therapist, and the interpreter. Topcu and Mosko (2025) noted that as interpreters are likely to influence the emotional tone, meaning, and trust of the therapeutic interaction, psychotherapy conducted through an interpreter needs to be well-coordinated.

Therefore, therapy approaches in this setting should be flexible, sensitive to linguistic differences, and culturally aware.

Common Mental Health Issues in This Context

In the context of multilingual primary healthcare, mental health problems are typically a reflection of broader social and economic stresses in the populace.

Depression

Depression is one of the most prevalent psychological conditions in rural health care settings. Patients frequently complain of sleep difficulties, fatigue, a loss of interest in daily life,and persistent sorrow. However, physical symptoms like headaches, body aches, or general weakness can also be signs of mental distress.Language limitations may prevent clients from communicating complex emotional problems. When someone tries to describe discomfort in a foreign language, they might not be able to find the right words, which could lead to an inaccurate or incomplete account of the symptoms.

In order to enhance emotional expression during a therapeutic session, a client should be permitted to speak in their native tongue, according to Dewaele and Costa's (2013), multilingual clients are more likely to communicate emotional experiences in their original language.

Stress and Anxiety

Due to financial difficulties, agricultural uncertainty, family responsibilities, or migration concerns, the majority of patients visiting rural primary health centers experience ongoing stress. Another issue may be the social isolation of migrant workers who do not speak the most widely spoken language in the region, as well as a lack of access to services.According to studies, language problems can cause poor communication in interactions between patients and therapists, resulting in miscommunication and a lack of participation in therapy.

Trauma and issues with adjustment

Clients in need of assistance may have experienced additional traumatic events such as spousal abuse, workplace exploitation, or other migration-related issues. It might be challenging to discuss traumatic events when there are linguistic barriers. Emotion levels during therapy may be impacted by the fact that certain memories have a strong connection to the language in which they were first rehearsed.

Important Limitations in A Multilingual Therapy Setting

Offering psychotherapy in low-resource, multilingual healthcare settings presents a number of practice problems.

First of all, there are not enough qualified interpreters in rural health centers. Family members frequently translate during sessions, which might compromise confidentiality and prevent open discussion of delicate topics.

Second, the therapy session is limited due to the large number of patients. Long-term psychotherapy is challenging, and mental health sessions can only last 20 to 30 minutes. Third, patients may be reluctant to disclose personal issues in the main health centers due to a lack of privacy. Joint consultation areas may eliminate private conversations. Fourth, stigma around mental health is another barrier to getting care. Rather than being a mental health problem, psychological anguish can be perceived as a personal weakness, spiritual imbalance, or family problems.

Finally, a lack of multilingual counseling training would suggest that the majority of therapists lack professional training in working with interpreters or modifying therapy to accommodate linguistic variety.

Strategies of Low-Resource Psychotherapy

Multilingual psychotherapy ought to be methodical, practical, and adaptable to the limited resources. The suggested strategy will combine culturally appropriate communication techniques, supportive counseling, and brief cognitive behavioral therapy (CBT). Before beginning therapy, the therapist should administer a brief language preference test to determine the client's preferred language. When expressing their emotional experiences, clients should be encouraged to use the language that makes them feel most at ease.

If the therapist and client do not speak the same language, a trained interpreter or multilingual community health professional should be present whenever possible. Only with the client's permission may informal interpreters, such as family members, be used.

Prior to the session, the therapist must quickly explain the goals of the session to the interpreter and make clear what is expected of them in terms of confidentiality and translation accuracy.

Interpreters' function in therapy

There are several rules that will be helpful to guarantee good communication whenever interpreters take part in therapy.

1. The therapist should speak directly to the client rather than the interpreter.
2. Short, clear sentences should be used to reduce translation errors.
3. The interpreter should translate meaning rather than word-for-word language when necessary.
4. Cultural expressions or idioms should be clarified to ensure accurate understanding.
5. Confidentiality agreements should be clearly explained.

Session Structure

The intervention will consist of 4-6 scheduled sessions, each lasting about 30-40 minutes. Depending on the services being provided, sessions are conducted either weekly or every two weeks.

Session 1-Psychoeducation and Engagement.

Session 2-Behavioral Activation.

Session 3-Cognitive Awareness is covered.

Session 4- Problem-Solving Techniques,

Session 5-Stress Management Strategies

Session 6-Preventing Relapses

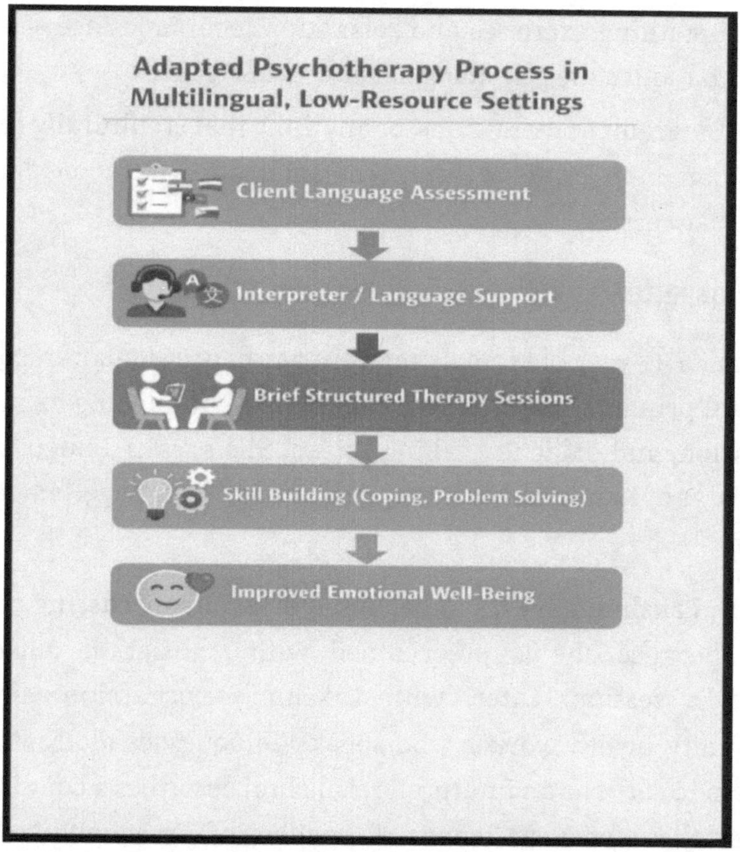

Figure 1: Adapted Psychotherapy Process in Multilingual,Low Resource Settings

Important Therapeutic Methods

Additionally, a number of techniques perform particularly well in multilingual and low-resource settings:

1. Psychoeducation by providing information on stress, emotional, and mental health in simple language and visuals.
2. Behavioral activation through encouragement of constructive activities that improve mood and social connection.
3. Helping clients develop useful coping strategies to handle everyday obstacles.

4. Breathing exercises and relaxation techniques are easy ways to reduce the physiological effects of stress.
5. Diagrams and drawings, or anything that is culturally familiar, can help improve comprehension and overcome language barriers.

Case Vigenette

Lakshmi, a 34-year-old female migrant agricultural laborer, comes to the rural primary health center complaining of ongoing exhaustion, depression, and difficulty falling asleep. She speaks Telugu, but her knowledge of Kannada, the therapist's primary language, is somewhat limited.

Initially, Lakshmi appears to be closed off while discussing personal issues because she is preoccupied with translation during her husband's session. Later, with Lakshmi's permission, a female community health worker who speaks Telugu goes along with this program to serve as an interpreter. Lakshmi describes a condition she had that she refers to as 'manasu lo baadha', which roughly translates to "pain in the heart/mind." Instead of imposing a clinical diagnosis, the therapist explores this cultural presentation to better understand her emotional experience.

Using behavioral activation techniques, Lakshmi resumes going to the women's self-help group meetings. Her financial issues from seasonal work are resolved with the help of problem-solving exercises. Sleep issues can be resolved with breathing exercises. After several sessions, Lakshmi reports feeling optimistic and supported emotionally. She talks about how the freedom to speak Telugu allowed her to express emotions that she had previously been unable to.

Cultural, Social, and Ethical Aspects

Confidentiality must be clearly conveyed to both the client and the interpreter; the interpreter must be aware that protecting confidentiality is his or her responsibility. The client must provide informed permission in a language they can understand, and the interpreter must be aware of their role in psychotherapy.

Cultural factors must also be taken into account; the therapist must understand the acceptability of various coping mechanisms for stress and mental illness and refrain from forcing foreign coping mechanisms on his or her client's culture.

In a smaller community where the therapist may come into contact with the client outside of the healthcare setting, the therapist must uphold professional boundaries and show respect for the client's behavior.

Conclusion

Language limitations are another significant issue with the delivery of mental health care in multilingual communities. Communication issues can limit the expression of emotions, improve or reduce trust, and affect therapy outcomes when the therapist and clients do not speak the same language. Despite these challenges, tailored interventions can provide substantial psychological support. Brief cognitive-behavioral therapies, supportive counseling, and culturally sensitive communication techniques may be useful in multilingual and low-resource health care settings. Increasing the number of qualified interpreters available, improving multilingualism in mental health education, and developing culturally adaptable therapeutic approaches would all help to expand access to quality psychological care.

References

Bauer, A. M., & Alegría, M. (2010). Impact of patient language proficiency and interpreter service use on the quality of psychiatric care: A systematic review. *Psychiatric Services, 61*(8), 765-773.

Dewaele, J. M., & Costa, B. (2013). Multilingual clients' experience of psychotherapy. *Language and Psychoanalysis, 2*(1), 31-50.

Fan, S., & Prosek, E. A. (2025). Bridges or barriers? A systematic literature review of multilingualism in counseling. *International Journal for the Advancement of Counselling.*

Topçu, B., & Mösko, M. O. (2025). Building trust and relationship across language barriers: A qualitative study of interpreter-mediated psychotherapy. *International Journal for Equity in Health.*

Verkerk, T., Zijlstra, B., & colleagues. (2021). Language choice in psychotherapy with multilingual clients. *Language and Psychoanalysis.*

Chapter 41

Building Therapeutic Alliance in High Volume, Low Resource Clinics

– Karen Sadhana Wilkinson

Introduction

High-traffic, resource-limited clinical settings represent a substantial segment of mental health service frameworks in developing and densely populated areas. These environments typically comprise government outpatient facilities, primary health centers (PHCs), and non governmental organization (NGO) clinics functioning within economically challenged communities. This chapter outlines a government-supported urban outpatient facility located on the outskirts of a metropolitan area, where a solitary mental health provider is tasked with managing around 40–60 clients daily.

The clientele in these situations exhibits marked socioeconomic fragility. Individuals often belong to lower-income households, engage in informal or precarious employment, and possess limited educational and health literacy. A considerable portion includes migrant groups, first-generation urban dwellers, and those facing ongoing financial, familial, and job related stressors. Awareness of mental health issues is typically low, with psychological distress frequently articulated through physical manifestations.

The infrastructural challenges are evident. Therapeutic exchanges occur in semi-private or communal areas, often divided by makeshift barriers or curtains. The time allocated for each appointment is severely limited, generally spanning from 10 to 20 minutes. Despite these constraints, the necessity for psychological support remains both pressing and broad, requiring the development of context-sensitive and resource-efficient therapeutic methods. (World Health Organization [WHO], 2021; Patel et al., 2010)

Common Psychological Issues

Anxiety Disorders

Anxiety-related issues are widespread within this population, often appearing as generalized and persistent concerns related to financial insecurity, health worries, and family responsibilities. Due to a lack of psychological awareness, these issues are frequently expressed as physical symptoms, such as headaches, gastrointestinal problems, heart palpitations, and chronic tiredness. (Beck, 2011).

Depressive Symptoms

Both clinical and subclinical depression are highly common and often linked with ongoing psychosocial challenges. Clients may experience anhedonia, reduced motivation, irregular sleeping patterns, and pervasive feelings of hopelessness. The enduring nature of stressors intensifies the severity and longevity of depressive symptoms. (Cuijpers et al., 2007).

Adjustment and Stress-Related Conditions

A notable group of individuals faces difficulties with adjusting to life changes, including migration, job instability, academic pressures, and relationship breakdowns. These challenges frequently lead to emotional instability, irritability, and weakened coping strategies. (WHO, 2010)

Limitations

Temporal Constraints

The elevated client,therapist ratio enforces strict limitations on session lengths, thus restricting the possibilities for thorough assessment, formulation, and intervention

Impaired Confidentiality

The lack of fully private environments hinders open communication, especially regarding delicate or stigmatized matters such as domestic violence or substance abuse.

Stigma and Restricted Mental Health Awareness

Dominant sociocultural views often perceive mental illness through biomedical or supernatur al lenses, thus obstructing psychological involvement and treatment adherence.

Linguistic and Cultural Diversity

Various linguistic backgrounds demand flexible communication techniques, while cultural norms shape symptom portrayal, help-seeking behaviors, and expectations of therapy.

Resource Limitations

The shortage of standardized evaluation tools, constrained follow-up systems, and absence of multidisciplinary cooperation further inhibit therapeutic effectiveness

Low-Resource Therapy Plan

Session Structure

Overall Format:

1. Total Sessions: 3–5
2. Duration per Session: 15–20 minutes
3. Therapeutic Orientation: Brief, structured, and alliance-centered intervention model
4. Clinical Priority: Rapid alliance formation, symptom stabilization, and functional coping within constrained conditions

This sessional design is informed by brief intervention frameworks and scalable psychological care models developed for low-resource settings (World Health Organization [WHO], 2016; Patel et al., 2010).

Session 1: Engagement, Alliance Formation, and Rapid Assessment

Primary Focus is establishing a therapeutic alliance under temporal and environmental constraints

Objectives:

1. Facilitate immediate emotional safety and trust
2. Elicit presenting concerns and contextual stressors
3. Normalize distress to reduce perceived stigma

Techniques Used:

1. Empathic attunement and reflective listening (Rogers, 1957)
2. Validation and normalization strategies
3. Use of culturally congruent communication styles

Rationale

The therapeutic alliance is a robust predictor of treatment outcomes, even in brief interventions (Norcross & Lambert, 2011). In high-volume clinics, the ability to establish rapport within minutes becomes a critical clinical competency.

Outcome Goal

Client perceives the therapist as trustworthy, understood, and supportive, thereby enhancing engagement and retention

Session 2: Psychoeducation and Symptom Reframing

Primary Focus is enhancing psychological insight and reducing fear associated with symptoms

Objectives:

1. Provide accessible explanations of anxiety, stress, and depression
2. Externalize symptoms to reduce self-blame
3. Improve mental health literacy

Techniques Used:

1. Use of analogies (e.g., "overactive alarm system")
2. Simplified cognitive-behavioral explanations (Beck, 2011)
3. Linking somatic complaints to emotional processes

Rationale

Psychoeducation serves as a fundamental component in enhancing understanding and managing mental health challenges.

Session 3: Emotional Regulation and Immediate Coping Skills

Primary Focus is providing clients with effective tools to handle acute distress ***Objectives***:

1. Decrease physiological arousal
2. Improve perceived control over emotional experiences

Techniques Used:

1. Diaphragmatic breathing
2. Grounding techniques (e.g., sensory awareness methods)
3. Brief relaxation exercises

Rationale

Strategies for emotion regulation are fundamental to various therapeutic frameworks, including CBT and dialectical behavior therapy (Linehan, 1993). These methods are especially beneficial in low-resource environments due to their straightforwardness and immediate usability.

Outcome Goal

Client acquires at least one coping skill that can be used independently

Session 4: Structured Problem-Solving and Cognitive Reorientation

Primary Focus is tackling external stressors that contribute to psychological distress ***Objectives***:

1. Identify specific, manageable issues
2. Shift from emotional overwhelm to solution-oriented thinking

Techniques Used:

1. Stepwise problem-solving approach (Cuijpers et al., 2007)
2. Creation and assessment of alternative solutions
3. Basic cognitive restructuring (Ellis, 1962; Beck, 2011)

***Rationale*:**

Problem-solving therapy has shown effectiveness in alleviating depressive symptoms, particularly in resource-limited settings (Cuijpers et al., 2007). It is highly flexible and culturally neutral.

Outcome Goal

Client formulates actionable strategies to tackle real-life stressors

Session 5: Behavioural Activation and Relapse Prevention

Primary Focus is maintaining therapeutic progress and preventing relapse ***Objectives:***

1. Enhance participation in rewarding activities
2. Reinforce previously acquired strategies
3. Recognize early warning signs of relapse

Techniques Used:

1. Activity scheduling (Jacobson et al., 2001)
2. Reinforcement of positive behaviours

Rationale

Behavioral activation is a research-backed intervention for depression that promotes engagement in meaningful activities, thereby supporting recovery and preventing relapse.

Flexibility Principle in Low-Resource Contexts Due to irregular follow-up and high dropout rates in such settings, each session is designed as a self-contained therapeutic unit. This modular approach ensures that even a single encounter delivers measurable benefit, aligning with scalable care models such as WHO's Problem Management Plus (WHO, 2016).

Key Techniques

Accelerated Therapeutic Alliance Formation

In light of time limitations, the therapist emphasizes the swift creation of rapport through micro-skills such as empathic attunement, reflective listening, and culturally appropriate communication. The initial moments of the session are deliberately used to cultivate trust and psychological safety. (Rogers, 1957; Norcross & Lambert, 2011)

Psychoeducation

Clients receive concise and culturally relevant explanations regarding their symptoms. Analogical reasoning (for instance, likening anxiety to an overactive alarm system) is utilized to improve understanding and diminish stigma. (WHO, 2010)

Grounding and Regulation Techniques

Short, easily applicable strategies such as diaphragmatic breathing and sensory grounding exercises are introduced to provide immediate symptom relief.

Structured Problem-Solving

Clients are led through a methodical problem-solving process that includes identifying the problem, generating alternatives, assessing consequences, and choosing actionable solutions.

Behavioural Activation

For individuals displaying depressive symptoms, gradual involvement in rewarding activities is promoted to counteract behavioural withdrawal and improve mood regulation. (Jacobson et al., 2001)

Case Vignette

Adeline, a 32-year-old domestic worker, reported ongoing fatigue, physical complaints, and increased irritability. She linked her condition to physical weakness, with limited insight into psychological factors. Her stressors included financial uncertainty and conflicts at work.

In the first session, the therapist utilized empathic listening and normalization to build rapport. Psychoeducation was offered to reframe her physical symptoms as responses to stress. A straightforward breathing exercise was introduced. In later sessions, structured problem-solving was employed to tackle her workplace challenges, while Behavioural activation strategies promoted participation in restorative activities such as evening walks. Although the intervention was brief, Adeline noted a significant decrease in distress and an enhancement in coping abilities.

Ethical and Cultural Considerations

Confidentiality

Ensuring confidentiality in shared environments requires adaptive approaches, including adjusting vocal tone, careful scheduling, and employing non-specific language when necessary.

Informed Consent

Consent processes should be streamlined and presented in clear language, guaranteeing understanding regardless of literacy levels. In such situations, verbal consent may be preferred.

Boundary Management

Due to the community-oriented nature of services, therapists might meet clients outside of clinical environments. It is crucial to uphold professional boundaries while honoring sociocultural norms.

Cultural Responsiveness

Interventions should be consistent with the client's cultural context, integrating indigenous belief systems, family dynamics, and culturally accepted coping strategies.

Conclusion

The act of conceptualizing psychotherapy in a high-volume, low-resource environment highlights the need for clinical flexibility, accuracy, and cultural sensitivity. It questions the traditional view that associates therapeutic effectiveness with length and intensity, instead illustrating that well-structured, brief interventions can produce significant results. Key to this process is the acknowledgment that the therapeutic alliance, even when formed within limited time constraints, acts as a crucial agent of change. This exercise emphasizes the necessity for mental health practitioners to merge theoretical depth with practical innovation, thus ensuring that psychological care is accessible, fair, and contextually relevant. (Norcross & Lambert, 2011)

References

Beck, J. S. (2011). *Cognitive behavior therapy: Basics and beyond* (2nd ed.). Guilford Press.

Cuijpers, P., van Straten, A., & Warmerdam, L. (2007). Problem-solving therapies for depression: A meta-analysis. *European Psychiatry, 22*(1), 9–15.

Ellis, A. (1962). *Reason and emotion in psychotherapy.* Lyle Stuart.

Hofmann, S. G., Asnaani, A., Vonk, I. J., Sawyer, A. T., & Fang, A. (2012). The efficacy of cognitive behavioral therapy: A review of meta-analyses. *Cognitive Therapy and Research, 36*(5), 427–440.

Jacobson, N. S., Martell, C. R., & Dimidjian, S. (2001). Behavioral activation treatment for depression: Returning to contextual roots. *Clinical Psychology: Science and Practice, 8*(3), 255–270.

Kazdin, A. E. (2017). *Research design in clinical psychology* (5th ed.). Pearson.

Linehan, M. M. (1993). *Skills training manual for treating borderline personality disorder.* Guilford Press.

Miller, W. R., & Rollnick, S. (2013). *Motivational interviewing: Helping people change* (3rd ed.). Guilford Press.

Rogers, C. R. (1957). The necessary and sufficient conditions of therapeutic personality change. *Journal of Consulting Psychology, 21*(2), 95–103.

World Health Organization. (2010). *mhGAP intervention guide for mental, neurological and substance use disorders in non-specialized health settings.*

World Health Organization. (2016). *Problem management plus (PM+): Individual psychological help for adults impaired by distress in communities exposed to adversity.*

World Health Organization. (2021). *Guidance on community mental health services: Promoting person-centred and rights-based approaches.*

www.ingramcontent.com/pod-product-compliance
Lightning Source LLC
LaVergne TN
LVHW100250210926
848480LV00003B/878